ARTHUR SCHWARTZ received his Master's degree in psychiatric social work from Boston University and his Ph.D. in sociology from Columbia University. A co-founder and former co-director of the Clinic for Treatment of Sexual Dysfunction and Marital Conflict of the University of Chicago, he is the author (with Israel Goldiamond) of *Social Casework: A Behavioral Approach* and (with Mary Rogel and E. Spencer Parsons) of the forthcoming *Human Sexuality*. He currently teaches in the University of Chicago School of Social Service Administration and conducts a private practice in therapy.

THE BEHAVIOR THERAPIES

Treatment Approaches in the Human Services

FRANCIS J. TURNER, Editor

THE BEHAVIOR THERAPIES

Theories and Applications

Arthur Schwartz

THE FREE PRESS
A Division of Macmillan Publishing Co., Inc.
NEW YORK

Collier Macmillan Publishers
LONDON

The Free Press
A Division of Macmillan Publishing Co., Inc.
866 Third Avenue, New York, N.Y. 10022

Collier Macmillan Canada, Ltd.

Library of Congress Catalog Card Number: 81-67422

Printed in the United States of America

printing number

1 2 3 4 5 6 7 8 9 10

Library of Congress Cataloging in Publication Data
Schwartz, Arthur.
  The behavior therapies.

  (Treatment approaches in the human services)
  Includes bibliographical references and index.
  1. Behavior therapy. I. Title. II. Series.
RC489.B4S38   616.89′142   81-67422
ISBN 0-02-928150-4   AACR2

Contents

Foreword

Dr. Arthur Schwartz has made a major contribution in writing this book. It will be welcomed and appreciated by our colleagues in social work. It will also be welcomed by our colleagues in other helping professions. This for several reasons.

The book is a rich and scholarly discussion and analysis of a wide range of therapeutic approaches and applications that are included under the general heading of behavior therapy. This of course has been done by other authors. What makes Dr. Schwartz's book so attractive is that he approaches this complex body of knowledge with the searching humility of both the scholar and the practitioner. This results in a book which presents a balanced position on behavior therapies—a most welcome perspective. He is not arguing, as others before him have done, that this is the only responsible approach to therapy. Nor is he taking the position that one must be either for or against behavior therapy and there is no in-between position. Rather, throughout the book he reflects the position, clearly stated in the first chapter, that the responsible practitioner in today's world is one who seeks out interlocking theoretical approaches to practice.

The task of seeking to understand the human being in interaction with society is overwhelmingly complex. Thus to adopt a fixed and narrow theoretical position is limiting in a manner bordering on the irresponsible. The various theoretical positions currently influencing psychotherapeutic practice are not mutually exclusive. Most practitioners are finding that there are commonalities among all of them and much more mutual compatibility than is believed in some academic and practice circles.

There are few contemporary social workers who lack some beginning understanding of the important contribution behavior therapies have made to practice. There are certainly many who do not fully understand the breadth of these contributions. There are also those who fear that in moving to a behavioral approach to practice they will have to reject all other bases of practice.

Arthur Schwartz's book helps in all these areas. He helps the reader understand the broadly diverse cluster of techniques and the various components and uses that are encompassed by these approaches. He also helps the practitioner understand how these approaches can be and are linked to other approaches to therapy. Finally he identifies the types of client problems and situations in which the various techniques are useful and also those in which they are not effective.

It is essential that today's practitioner in the human services be both knowledgeable and skillful in at least some of the behavioral techniques. It is an area where the literature is vast and complex, as the rich bibliography of this book attests. It is this very richness that deters some social workers from moving into this approach and practice. This book admirably condenses a vast amount of knowledge in a manner that can be used and understood by practitioners or senior students. It is not a how-to-do-it book but a theoretical research-based presentation enriched with practice wisdom which helps the reader to apply this knowledge.

In addition to presenting the material well, Dr. Schwartz also reminds us that not only has behavior theory greatly expanded our repertoire of therapeutic techniques; it has also enriched other approaches to practice. For example, behavior theory gives us a much more precise understanding of the effect of environment on behavior—something very essential to social work practice. It has also helped us see the importance of being much more concrete and precise in our practice than the psychodynamic tradition required. This in turn helps us to develop a practice based on empirical data, the true mark of the scientific clinician in the 1980s.

Francis J. Turner

Acknowledgments

I wish to thank Dr. Frank Turner of Laurentian University, Sudbury, Ontario, for inviting me to contribute to this series, and for his comments, feedback, and foreword. Gladys Topkis, senior editor at The Free Press, was extremely constructive in her suggestions, which helped bring the book to its final form. My thanks also go to Charles Smith and Bill Martin, also of The Free Press.

The staff of the Regenstein library at the University of Chicago offered a level of assistance that is too often taken for granted. I am particularly indebted to Patricia Wilcoxen, head of circulation services.

Dean Margaret K. Rosenheim of the School of Social Service Administration at the University of Chicago aided the work by providing an environment that encouraged the writing of this book. Dorothy Van Steele helped smooth over many problems, and Gwen Graham typed part of the manuscript. My thanks also go to Don Davis for his generous help.

My friend Ethel Schenk not only assisted with the typing, correspondence, and the innumerable other tasks that had to be done, but she also provided an encouraging word when it was needed.

Finally, my wife Ruth—as usual—proved to be my strongest supporter and my most astute critic, helping me at all phases of the writing of this book.

I am grateful to all of these people and to others whose names I may have inadvertently omitted from these acknowledgments.

Chapter 1

Introduction

The purpose of this book is to provide an overview of the behavioral approaches to therapy. The behavior therapies, as a group, are controversial. People either advocate them with an almost religious fervor that disqualifies them as objective judges or condemn them as inhumane, with equal fervor and equal damage to objectivity. It is rare indeed to find nonpartisan and dispassionate discussions of these new therapies. This is unfortunate, for the truth lies between the two extremes.

The behavior therapies are not inherently mechanistic and inhumane. Like all therapies, they can be so if applied by an insensitive and unfeeling person. They are not all-powerful, but there is a substantial body of evidence that behavioral procedures can be effective in treating some (but not all) problems. There is also increasing awareness among behaviorists that while the behavior therapies represent great advances in some areas, these advances do not automatically negate the value of other therapeutic approaches. In particular, there is a growing body of opinion that the behavioral and the psychodynamic approaches are not so imcompatible as was previously thought. In fact, a careful consideration of all the various treatment approaches shows that they share at least some commonalities.

1

We suspect that many of the alleged differences may exist more in theory than in actual practice in the office or clinic, that there is far more similarity among therapists in what they actually do than in what they say they do. Fiedler (1950) found more agreement among experienced therapists of different orientations than between experienced and inexperienced therapists with the same orientation. Even Carl Rogers, who identified three "currents" in the American psychotherapeutic field—the psychodynamic, the behavioral, and the existential—stated that these currents, while separate and distinct, often tend to overlap (1964). A capable and concerned therapist can adapt and utilize aspects of one approach while retaining a primary emphasis on another approach. We shall illustrate this observation throughout this book and expand upon the commonalities—and the possibilities of a future rapprochement—in the final chapter.

The Fragmentation of Human Functioning

In this book the word "behavior" is used in its broadest sense, following B. F. Skinner's definition of behavior as "the movement of an organism in space with respect to itself or any other useful frame of reference" (Skinner, quoted in Evans, 1968, p. 8). In practice, though, behavior is specified as precisely as possible.

Humans can be described in three ways. We can talk about what they are doing, their "behavior." We can talk about what they are feeling, their "affects," their "emotions." We can also talk about the way they think, their "cognitions." It is obvious that there are therapies which seem to concentrate upon one or another of these areas. Behaviorists tend very much to concentrate on behavior, in the belief that a change in behavior produces change in affects and cognitions. They do not deny that other approaches are possible. They agree, for example, that it is entirely possible to help a person to change his behavior by first changing the way he feels or thinks or perceives (Ellis, 1977a). However, behaviorists feel that the most economical, speedy, efficient, and effective way to intervene is to change behavior first. This point of view is supported by some non-behaviorists, such as social psychologist Leon Festinger (1964). Furthermore, many behaviorists would say that since behavior is the only one of the three categories that is observable and describable, then change in behavior is all that is necessary.

Some Characteristics of the Behavioral Approaches

Among the main contributions of the behaviorists are their marked empiricism and their emphasis on procedures that can be specified and measured. In this book we shall discuss some of these procedures, alerting our readers to the positive contributions of the behavioral methods but, at the same time, we hope, maintaining a critical stance, pointing out where some of these procedures either are ineffective or have not yet fulfilled the expectations of their developers.

Behavior theory and practice evolved from experimental psychology, as contrasted with psychoanalytic theory, which has its roots allegedly in medicine but, actually upon closer examination, in philosophy. There is an emphasis in all the behavioral approaches upon specification of the problem in terms that can be agreed upon by two or more observers and on spelling out the procedures used to resolve the problem. There is also a high priority on researching the efficacy of the intervention procedures. These characteristics tend to differentiate the behavioral approaches from much psychotherapeutic practice, as we shall illus-

trate throughout this book. Thus a psychodynamically oriented therapist might define his aim as "to enhance ego
functioning." This goal would be too general for a behaviorist who would want to spell out treatment goals by helping the patient to specify what "enhanced ego functioning"
meant in terms of his own observable behavior and the specific conditions (time, place, etc.) under which these behaviors would occur. Beginning, then intermediate goals would
be set to work toward behavioral changes. The patient's
behavior would be monitored and measured against his
"baseline" behavior, and the occurrence of new or improved behaviors would confirm that "ego functioning"
was actually being "enhanced."

The behavioral approach is characterized by questioning
and rejection of the "disease" concept of mental illness, as
well as of the so-called drive theories of causation of psychological problems. These theories postulate that the
symptom is merely the external expression of an underlying
problem and that if the presenting problem is treated without consideration of the underlying problem, the individual
will sooner or later manifest other problems. This is the
concept of "symptom substitution."

Symptom substitution will be discussed in detail later in
this book, but for the moment we can say that it is a reflection of Freud's theory of libido. Oversimplifying somewhat,
the theory states that if energy is blocked at one point it will
seek exit at another point. The late George Klein (1973), a
psychologist at the Menninger Clinic, pointed out that
Freud was working within the context of nineteenth-
century Newtonian physics, which postulated closed systems. If Freud were alive today, says Klein, he would be
interested in open-systems theory and feedback loops
(Schwartz, 1977) rather than in what is sometimes disparag-
ingly called the "hydraulic theory" of personality.

To a behavior therapist, the problems with which a client
comes to the therapist, such as chronic lateness for work,

or premature ejaculation, or stuttering, are seen as problems in their own right. Furthermore, they are seen as *learned* phenomena. He knows that any behavior, no matter how dysfunctional it seems, is producing some positive consequences for the client. In a sense, these "consequences" may be said to be the "meaning" or the "function" of the stuttering for the individual.

Stuttering, for example, is an adaptation which has consequences for the individual. A person who stutters may feel humiliated when he speaks, but he may also get the rapt attention of polite listeners, no matter how boring or inconsequential his statements are. It may be the way in which he controls people's attention, or receives reinforcement, or manages to avoid people or keep them at a distance. His selection of the precise symptom and its function may or may not be readily apparent, but the behavior certainly is not meaningless. In this sense the behaviorists agree with Freud's observation that all behavior is meaningful and all behavior is determined. Helping the client to eliminate the stuttering without helping him to find alternate ways of obtaining the listener's attention (a reinforcer for his behavior) may very well result in either a return of the stuttering or the appearance of another, functionally similar behavior. This is not the same as "symptom substitution."

The "symptom substitution" argument has long outlived its usefulness (American Psychiatric Association Task Force on Behavior Therapy, 1973). As Bandura (1969) has observed, the concept cannot be tested because of lack of agreement on the meaning of the terms "symptom" and "underlying cause." The argument as it persists in this "simplistic, mechanistic, and reductionistic form . . . ," merely serves to get in the way of a dialogue between behaviorists and non-behaviorists (Schwartz and Goldiamond, 1975). However, behaviorists do agree that the elimination of some problems may result in the appearance of other problems if there is not a complete assessment of the "person in the situation."

To regard stuttering and other "symptoms" as learned behavior implies that they can be unlearned and that more adaptive and functional behaviors can be learned. Rather than work toward "curing" a particularly maladaptive behavior, the behavior therapist focuses on helping the patient to learn more adaptive speech patterns. The behaviorist might say that his approach is not only optimistic but efficient (a rather distasteful word that is becoming increasingly necessary to discuss in psychotherapy today, considering the increased demands for accountability). The behaviorist would say that his work is characterized by a parsimony of conceptualization, which makes for a parsimony in intervention efforts, which produces the maximum result. We shall discuss in the course of this book instances in which we believe this claim is true, instances where we believe it to be false, and above all instances where we believe that the claim is premature but may be true in the future.

The behaviorist tends to downplay concepts of personality, particularly trait psychology. That is, he rejects the idea that only a particular "kind" of person tends to engage in a given behavior, such as "stuttering," and another "kind" in premature ejaculation. He believes that while there are similarities among individuals, and certainly similarities in their adaptive styles (Shapiro, 1975), the personality theories have so far not proved useful in explaining and predicting phenomena. He would state, rather, that a wide variety of people with many different "personalities" can exhibit the same symptom, be it stuttering or obesity or marital problems or existential crisis. The correlations found to date between specific personality types and specific "psychological problems" have been of such a low order that we can predict very little from them. If personality theory does not enable one to predict, which is one of the main contributions a theory has to offer, then personality theory tends not to lend itself to therapeutic intervention that can be validated through research.

THE PRIMACY OF THE ENVIRONMENT

In contrast to the dynamic psychologist, who emphasizes looking deep within the individual for the "reasons" that he is engaging in certain behaviors, the behaviorist tends to emphasize the individual's environments. The reader will note that the word "environments" is plural. Each individual has more than one environment (cf. Merton, 1957, on "role sets" and "status sets") and tends to operate differently under the demands of different environments. The behaviorist would say that the way a person behaves is less a function of his innate personality traits than a response to certain kinds of environmental stimuli or cues and to the demands that these environments present. For example, most social work students behave differently in the classroom and in field work in an agency setting.

One element that is common to all helping orientations is an interest in the client's history. The behaviorist tends to concentrate upon the here and now and to go backward in a patient's history only far enough to understand the present situation. The analytically oriented therapist may take the opposite view, using a genetic approach, but both he and the behaviorist emphasize that the past of the patient is important. The psychodynamic therapist might call it experience or developmental phases, the behaviorist a history of conditioning or learning; but both would agree that what happens when one is a child affects what happens later in life (Evans, 1968). They may disagree, however, on the mechanism by which this happens. The psychoanalyst might say that the person acts this way because he has severe superego lacunae (gaps in the development of the supergo); the behaviorist might say that the client manifests a behavioral deficit or, more likely, that he himself simply does not understand, at this point of our knowledge, the mechanisms by which this happens. Furthermore, he would attack the concept of "superego lacunae" as a "mentalistic" explanation, regarding it as worse than no explanation at all, for it appears to explain what it does not in fact explain and, furthermore, has the negative effect of cutting off further explorations.

EMPHASIS ON THE "OBSERVABLES"

The behaviorist tends to concentrate upon observable behavior, such as skin flushes or the verbalizations of the client, keeping the use of inferences to the minimum or avoiding them altogether. It must be pointed out that the various behavioral points of view differ widely in this respect. The "radical" behaviorist would state that all behaviors are governed by external events which are observable, thus leading one therapist to observe that a radical behaviorist is "one with no invisible means of support" (Mahoney, 1974, p. 14). This view has remained fairly consistent since the days of the early behaviorists but has been challenged by a number of contemporary theorists. Behaviorists also differ from therapists of other persuasions in the extent to which they demand explicit descriptions of the behavior, as well as of the conditions governing the behavior. Behaviorists work with their clients toward pinpointing the problem, delineating specific goals of therapy, and articulating the procedures to be used. In fact, the behavioral approach has also been called a "procedural approach."

The psychodynamic approaches tend to be heavily theoretical; practitioners and researchers tend to isolate aspects of the theory and look for evidence to substantiate them. This is called a "hypothetical-deductive" approach. The behaviorist tends to start with the laboratory approach and induce his theory from his clinical observations. This dichotomy may be somewhat artificial, for many observers have long called for a clinically based science of psychoanalysis (Klein, 1973).

Both approaches are deterministic. While the behavior therapist tends to reject internal drive theories and the abstractions of mentalistic terms, he does believe that behavior is determined primarily by learning, by the patient's history of learning, and by the current external environments in which the individual is operating. The psychodynamic therapist tends to place much more emphasis on inner drives and biological factors. Nevertheless, both would agree that the parameters of human choice are limited because behavior is determined.[1]

Historical Overview of Behaviorism

"Behaviorism" is not a unified body of theory and practice but, in fact, a group of "approaches" with divisions

[1] Our view is that one most certainly can change affects and cognitions by changing behavior. In fact, whenever possible we work on helping the client to change his behaviors first, and this is the approach stressed throughout this book. However, we reject the concept of viewing a person as divided into behaviors, affects, and cognitions. That there is a unity of body and mind is advocated by such disparate theorists as Freud, Piaget, and Skinner (if not by their overzealous disciples), who agreed that eventually the explanations for our behaviors, affects, and cognitions will be found in our internal biochemistry. However, we do feel that there are advantages in focusing on and attempting to intervene in one area—behavior—if the therapist bears in mind that the other two are intimately involved. It is our view that one can help to change behavior rapidly and quite effectively, but that often behavior change will be temporary and transient unless there are also changes in the affects and the cognitions. We also feel that the individual must learn ways of handling himself in future situations, so the behavioral approaches as described in this book also have an important teaching, preventive aspect.

and schisms, some minor and some as large, and often as acrimonious, as schisms among the older orientations. The four main developments are discussed in Chapters 2, 3, 4, 5, and 6 and illustrated in Chapter 7; in Chapter 8 we offer some speculations on future developments, divisions, and reconciliation of views.

While behaviorism has had a long history, when we think of behaviorism we usually begin with the work of the Russian physiologist Ivan Pavlov (1849–1936). Most readers are probably familiar with Pavlov's experiments. Briefly, Pavlov found that hungry dogs would salivate (an unconditioned response) when presented with meat powder (an unconditioned stimulus). When Pavlov repeatedly paired the meat powder with a neutral stimulus such as a bell or a tone or a light and then later presented this originally neutral stimulus without the meat powder, the bell (or the light or tone) would itself produce salivation, a conditioned response.[2] By extension into the real world from the laboratory, many neutral stimuli could be conditioned to produce a variety of responses in humans as well as in animals. We shall devote Chapter 2 to this model, called the classical or respondent or stimulus-response or Pavlovian model.

The kind of behaviorism associated with Pavlov made its earliest and perhaps most meaningful entry into the United States in the 1920s under the influence of the American psychologist John Watson. Watson's view of behaviorism was almost a complete environmentalism, clearly opposed to the introspectionism then in vogue in psychology. Behav-

---

[2] The original term, infrequently used today but more accurate, was "conditional response," indicating a changing rather than a fixed process. The term became "conditioned response" through translation error. For an interesting account of the history and controversy over which term is correct, see Franks (1970), especially pp. 113–114.

iorism was also placed in false juxtaposition to the intrapsychic emphasis of the new and growing Freudianism. Watson himself eschewed the study of emotion because he could not see it and thus could not measure it. In his view, innate emotions were limited to love, anger, and fear; the rest of the gamut of emotional responses in human feeling was learned behavior and thus was capable of being changed.

The writings of Watson were greeted with much enthusiasm in the 1920s. This was the era of a booming economy, a naive faith in the boundless future of the United States and, by implication, the unlimited possibilities for people to develop their own potential. The "sky was the limit" economically as well as psychologically. In Russia, the spread of Marxism, an extreme environmentalist view, was a parallel trend.

The 1920s, the time that Einstein was producing his precedent-shattering theories, were also characterized by an almost religious belief in "science." This belief in "science" and the emphasis on environmentalism provoked Watson into such statements as "Give me a dozen healthy infants and I shall produce the conditions that will produce what you want—doctors, lawyers, criminals, what-you-will" (Watson, 1924). In retrospect, of course, this seems naive and grandiose, but the atmosphere at that time encouraged the conviction that here, at last, was the possibility of developing a science of human beings. There was the hope that, by applying scientific principles to the rearing of children, one could produce a generation that would reap the rewards of the new prosperity. A "scientific era of child rearing" arose. Infants were fed not on demand but on a rigid schedule. Children were treated not as children, individuals with their own developmental needs and patterns, but as small adults.

The hopeful tone of Watson's approach, consonant with

the optimism of the 1920s, was soon to confront the realities of the 1930s, a decade which brought economic and accompanying psychological depression and was followed by World War II. Moreover, the application of the "scientific" principles he propounded was often rigid, unquestioning, and ultimately stifling. Behaviorism as proposed by Watson did not vanish but vastly diminished in importance. Some of the hopes, the wishes, and the pretensions of this early approach have still not yet been laid to rest.

With the introduction of Pavlov's thought to the United States, primarily through the writings of John Watson, there was a move toward applying the principles of Pavlovian respondent conditioning to human problems. Watson and Rayner (1920), in one of the first attempts, exposed an infant named Albert to a white rat, to which he showed no fear. They then paired the appearance of the rat with a loud noise (an unconditioned stimulus), to which the child responded with fear. When the rat was later presented without the noise, the hapless child also responded with fear, demonstrating that Watson and Rayner had successfully conditioned the child to respond with fear to a previously neutral stimulus. This fear later generalized (spread) from the rat to a number of furry objects, such as a rabbit, a fur coat, a dog, cotton, wool, and even Watson's hair, but did not generalize to non-furry objects. Watson and Rayner thus demonstrated that fears could be learned.[3]

Mary Cover Jones, a student of Watson, later succeeded in deconditioning children's fears by a process she called the "Method of Direct Conditioning." She reduced the fear of a rabbit in a boy named Peter by putting a caged rabbit near his chair while he was eating candy. When he cried, she moved the rabbit away and then—over a period of time—moved the rabbit closer and closer, until Peter finally

[3] Needless to say, many of us today would consider this kind of research, upon a subject unable to offer consent, as highly unethical. Behaviorist

lost his fear of the rabbit and could even play with it (Jones, 1924, described in Reese, 1978, p. 191).[4]

These isolated applications of Pavlovian conditioning principles were frequently replicated, but with very little influence on the mainstream of therapy. More influential was the publication of *Personality and Psychotherapy* by Dollard and Miller (1950), an effort to relate stimulus-response theory to psychoanalytic concepts such as transference, repression, free association, etc. Other behavioral works that opposed the then-dominant theories of psychoanalysis were Andrew Salter's *Conditioned Reflex Therapy* (1949) and the pioneer work by O. H. Mowrer, *Learning Theory and Personality Dynamics* (1950). These early applications of behavioral work were considered interesting, but they made comparatively little impact until publication of the studies by Hans Eysenck (1952) in which he claimed that neurotic clients who were not treated by psychotherapy fared just as well as those who had received treatment by psychotherapists. Eysenck's studies are rather dubious for a number of reasons, particularly the weakness of the data and the differential criteria that he seemed to use in comparing "treated" neurotics with "untreated" neurotics, to the detriment of the former (see the devastating analysis by Bergin, 1971). Yet these studies, questionable as their findings later turned out to be, gave impetus to the work of Joseph Wolpe, particularly his *Psychotherapy by Reciprocal Inhibition* (1958), by adding to the growing mistrust and questioning of the psychoanalytically oriented therapies.

---

researchers and practitioners today observe all the safeguards of human subjects now rigorously demanded by law and by professional dictates. Yet these old researches are still cited as evidence that the behavioral approaches are inhumane procedures performed by inhumane experimenters.

[4] For a good overview of the early influences see Levis (1970).

CONTEMPORARY "BEHAVIOR THERAPY": JOSEPH WOLPE

The classical conditioning model of Pavlov and Watson has influenced us most through the work of Joseph Wolpe (1915–   ), a South African-born psychiatrist currently practicing in the United States. Wolpe formulated a theory called "reciprocal inhibition through systematic desensitization" (Wolpe, 1958). Initially he worked primarily with the phobias, but he has recently expanded his scope to include the treatment of a whole range of disorders, following a series of earlier experimentalists, such as Mary Cover Jones, who used the classical conditioning paradigm to "decondition" people with psychological problems. Wolpe's approach basically counterposes anxiety responses with non-anxiety responses, for he believes that an individual cannot experience both anxiety and non-anxiety (relaxation) simultaneously.

Wolpe is a prolific writer whose work has influenced much of contemporary American therapy; for example, it is the basis of much of the Masters and Johnson approach to the treatment of sexual dysfunctions. Other respondent therapies include the conditioned reflex therapy of Andrew Salter (1949) and the implosion therapies of Stampfl and Levis (1967, 1968) as well as the various aversive treatments such as conditioned reflex treatment for alcoholism, homosexuality, and other behavior deviations. We shall discuss these further in Chapter 2.

OPERANT CONDITIONING: B. F. SKINNER

The main approach in American behaviorism today is not Wolpe's approach, based on classical conditioning, but the operant conditioning views associated with B. F. Skinner (1904–   ), Professor Emeritus of Psychology at Harvard

University. These are discussed at length in Chapters 3 and 4.

The Skinnerians tend to view behavior not solely as a conditioned response to an antecedent stimulus (the Pavlovian approach) but within an A–B–C framework. Antecedent conditions or stimuli (A) affect behavior (B), but the behavior does not follow these antecedent conditions automatically, as in the Pavlovian scheme. Whether or not a given behavior will occur under any antecedent conditions is determined by the consequences (C) of that behavior. Those behaviors which produce desirable effects (C) for the actor will be reinforced and will tend to occur again. Consequences that are unpleasant to the actor will lower the rate of behavior (the behavior is said to be punished). For example, a professor is conducting a seminar (A). One student makes a comment (B). If the professor smiles and shows approval of the comment (if he says "good"), then the approval is the consequence (C) and the student will be more likely to make a comment in the future. However, if this student makes a comment (B) and the professor disputes it and shows dissaproval (C), then the consequence is unpleasant and punishing for the student, and he will be less likely to make a comment in the future. While the idea that the consequences of behavior affect the rate and frequency of its occurrence has been known for a long time it is primarily due to the work of B. F. Skinner and his adherents that the orientation known as operant conditioning has assumed a major role in contemporary psychology (Reese, 1978, p. 3).

The difference between the two "rather different traditions" has been delineated by Stuart (1977). Stuart calls the Pavlov-Watson-Wolpe approach, based on classical conditioning procedures and using a combination of desensitization and aversive procedures, "behavior therapy." He calls the Skinnerian operant approach "applied behavior analysis," which attempts to strengthen some responses and weaken others primarily "through the rearrangement of the environmental contingencies that control their occurrence". "Applied behavior analysis" means looking at the individual's interactions with all of the factors—the contingencies—within this A–B–C conception. These contingencies include the individual's interaction with all of his environments (the "individual-in-the-situation" concept familiar to social workers) and some internal factors and history, as well as (in the opinion of some authors) such items as imagery and "private events" (Schwartz, 1977). Stuart claims that both approaches basically rely on data-based research. In actual practice there tends to be increasing overlapping between these two approaches.

SOCIAL LEARNING: ALBERT BANDURA

Another important development in the behavioral approaches is the social learning approach of Albert Bandura (1925–   ), Professor of Psychology at Stanford University. Bandura (1969, 1971) observed that learning often takes place without immediate reinforcement (or punishment) of the behavior and concluded that behavior can be learned by imitation or "modeling." That is, a person can learn "vicariously" while watching someone else do something and observing the consequences of the behavior for that person (Schwartz, 1977). For example, we can learn to serve better in tennis by observing a tennis pro and noticing how he holds his racquet, throws the ball, follows through, and so forth. We would then imitate or "ape" him, modeling our behavior after his. Similarly, if we observe others engaging in behavior that is rewarded, or is punished, we would imitate the behavior in the first instance and avoid it in the second, thus showing that an abstraction such as a "standard of behavior" may be learned vicariously.

The Cognitive Behaviorists

A strict behavioral approach examines only a part of the artificially segmented human. As we have noted, it is becoming apparent to many behaviorists that cognitive processes and feelings are interwoven with behaviors. Cognitive behaviorists, such as Michael J. Mahoney (1946–), Donald Meichenbaum (1940–), Albert Ellis (1913–), and Aaron T. Beck (1921–), work toward helping their clients understand the meanings of their behaviors through an understanding of the *thought processes* that accompany behavioral changes. For example, some people distort the nature of reality and then act as if their distorted perception *were* reality. Others do not engage in certain activities because they give themselves messages, sometimes without full awareness and usually subvocally, that they are not capable of engaging in those activities. Examining the way people think about situations and the way they act in accordance with these thoughts (cognitions) can help effect behavioral and other changes. Evidence is beginning to show that without cognitive changes, changes in behavior may not be maintained. While behaviorists have always been concerned with thoughts and feelings, they have tended to downplay them in favor of behavior-contingency analysis. Needless to say, this new development has produced even more schisms among behaviorists.

Behaviorism in Social Work

All behaviorists, as we have noted, are very much concerned with data, with careful specification and definition of problems, change goals, and intervention procedures, and with evaluation and accountability. These are all steps toward empirically oriented casework (Schwartz and Goldiamond, 1975, p. 1).

In behavioral analysis we look at the relationship of the individual to all of the relevant environmental factors which influence behavior, in addition to variables within the individual (particularly his history of conditioning); all of these conditions are called the "contingencies" (Schwartz and Goldiamond, ibid.). This concept is identical with the long-standing social work concept of the "individual in the situation" (Schwartz and Goldiamond, 1975, p. 2).

Above all, client problems are seen by behaviorists primarily as "problems in social functioning" (Schwartz, 1977). This means emphasizing problems in relationships of individuals with their environments or with other individuals over problems within themselves.

To behaviorists the individual is an actor in a system which is constantly changing. Likewise, the focus of concern of social work is not the individual *or* the system but both, especially where they interplay and interact. The recent dichotomy in social work education on whether to emphasize study of the individual or study of social action is, in our opinion, artificial.

If one views behaviorism as emphasizing the study of the individual in the situation and of the individual's interactions with the many environments that affect his behavior, then social work has always been "behavioristic." Certainly the early social workers, as the direct descendants of the social reformers, were primarily environmentally oriented, whether their governing theoretical orientation was theological or Marxist. With the introduction of psychodynamic thought into social work (Borenzweig, 1971), the emphasis began to switch to inner dynamics with a corresponding de-emphasis on the study of the environment. While lip service has certainly been paid to the interaction of the individual and the environment, it is generally agreed that the advent of Freudian psychology has tended, for better or for worse, to focus the attention of the profession of people's internal processes. It is not our wish to reignite the running controversies of environment vs. heredity (nature vs. nurture) that have afflicted social work and many other professions. Nevertheless, we shall state our view that environment has been minimized in social work, although the trend may now be changing (see Germain, 1973; Grinnell, 1974; Grinnell and Kyte, 1974, 1975).

It is very seldom that a single individual can be credited with introducing an orientation into a discipline, but this is the case with Professor Edwin J. Thomas of the University of Michigan, who, after completing his own doctoral work in psychology, has assiduously applied the findings of the social and behavioral sciences and, in particular, the teachings of Wolpe and Skinner to the practice of social work. An early publication was a transcription of his lectures (Thomas and Goodman, 1965). In 1967 he edited a volume on *The Socio-Behavioral Approach and Application to Social Work*. Contributors include Sheldon Rose, whose later works formed the foundation of a behavioral approach to group work; Richard B. Stuart, who applied these principles to casework and psychotherapy; and others who have applied it to various aspects of social work practices, such as Rosemary Sarri, Robert Vinter, and Roger Lind.

For a long time the University of Michigan was the central training place for behaviorists. Recently, though, there have been independent establishments of practice throughout the country. The first behavioral track in social casework was established at the University of Chicago by Arthur Schwartz, simultaneously with programs in group work started by Sheldon Rose at the University of Wisconsin. Today many schools of social work have behaviorists on their faculties, and behavioral principles are being applied in many areas of social work practice. A recent bibliography listed over two hundred references (Shorkey, 1978). In addition, introductory texts have been published

by Arkava (1973), Fischer and Gochros (1975), and Wodarski and Bagarozzi (1979). An encyclopedic handbook
has been written by Gambrill (1977). An application specifically to casework is the work by Schwartz and Goldiamond
(1975) while Rose (1973, 1977, 1980) has written three fine
volumes applying these principles to groups. Throughout
this book we shall make references to social work applications and, in the last chapter, discuss some of the ethical
and practical problems and promises of this approach for
social work. In particular, we shall elaborate on its compatibility with other philosophies and methods of helping.

The Organization of This Book

Chapters 2, 3, 4, and 5 focus on the main trends in behaviorism today: The classical, Pavlovian approach; the
Skinnerian or operant-conditioning approach; the social-
learning approaches (primarily of Bandura) and the development of cognitive behavioral approaches. Chapter 6 illus-
trates the use of these four behavioral approaches in
treating depression, a condition that is almost epidemic today, at least in the major urban centers where most therapy
is done. It also briefly alerts the reader to newer, nonbehavioral techniques, such as developments in the biochemical
area. We believe that depression as a clinical entity is one
area in which all theories may eventually coalesce in a unified theory. Then, in Chapter 7, we present recent extensions of the behavioral therapies to new target conditions
and new client groups.

The final chapter assays the current state of theory and
research in the various behavioral approaches as well as the
promises, the problems, and the unresolved questions of
behaviorism. It discusses the commonalities, differences
and future directions of possible rapproachement of behaviorism with the other helping modalities and theories.

The appendix is intended to enable the reader to locate the latest research and intervention procedures. We intend this appendix as a working guide to practice, a way to enlarge upon the beginning which we hope this book will provide.

Chapter 2

Respondent Conditioning: The "Stimulus-Response" Therapies

We have noted that Joseph Wolpe, a prolific writer, was a pioneer in the development of the behavior therapies in the United States. Wolpe started his work with animal neuroses, later generalizing from his studies with animals to therapy with humans (see Wolpe, 1976, for a description of his early work). Wolpe claims that the conditions he studied in animals are truly neuroses and therefore have applicability for the study of human neuroses. Needless to say, some people have interpreted this assertion to mean that Wolpe equates humans with cats and rabbits. This is a misinterpretation of Wolpe's statement. His view is that there are commonalities among species and that by studying animal neuroses we have a model for the treatment of human neuroses. Wolpe certainly does not demean or dehumanize humans. In fact he holds the optimistic view that if humans can be conditioned to be neurotic, then they can be reconditioned to be "not neurotic," as was the case with his original sample of neurotic cats. Neurotic behavior, being learned behavior, can be unlearned.

Wolpe states that many so-called neurotic problems are habits, which he defines as "consistent ways of responding to defined stimulus situations" (Wolpe, 1969). These habits are acquired through learning; that is, by conditioning. "Bad habits," being learned, can be unlearned, and more adaptive patterns learned. Wolpe's emphasis on learning was in direct contradiction to the emphasis on pathology as a result of the disturbances of drive theories then espoused by the predominant psychodynamic therapists.

Another factor in neurosis is primary stimulus generalization. If a stimulus triggers a fear or an anxiety response in the individual, it is possible that this fear-anxiety response can generalize to other, originally neutral, stimuli, making them also capable of producing anxiety. Thus, a fear of snakes may generalize to a fear of frogs, cats, dogs, heights, airplanes, or a number of originally dissimilar subjects, objects, or situations, all of which ultimately can acquire the common property of producing fear and anxiety.

Wolpe states that when a stimulus becomes noxious to an individual, one reaction is anxiety, "an individual organism's characteristic pattern of autonomic responses to noxious stimuli stimulation. As a result of conditioning a great many cues to condition an anxiety are established" (Wolpe, 1973, p. 16). In other words, when people characteristically respond to unpleasant and threatening situations with anxiety, a pattern tends to develop whereby they will respond to many "cues" which will trigger anxiety.

If a stimulus automatically produces anxiety, Wolpe's aim is to teach the individual to produce a response *inhibiting* the anxiety, since such a response cannot occur simultaneously with the anxious response. Relaxation is such an inhibiting response. One cannot be anxious and relaxed simultaneously; the human nervous system simply cannot process two such conflicting states simultaneously. To oversimplify Wolpe's technique, the individual is taught some relaxation procedures and then is systematically exposed by progressive increments or steps to the feared object. Gradually the feared object loses its ability to produce anxiety. Thus the individual is "desensitized." In Wolpe's words, "If a response inhibiting anxiety can be made to occur in the presence of that anxiety-evoking stimulus, it will weaken the bond between the conditioned stimulus and the anxiety it provokes" (Wolpe, 1969, p. 15).

In other words, if you can learn to feel relaxed in the presence of something that usually brings on anxiety—e.g., the sight of a snake—then you are weakening the power of the sight of the snake to produce feelings of anxiety. You become "desensitized." It is precisely these anxiety responses that produce the maladaptive habits sometimes called "neuroses," in particular the neurosis of phobia, a maladaptive habit in which the person feels much anxiety. The exact source or sources of a phobia may not be obvious or apparent; many cues other than the original phobia-producing cues can acquire the ability to produce anxiety.

We reiterate that throughout Wolpe's system, anxiety is viewed as a *learned* phenomenon. Unlearning the anxiety involves producing a response that will weaken the link between the anxiety and the stimulus. This procedure need not be on a conscious level; awareness most certainly is not a central feature of the mechanisms of this conditioned pairing. It is precisely these maladaptive habits, in particular the neuroses, that are the domain of behavior therapy, especially behavior therapy as viewed by Joseph Wolpe.

According to Wolpe, problems that are treatable by behavior therapy also include maladaptive patterns without anxiety responses, such as temper tantrums, nailbiting, and eneuresis, and the psychoses, in particular schizophrenia. In his earlier works, Wolpe stated that schizophrenia had an organic basis, and he tended not to treat it. However, in his later work (1973, 1976) he asserted that some of the maladaptive patterns accompanying schizophrenia were learned, that they had anxiety components and could be treated through conditioning procedures.

Reciprocal Inhibition through Systematic Desensitization

Wolpe's main therapeutic technique is called "reciprocal inhibition through systematic desensitization." Systematic desensitization, which will be described below, is a procedure where the individual is taught to relax, and then slowly (systematically) exposed to the stimulus, such as a snake, which causes his anxiety.

When he sees a patient, Wolpe first takes a complete history and then applies several standardized tests such as the Willoughby Personality Schedule, a Fear Inventory, and a Bernreuter (an instrument to determine "self-sufficiency"), which he uses to assess subsequent changes in the client. According to Wolpe, systematic desensitization is a specific set of procedures that must be followed exactly as outlined in his writings, beginning with the administration of the tests mentioned above and then proceeding to include the following elements: (1) Training in deep muscle relaxation; (2) development of a scale of subjective anxiety; (3) building an anxiety hierarchy; and (4) relearning.

Even within this uniform approach, the treatment of each client is highly individualized. The therapist first analyzes the client's presenting problem and the circumstances around the onset to find out what events might have modified the reaction. Information is obtained on the client's past and present family life, his education and school experience, sex life, the history of emotionally warm and loving experiences, and his present social relationships. A medical examination may be necessary if there is any suggestion that there are physical complications.[1] Another concern, of course, is to determine whether the client has taken any drugs. Certainly the anti-anxiety drugs (tranquilizers) are counterindicated during the application of systematic desensitization. Not only will the tranquilizers tend to mask the anxiety but any learning that occurs while the client is on the drug may be lost if he stops taking the medication.

STEP ONE: DEEP MUSCLE RELAXATION

Relaxation techniques have applicability in a great variety of situations and are compatible with a number of the helping psychotherapies.[2] Wolpe ingeniously adapted and simplified the procedures of Jacobson (1938), positing relaxation as the response that should occur primarily in antagonism to the response of anxiety.

While there are a number of procedures in use today for muscle relaxation, most of them are essentially variations of Wolpe's adaptations of Jacobson's approach. The first step is to draw the client's attention to the various muscle groupings. He is then instructed first to tense and then to relax the muscles. For example, the client is asked to stretch out his right arm and make a very tight fist. When he does so, he will be asked to pay attention to the strain in the forearm muscles, in the hand, in the knuckles. After five to seven seconds, he will be told to relax, to "let go" very quickly, and to notice the feeling of relief. He will be asked to do this for the other fist, then both fists together, and

---

[1] While Wolpe states that this is optional (1973), it is the belief of this author that physical examinations are mandatory in all cases of psychotherapy (see Chapter 3).

[2] For example, Benson (1977) has indicated the usefulness of relaxation procedures for the treatment of high blood pressure and for the prevention of heart attacks.

then to flex the biceps (drawing the upper arm up until the biceps feel tense) and then to relax the muscles.

The various muscle groups of the body, including the face, forehead, eyes, neck, chest, shoulders, and the rest of the body, may be grouped into a number of clusters. The number of groupings itself is less important than a consistent and easily understood set of explicit procedures that may be learned by the client and used both inside and outside the session to produce a relaxation-like response. In addition to Wolpe (1973), Bernstein and Borkovec (1973) and Cautela and Groden (1978) are excellent manuals for relaxation procedures, the latter especially for use with children.

While Bernstein and Borkovec (1973) insist that these relaxation procedures must be taught to the individual client in the therapy situation, Wolpe and others (among them the present author) have experimented with the use of tape recordings. My experience has been that if I spend part of one session illustrating the taped procedures and then give the client a tape, the client can practice at home at convenient times and learn the procedures in a very short period.[3]

STEP TWO: THE DEVELOPMENT OF A SCALE OF SUBJECTIVE ANXIETY

The second step in systematic desensitization is the development of a scale of subjective anxiety. After carefully reviewing each individual's history, Wolpe develops scenes and situations involving the problem situation and asks the client to tell him on a scale of 0 to 100 the degree of anxiety

[3] An excellent tape may be obtained from John Marquis, Ph.D., Self-Management Schools, 745 Distel Drive, Los Altos, California 94022. Tapes are also available with women's voices, in Spanish and in other foreign languages, from BMA Audio Cassettes (Guilford Publications, Inc.), 200 Park Avenue South, New York, N.Y. 10003.

he feels in each. For example, if a client fears birds, he might rate a scene in which he sees a picture of a bird in a book at a discomfort level of 10 (low) while a scene in which a bird perches on his head may be rated at 95 or even 100 (extreme anxiety). Wolpe has called this rating a "subjective unit of discomfort" (SUDS).

STEP THREE: THE BUILDING OF A HIERARCHY

The third step is the building of an anxiety hierarchy. Wolpe constructs, with the client, a continuum of scenes ranging from the least threatening to the most threatening; the order of presentation of these scenes is determined by the number of SUDS produced in the client.

There generally tend to be two kinds of hierarchies, although any hierarchy can combine the two types (Paul and Bernstein, 1973, p. 19). The "spatial-temporal" hierarchy focuses upon the distance of the client from the anxiety-eliciting stimulus in either time or space. It begins with those imaginal items that produce the least anxiety; the client will approach the anxiety-producing event in imagination, either by getting closer in time (e.g., taking a pending examination) or in distance (e.g., gradually approaching a snake). The following example of a hierarchy utilizing time and distance is used by many therapists with clients who have a fear of taking examinations (this hierarchy is similar to one which may be found in Wolpe, 1973, p. 117):

1. Seven days before taking a written final examination
2. Six days before taking the examination
3. Five days before taking the examination
4. Four days before taking the examination
5. Three days before taking the examination
6. Two days before taking the examination
7. The day before the examination

8. Trying to sleep the night before the examination
9. Waking, realizing this is the day of the examination
10. Eating breakfast the day of the examination
11. Leaving the house the day of the examination
12. Getting into the car to drive to the examination
13. Driving to the examination
14. Parking the car in the university parking lot
15. Walking toward the building
16. Opening the door of the building
17. Walking through the hall toward the examination room
18. Reaching for the doorknob of the examination room
19. Walking through the door of the room
20. Sitting in the chair
21. Seeing the instructor with the examination blue books
22. The instructor walking toward my seat with the blue books
23. The instructor putting the blue book on my desk
24. Opening the blue book
25. Starting to write in the blue book

The number of steps and the exact nature of the steps should be, of course, individualized for each client through "trial and error." There should not be too many steps, but on the other hand, too few will not allow sufficient opportunity for relearning.

The second type of hierarchy focuses around some common feature or theme of the anxiety-eliciting stimulus, such as a fear of pointed objects or a fear of loneliness or a fear of medical examinations. The construction of the hierarchy in these cases can be a difficult undertaking. Standardized hierarchies may or may not be similar to the client's fear. However, it may be helpful to the therapist to consult some of the standard hierarchies for ideas. Standard hierarchies may be found in Wolpe (1973), Bernstein and Borkovec (1973), Paul and Bernstein (1973), and Marquis *et al.* (1974).

STEP FOUR: RELEARNING

The last step is the actual counterposing of the anxiety-provoking stimuli—the scenes from the hierarchy—with the relaxation response. The number of muscle groups involved, the order in which they are presented, and the speed of the tension release are all aimed at producing the same effect, a learned relaxation that will be inconsistent with the patient's anxiety response. The muscle-tensing exercises have a positive effect upon the client, teaching him that he can voluntarily control his muscles to counteract the sensations of anxiety and tension (Bernstein and Borkovec, 1973, p. 20).

In actual therapy, relaxation training begins each session; the client systematically tenses and relaxes the muscle groups. When the client is in a relaxed state he is presented with a neutral scene, to get an idea of his ability to imagine scenes and to weed out any possible complicating problem (Wolpe, 1973). After the test scene, the therapist presents the least anxiety-producing item in the hierarchy. The client is asked to raise a finger when the scene is in his mind. The therapist times the scene's duration, usually from 5 to 7 seconds, and then tells the client to erase the scene from his mind and rate the scene according to the number of SUDS it elicited; then to relax. After 30 seconds of relaxation the process is repeated until the item receives a zero SUDS level. The client then advances to the next item in the list and proceeds until he is deconditioned to all the items on the list. If a client expresses anxiety so high that a zero SUDS is unattainable, it may be sufficient to bring him to a SUDS of under 25 so that movement along the hierarchy can be facilitated. According to Wolpe, this is rarely necessary (Wolpe, 1973).

During the treatment with relaxation exercises, the client does two homework assignments. First, he writes down the situations that cause him to be tense and tries to identify those elements of his environment that are stress producing. The second assignment is to have at least two daily 15 or 20-minute sessions of tension-release practice to facilitate his learning the skill.

A client who finds it difficult to relax can be helped by presenting imaginal scenes that have a calming effect on which he can focus. Sometimes the client may be taught additional breathing exercises. Sometimes hypnosis is used. Sometimes some of the tranquilizers are used (specifically for the session, not for the general state of anxiety). Deep relaxation can be facilitated by the use of a muscle-relaxant drug called Brevital (methohexital sodium). Needless to say, tranquilizers and muscle relaxants should be used only under medical supervision.

Of course, the process requires the client's cooperation. If the client decides not to focus or not to imagine the scenes in the hierarchy, the entire procedure will be useless. As we shall develop below, sometimes phobias are maintained by their consequences (in analytic terms, their "secondary gains"); while the client is consciously seeking treatment, he may unconsciously wish to avoid the new situations he would have to face if he no longer had the phobia. For example, one client had a fear of flying which kept him from visiting his family, who lived 2,000 miles away. Once he got rid of his fear of flying he no longer had an "excuse" to avoid the visits and thus had to face the larger problem, his disturbed relationship with his family.

If the first item on the list produces too much anxiety, too much distress for the client, the therapist should substitute an even weaker item. The therapist may have to experiment with the spacing between adjacent items, using the SUDS scale as a guide. According to Wolpe (1973), the difference in anxiety ratings between any two adjacent items should be not more than 5 to 10 SUDS on the subjective scale. If the items are too close together, progress will be too slow;

if they are too far apart, progress may stop and the client may, paradoxically, become much more sensitized to the stimulus. It is better to err in the direction of listing steps that are too small rather than ones that are too large.

In some instances the hierarchy may need to be revised. During this entire process the therapist and client must be in communication; feedback from the client is essential (Wolpe, 1973). The adequacy of a hierarchy often depends to a great degree on how skillful the therapist is and how good the rapport is between therapist and client.

It may be necessary for the last scene in a patient's hierarchy to be repeated a number of times to prevent a recurrence of the anxiety reaction. It may also be wise near the end of therapy to re-present any items that did not elicit a zero SUDS rating.

If at any time during the procedure the client's anxiety level becomes manifestly too high, the presentation of the scenes should be stopped and the client encouraged to relax. It goes without saying that the client should leave the session in a relaxed state of mind even if it means not pushing the hierarchy to its ultimate, for the relaxation will last and generalize for some while (Bernstein and Borkovec, 1973, p. 55).

It is possible to work on two or more hierarchies either in succession or concurrently. Paul (1969) thinks that they should be presented in sequence rather than concurrently, to reduce the generalization of anxiety over related items.

Systematic Desensitization: A Discussion and Critique

Systematic desensitization is without doubt the most thoroughly researched therapeutic procedure in *any* psychotherapeutic school. There have been literally hundreds of studies involving various aspects of systematic desensitization.

While Wolpe insists that his four phases of systematic desensitization account for the majority of the effects, some workers challenge this assumption. Paul (1966), for example, postulates that the attention and the positive expectations the therapist generates explain why the therapy seems to work. This "placebo" effect, he claims, accounts for almost all success in insight therapy and at least 50 percent of the success of systematic desensitization. Similarly, Franks and Wilson (1976) summarized four studies and concluded that systematic desensitization was no more effective than a convincing placebo. They stated that success in treatment is related to factors such as the increased optimism and motivation of the client, his compliance in following procedures, and modification of his cognitions.

There seems to be general agreement that systematic desensitization is indeed effective. But there is disagreement as to exactly what mechanisms account for the effectiveness of the procedure. Wolpe states that the procedure works through reciprocal inhibition and the learning of new responses that inhibit anxiety. Other therapists have disagreed, offering several possible alternatives. Kazdin and Wilcoxon (1976) suggest that the success of the process is not due to reciprocal inhibition but to "counter-conditioning," the pairing of anxiety-provoking stimuli with *any* nonanxiety response. They state that while relaxation and a hierarchy may facilitate fear reduction, they are not absolutely essential. *Any* response counteractive to anxiety, such as just relaxing the muscles instead of tensing, or thinking a "nice thought," or imagining or taking a positive action, is enough to counteract the noxious effect of the anxiety-producing stimulus. Wolpe disputes this view, and the research data are, admittedly, contradictory.

Another explanation is that the anxiety drops because the noxious stimulus is not being followed by aversive consequences (Kazdin and Wilcoxon, 1976). As we described above, if the presentation of a feared object, such as a snake, does not produce anxiety, or produces smaller and more tolerable amounts of anxiety, then the effect of the noxious stimulus, the snake, will be extinguished. Extinction, in the respondent conditioning model, means that the stimulus no longer elicits a response. For example, presenting a tone to a dog without the meat powder will mean that the dog eventually will not salivate to the tone. In this case, the conditioned response is said to have been extinguished.

Still another explanation for the effectiveness of systematic desensitization is that anxiety is reduced by a direct experience of graduated exposure to the phobic stimulus. This can be done in either of two ways. One is by "shaping," the process by which, step by step, the desired behavior is approached. Shaping is a procedure whereby the elements in behavior that are part of the final desired behavior are reinforced, and those elements that are not like the final behavior are not reinforced. For example, if one were teaching a child to say the word "mother" one would reinforce the initial sound "m" and not reinforce, let us say, "d." We would then reinforce the sound "mo," then "moth" then, finally "mother."

The patient's contact with the phobic stimulus is increased through shaping and reinforcement of approach behavior. As the client more and more approaches the feared object, he is reinforced (either physically or symbolically) by the therapist and by the very action of approaching the feared stimulus. This tends also to shape antiphobic behavior. (Shaping is discussed in Chapter 3.)

Another way in which exposure works is through social modeling combined with gradual exposure to the stimulus that produces the phobia. The therapist or other individuals (significant others) in the client's life may model these approach behaviors; the client learns by observation and imitation or modeling (discussed in Chapter 5).

An example of operant shaping is to take a child who is afraid of dogs and give him some dog biscuits. Have him throw the first biscuit thirty feet away, then the second twenty feet away, until gradually the dog approaches the child and even takes the biscuit from his hand. A more effective procedure might be to have the dog stay in one place and the child gradually approach it. As the child gets nearer and nearer to the dog by throwing the biscuits, he is reinforced both by the therapist and by the situation of being close to the dog without feeling fear. In social modeling, the therapist would approach the dog first, demonstrating behavior to the child that he could imitate.

Another explanation, related to some of the cognitive-behavioral procedures discussed in Chapter 5, is that systematic desensitization is actually the learning of a coping skill. Anxiety reduction is consciously mediated through *in vivo* (real life) exposure, and the anxiety itself is a cue for the individual to make a non-anxious response, either of a physical nature such as muscle relaxation or a cognitive one, where the individual gives himself different reassuring messages. The individual can use the fear as a cue-controlled relaxation, learning to go through the relaxation procedures to produce a relaxed response in the face of stress-provoking stimuli. He could also learn to give himself helpful instructions to cope with the stressful situation (Meichenbaum, 1977), saying to himself, "I will not be anxious" or "I am capable of handling the situation" or "I can do X, or Y, or Z to handle that." These self-instructions often are most effective when they are paired with a cue-controlled relaxation, with the person simultaneously relaxing.

Although the explanations for the phenomenon vary, it should be noted that none of the critics who espouse these alternative explanations denies the demonstrated fact that the therapy does indeed work. It is our feeling that much of the success or failure depends upon the client's expectation of what he will feel in the situation. Certainly if a client feels he can handle it—if his "self-efficacy" (Bandura, 1977a) is high—he will be more capable. Coping skill (or "self-control" measure) is a concept that will be discussed in Chapter 4.

These experiments we have described show that whether or not the procedures themselves have an effect, the presence of the therapist clearly does. The therapist who conveys to his clients, either overtly or covertly, confidence in his treatment techniques and conviction that change can occur will indeed facilitate client improvement. The effectiveness of the behavior therapy procedures, and other therapy procedures, will be greatly enhanced if the therapist is aware of the nonspecific aspects of the therapy, particularly the nonspecific factors of relationship (see Kazdin and Wilcoxon, 1976).

Variations on Systematic Desensitization

In Vivo Desensitization

One development in systematic desensitization that has usefulness both as a "real life trial" of the effectiveness of the imaginal systematic desensitization procedures and as a therapy in its own right is the procedure called *in vivo* desensitization. Here the feared object is not approached imaginally, as in systematic desensitization, but in actuality (Wolpe, 1973). For example, the individual who is fearful of heights and elevators is given an assignment to go up in an elevator to the second floor, then the third, then as high as he can tolerate the anxiety. When the anxiety becomes intolerable, he is instructed to leave the elevator. The next time, he may start at a floor or two below the highest he was able to tolerate and continue until he has reached the top floor of the building. Anyone who has overcome a fear of dogs by gradually approaching a dog while placating the dog with dog biscuits has used *in vivo* desensitization. The procedures may or may not also include relaxation procedures to counteract anxiety as the client gradually gets closer and closer to the feared object.

One advantage of *in vivo* desensitization is that the presentation of the feared object in real life facilitates generalization; that is, it is more likely that the results will not be limited to verbal behavior in the therapist's office. The gains have a much greater chance of persisting. In addition, this gradual approach can be combined with reinforcement procedures, such as a reward (Chapter 3), or with modeling (Chapter 5) by the therapist.

In vivo desensitization is similar to "shaping" but they differ in one crucial way. The former, in our view, involves extinguishing a fear by non-reinforcement. The latter, as we described in the example of the boy approaching a dog, involves reinforcing imitating and approach behaviors.

One problem with *in vivo* procedures is that they are less convenient for the therapist, who has to leave his office and get into the real life situation with the client. He cannot fit the client and the real life situation neatly into his office and the forty-five-minute session.

Flooding and Implosion

One explanation for the success of systematic desensitization is that the procedure works through extinction. If the presentation of a feared object, such as a snake, is not followed by anxiety, then the snake will cease to produce anxiety; extinction occurs. (Kazdin and Wilcoxon, 1976.) This has led to the formulation of two therapies based on extinction—*implosion* and *flooding*—both associated with the work of Stampfl and Levis (1967, 1968) and Levis and

Hare (1977). (For a critique, see Morganstern [1973] and the reply by Levis [1974].)

Implosion is done in imagination as is systematic desensitization; flooding is done *in vivo* with the stimuli actually physically presented. The logic behind both is as follows: If gradual exposure to a noxious stimulus will gradually desensitize the person and thus cause the noxious stimulus to lose its anxiety-producing properties, then a massive exposure to the stimulus will result in a rapid reduction in anxiety. The noxious stimulus will rapidly lose its ability to produce anxiety.

In practice, implosion consists of having the patient imagine a massive exposure to a feared object (for example, he would imagine snakes crawling up and down his back, all around him, being smothered in snakes) or flooding (in which actual snakes—nonpoisonous, of course—would be used).

In implosion and flooding there should be no chance for the individual to escape. He has to stay and face his anxiety. Some persons absolutely refuse to subject themselves, either in imagination or in real life, to a feared stimulus. Some clients will literally panic and leave the situation. Some will discontinue therapy. Needless to say, a careful assessment of the client is essential before either approach is used. These treatments are meant specifically for neurotic patients. With a borderline patient or a seriously disturbed patient (especially a psychotic) flooding and implosion most certainly should not be used.

An advantage of flooding and implosion, according to their proponents, is that one does not need to construct hierarchies or train the client in muscle relaxation, so that these procedures take much less time than systematic desensitization.

Stampfl's work is quite controversial. While Stampfl claims quick and lasting results, some critics have claimed that they could not replicate his results (Morganstern,

1973). Others attack flooding and implosion as aversive procedures, for they are indeed unpleasant to the client. Wolpe states that systematic desensitization is not only more effective but is not an aversive procedure. As Bandura (1969) points out, flooding is by far the less potentially noxious of the two because the physical stimuli can actually be presented in only a limited number of ways while implosion, where the stimuli are presented in imagination, can become hazardous because the therapist may unwittingly suggest possibilities to the patient that he had never thought of before.

Flooding and systematic desensitization might be compared by analogy to teaching a person how to swim. A person can sometimes be taught to swim by throwing him into water over his head. However, a person also may be taught to swim and to lose his fear of water by first wetting his toes, then his ankles, then his knees, then his legs, then his upper torso, etc. One who is thrown into water over his head may learn how to swim, but he may forever have a fear of or aversion toward the water. Similarly, both flooding and implosion procedures *may* reduce a fear, but there is also the risk of increasing the fear or even, in extreme cases, of inducing panic. Wolpe's point is, why use an aversive procedure when a nonaversive procedure is available?

Paradoxical Intention

A useful variation on flooding and implosion was devised not by behaviorists but by an existential psychiatrist, Viktor Frankl (1959). In the procedure called "paradoxical intention," the person is told to deliberately exaggerate the condition he fears. For example, if a client fears fainting, the therapist will ask him to try as hard as he can to imagine fainting or actually to faint. If a person has a fear of vomiting, he will ask the person to try to vomit. If a person is afraid of having a heart attack, he will ask the person to try as hard as he can to have a heart attack. This can be an extremely effective procedure, although many clients cannot overcome their anxieties and refuse to participate because of the feared aversive consequences. However, our experience has been that those clients who *do* undertake paradoxical intention find themselves unable to faint, vomit, have a heart attack, etc. Often clients will even break out in laughter at what they are trying to do in what is supposed to be a fear-producing situation. We have found paradoxical intention to be a most useful technique for some clients.

Assertiveness Training

Assertiveness training is a general term for a group of procedures by which people can learn to affirm themselves in situations where they were previously controlled or were manipulated by others. Assertiveness training has recently become popular, for this set of procedures has applicability for populations other than those defined as "clinical" or "disturbed." For example, many consumer interest groups, women's consciousness-raising groups, handicapped citizens' groups, and groups of older adults have utilized assertive training. These procedures, often used by individuals who shudder at any mention of "behaviorism," are actually one of the early contributions of Wolpe, who saw assertiveness training as a form of "reciprocal inhibition through positive counterconditioning." Wolpe defined assertiveness as "the proper expression of *any* emotion other than anxiety toward another person" (Wolpe, 1973, p. 81, emphasis added). The emotion can be any positive emotion incompatible with the anxiety, especially the performing of a task. It is the incompatibility of the competing emotion, plus the performance of a task, that weakens the conditioned bond. For example, rather than feel tense and intimidated by an overbearing sales clerk, one might first relax and then feel an emotion, such as competence. Then, rather than merely being browbeaten, one might speak directly and affirmatively to the sales clerk, stating exactly what one wishes, and persisting till one gets it.

Assertiveness training has evolved beyond the respondent techniques into a complex package of procedures utilizing many behavioral as well as nonbehavioral refinements (see Ferguson and Birchler, 1978). The main use of assertiveness training today is to help people learn to stand up for themselves, not to allow themselves to be imposed upon. Many people today experience frustration and feel put down; they generally respond with either aggression or submission, neither of which is a constructive way of handling problematic situations. Ferguson and Birchler point out that this is one of the heritages of the Judeo-Christian tradition which encourages us to "turn the other cheek" (Ferguson and Birchler, 1978).

Note that assertiveness is not synonymous with aggressiveness. Learning to stand up for your rights should not be misconstrued as pushing others around. There is a world of difference between protesting when someone pushes ahead of you in line and pushing ahead in line yourself to be first. The purpose of assertiveness training is the protection of one's own rights and prerogatives but not at the cost of curtailing another's rights and prerogatives.[4]

Treating Sexual Dysfunction

The sexual dysfunctions were once considered extremely unresponsive to treatment. However, since the innovations

[4] Good references are Ferguson and Birchler (1978), Gambrill and Richey (1975), and Gambrill (1977).

by Masters and Johnson (1966, 1970), techniques for treating these problems have become part of the armamentarium of many therapists. A number of these procedures, especially the basic "sensate focus" exercises, are forms of systematic desensitization.

In sensate focus, the couple is directed to abstain from sexual intercourse. They touch each other in a caressing manner but with no attempt to stimulate or sexually arouse the partner, then proceed through various steps to successful sexual intercourse. Through the sensate focus exercises the couple learn to reacquaint themselves with their own sexual and sensual cues without the necessity of "performing" (having sexual relations to live up to some standard, rather than for pleasure, for intimacy, for communication). This is another way of saying that for many troubled couples, sexual closeness and emotional intimacy have become anxiety-producing situations, with their partners becoming, in effect, "noxious stimuli." Gradual exposure to their partners, their "noxious stimuli," while following the procedures designed to decrease felt anxiety, enables the couple to engage in further exercises, which include conversation as well as touching. As a result, their sexual problems become more amenable to treatment. These procedures, which form the basis of the Masters and Johnson sex therapy treatment, as well as those of Helen Singer Kaplan (1974) and others, are derived from the innovations of Wolpe. In fact, in a recent work, Wolpe (1976, p. 20) refers to the "new sex therapy of 1974," citing his own work, which was done in 1954.[5]

---

[5] There is a caution to be observed about these new sex therapy procedures. They do have much value, but they tend to be applied in a stereotyped cookbook fashion to any client who complains of a sexual dysfunction. Frequently there are problems with intimacy, communication, relationship, and depression that are overlooked by the narrowly trained sex therapist in his eagerness to apply these new procedures. Those who are trained solely as "sex therapists" sometimes are not able to make an evaluation of what may be a much more complex inter-

The Aversion Therapies

Prior to and paralleling the work of Wolpe, the chief application of respondent conditioning theories was in the so-called aversion therapies. The aversion therapies were generally used to correct what we might call behavioral deviations, such as alcoholism, homosexuality, fetishism, and other deviant sexual activities as well as a number of phobias, eneuresis, and other problem behaviors. The theoretical model comes directly from stimulus-response psychology. An unconditioned stimulus which is repugnant to the patient (electric shock, chemicals, noise, a drug) is paired repeatedly with the unwanted behavior (a previously neutral stimulus) such as drinking, exhibitionism, etc. Eventually, when the patient engages in this behavior, he will experience unpleasant effects similar to those produced by the noxious stimulus even when the two are no longer actually paired. That is, he becomes conditioned to react to the undesired behavior as painful or aversive, and presumably he will tend not to engage in that behavior in the future.

At the Washingtonian Hospital in Boston, for example, Dr. Joseph Thimann practiced what was called "conditioned reflex therapy" for alcoholism. He would inject a patient with a nausea-producing drug and then, just before the drug took effect, would have him take a shot of his favorite whiskey. After drinking the whiskey, the patient would vomit. After a while, drinking the whiskey alone without the drug would produce the same effect of nausea and vomiting (Thimann, 1949). Thimann claimed complete

---

actional picture. While these procedures have value in their own right, treatment of sexual problems cannot be separated from the larger and often more salient elements of the interpersonal relationship. For a unified model, we suggest the reader look at Schwartz and Schwartz (in preparation).

abstinence of 51 percent of 275 patients in a follow-up of from three to seven years after discharge. (We must note that these figures did not include cases that he could not locate, so we can assume that the final percentage was lower.)

It must be emphasized that in this model the unpleasant effects are always paired with the undesired behavior so as to eliminate this behavior. This is an automatic, reflexive training which requires little, if any, thought or cooperation on the part of the person receiving the training. This can sometimes be an advantage; these therapies can be used when a client states that his behavior is "beyond his control." Unfortunately, it is also a shortcoming. Not only are the aversive therapies sometimes applied without the consent of the patient but they often merely remove a behavior, leaving a behavioral void which the client is not able to fill with an adaptive behavior (Skinner, 1953).

Even this "strict" behavioral approach was confounded by nonspecific (and nonbehavioral) factors. Dr. Thimann, for example, was aware that there were factors operating in addition to the stimulus-response procedures. He deliberately gave this therapy in unpleasant surroundings—an attic room of the old, now demolished Washingtonian Hospital, a Gothic-like structure. He said many times that "punishment" was part of the therapy; that he was experienced by some of the patients as a castigating father who punished them for their "sin" of drinking. We make this point to bring to the reader's attention once again the fact that while much of the behavioral literature seems to describe experimenters applying laboratory procedures in an unfeeling way and the explanations may seem oversimplified, the individuals performing the procedures are usually aware of some of the more nonspecific factors involved. However, they often either cannot specify these variables or dismiss them as relatively unimportant. The increased awareness of the importance of these factors is the basis of the current interest in cognitive-behavioral procedures (see Chapter 5).

The aversion therapies were used not only with alcoholics but with sexual behavior problems (Bandura, 1969, pp. 511–525). One variation is called "aversion relief therapy." In an example cited by Rachman and Teasdale (1969), a homosexual patient received electric shock (an aversive stimulus) while seeing slides depicting sodomy, but the shock was stopped (a relief stimulus) when pictures of attractive women were shown. The effect of this therapy, however, seems to be short-lived.

Many of the criticisms of the current behavior therapies are based on the erroneous belief that these therapies are essentially aversion therapies in one form or another. This is simply not true. The aversion therapies are used by a relatively few clinicians, and then only with extreme cases which do not respond to other means of intervention, particularly cases involving self-destructive behavior. In addition, these procedures are usually applied with full legal safeguards, including informed consent of the client, and often representation by legal counsel, as well as consent of family. Unfortunately, there were occasions in the past (prior to "informed consent" requirements) when these techniques were grossly misused. The bad reputation resulting from these abuses, though no longer valid, still clings tenaciously.

Except in certain extreme circumstances, described below, we are adamantly opposed to the use of aversive procedures, especially by psychotherapists outside of medical institutional settings. First of all, the use of chemical, electrical, and other aversive stimuli—in their own right—is an extremely complicated matter. There is need for continual medical—and legal—supervision and regulation. Furthermore, the reported results of aversive procedures are questionable and, in most cases, do not last very long. In addition, there is evidence that the use of any aversion stimuli (and other punishment procedures) makes clients aggressive and especially hostile toward the therapist (Rachman and Teasdale, 1969, p. 33). Needless to say, the anxiety created by the use of drugs as well as the dangerous side effects make these not only questionable therapies to begin with but puts them outside the realm of the nonmedical therapist. There are ethical reasons not to use aversion procedures as well as questions about their efficacy (see Chapter 4).

There are other procedures that can be used to treat the same problems through the reinforcement of positive behaviors rather than through the punishment of problematic behaviors. For example, in dealing with eneuresis, many parents continue to use the so-called "bell and pad" technique. In this procedure, first introduced by Mowrer (1938) and by Lovibond (1964), the sleeping child is wired to an electric circuit. At the first drops of urine the circuit is completed and a bell or some other loud device is activated to awaken the child so that he can complete urination in the toilet. This is obviously a punishment procedure, not only in the noise of the aversive stimulus and the rude awakening but because it deprives the child of sleep. There have been, however, reports of success with the bell and pad (see Kanfer and Phillips, 1970, pp. 123–127 for a comprehensive summary).

The operant techniques of Azrin and Foxx (1974), however, reinforce dryness rather than punish wetness. They use no aversive control and report a high degree of success. The child is doubly rewarded, not only by the attention of his parents but by having dry pants (Schwartz and Goldiamond, 1975, p. 251). We shall discuss these procedures further in Chapter 4.[6]

---

[6] See Doleys (1977) for a comprehensive review of the behavioral treatments of nocturnal eneuresis in children.

Part of the problem with the aversion therapies, particularly for problems such as alcoholism, is that they tend to work only as long as the individual is subjected to whatever unpleasant stimulus is constantly paired with the undesired behavior. However, when he is in his natural environment and can have access to alcohol without the paired electric shock, he usually begins drinking again. Hence the effects of the punishment procedures tend to fade very quickly. This is a technical objection which, when added to the moral and ethical drawbacks to the use of aversion therapies, should rule them out for most psychotherapists in general and for social workers in particular.

The Covert Procedures

A set of procedures generally associated with Cautela (1967, 1970, 1971) is based on the classical conditioning model but deals with covert imagery rather than with overt behavior. The chief form is an aversive procedure called "covert sensitization." The client imagines scenes in his life when he engaged in an undesired (or "undesirable" behavior). For example, the alcoholic will imagine himself going into a bar. At first the situation will be pleasant, but when he reaches for a drink he will experience an aversive response, such as nausea. He will become disgusted, leave the bar, and go into the fresh, open air where he is able to breathe deeply. This "escape" or "relief" scene is necessary for the therapy. Similarly, in the treatment of homosexuality, the client will imagine seeing a young man who looks very attractive and appealing. As he approaches the young man, he sees that the young man is covered with rashes and boils, he smells, etc. As the patient recoils, the young man will reach for the patient, who experiences an overwhelming feeling of disgust, which is terminated when the patient leaves the scene and again goes into the clean, open air.

This procedure can also be viewed as a self-control technique (an active coping strategy) but it is theoretically based on a classical conditioning model. The undesired behavior, such as drinking, homosexual behavior, fetishism, rape, etc., is paired with a noxious result, in this case nausea. It most certainly is aversive to the individual undergoing the treatment, and like many of the aversion therapies it has the effect of eliminating the behavior but does not help the client to learn constructive behavior to take its place. It does have the advantage that the aversive stimulus is presented only in imagination. Cautela has also developed procedures called covert reinforcement and covert extinction, which we shall not discuss here (see Cautela, 1970 and 1971).

Cautela's procedures share the difficulties of all imagery procedures: There are very few overt indicators as to what is actually happening other than the verbalizations and the affect of the client and, of course, his consequent behavior in the stimulus situation (e.g., will he drink in a bar?). If the client wishes to resist by not imagining the aversive procedures, the therapy is not useful and the therapist cannot help him.

Summary

The initial behavior therapies were based on a stimulus-response conceptualization of behavior. A primary influence was Joseph Wolpe, whose innovations posed a major counterinfluence to the predominantly psychoanalytically oriented therapies of the 1950s.

Wolpe advocates a learning model theory, regarding most neurotic problems as "habits." Exposure to threatening stimuli produces anxiety, which in turn is the basis of the neuroses, particularly the phobias. Wolpe's therapies are called "reciprocal inhibition" therapies, the best known of which is "systematic desensitization." A client is taught a series of muscle-tensing procedures which teach relaxation, incompatible with anxiety. Then a hierarchy of events connected with the threatening stimulus is constructed, along with a series of scenes which the client is to imagine and to pair with the relaxation rather than the anxiety response. The final step is the presentation of these scenes along with the relaxation, so that the stimulus is no longer anxiety producing to the client.

Systematic desensitization works, although there are disputes over the theoretical explanations of *how* it works. Explanations offered, in addition to Wolpe's *reciprocal inhibition*, are *counterconditioning* (*any* response, not necessarily relaxation, will counter the anxiety), *extinction* (if the noxious stimulus is not followed by anxiety, the stimulus loses its power to evoke anxiety), *exposure* (gradual exposure will also weaken the power of the stimulus), *social modeling* (approach behaviors by therapist are imitated by the client), the *learning of coping skills* (the anxiety is a cue for the person to engage in some other behavior, thus aborting the anxiety) and, finally, the effectiveness of the procedure may be due to *placebo effects* (improvements are due to suggestion).

Variations on these procedures are *in vivo desensitization* where the client is exposed to the threatening stimulus in real life (e.g., goes up in an elevator), *flooding and implosion,* where, instead of a gradual or slow exposure, the client receives a massive exposure (in flooding, there is exposure to a real stimulus, e.g., a harmless snake, while in implosion the exposure to the noxious stimulus is in the imagination).

Another procedure pioneered by Wolpe is *reciprocal inhibition through positive counterconditioning,* popularly known as *assertiveness training,* in which assertive (but not aggressive) responses are made to counteract anxiety.

Wolpe's views of reciprocal inhibition are the basis of many currently popular sexual therapies, particularly the "sensate focus" exercises of Masters and Johnson, in which couples gradually reapproach each other to unlearn maladaptive sexual practices and relearn more adaptive, more pleasurable, and less anxiety-producing sexual behavior.

Among the first of the therapies based on the respondent model were the *aversion therapies* in which certain behaviors, such as drinking alcohol, were paired with a distasteful event (such as electric shock, vomiting, noise, and others) so that the individual, over time, associated drinking—previously a pleasurable but undesired behavior—with an unpleasant result. Other applications of the aversion therapies were with sexual deviations, some conduct disorders, and the "bell and pad" method of treating nocturnal eneuresis.

The effects of aversion therapies are often short-lived and they also have serious ethical and technical shortcomings. In general, they are little used nowadays, for other, less aversive methods have been devised.

A series of therapies has been devised by Cautela, called the *covert procedures,* where the client imagines aversive consequences for such behaviors as drinking, homosexuality, etc. While these procedures do not involve the use of such potent and potentially abusable stimuli such as electricity, chemicals, and vomiting, they do require the utmost in cooperation from the client; if the client does not desire to imagine the images, then the procedures cannot work.

There has recently been a more reasoned and more accurate appraisal of the behavior therapy approach, in particular the contributions of Joseph Wolpe. The relaxation procedures have been "rediscovered"; there are newer applications and renewed recognitions of their usefulness (see Vattano [1978] for a useful overview). The distinctions between the respondent and the operant orientations, while convenient for a textbook such as this one, become blurred and indistinct in practice (Mowrer, 1956). With this caution in mind, let us examine the predominant orientation in contemporary behaviorism, operant conditioning, associated primarily with B. F. Skinner.

Chapter 3

Operant Conditioning

The predominant orientation in American behaviorism today is the approach associated with B. F. Skinner (b. 1904), professor emeritus of psychology at Harvard University. This model is variously called instrumental conditioning, type "R" conditioning (emphasizing the *response* rather than the stimulus), and instrumental conditioning. It is also called *operant conditioning* because the behavior *operates,* or has an effect, on its environment.

In the Pavlovian model, as we have seen, much behavior is viewed as a learned but conditioned response to stimuli in the environment. Since behavior is seen as automatic and reflexive, the therapeutic procedures tend to focus on changing this behavior itself—that is, changing the individual's learned conditioned response to the controlling stimuli which elicit the behavior. Using classical conditioning techniques, the early behavior therapists stressed elimination of fear or anxiety responses by deconditioning or positive counterconditioning (such as assertion training) or by altering the emotional responses that stood in the way of more adaptive behavior (Stuart, 1977). The various procedures of the behavior therapists focused upon changing the behavior and/or the emotional responses of the individual.

The operant conditioning view of behavior seems, at least at first, a little more complex, for behavior is seen not as just an automatic, conditioned response to environmental stimuli but as taking place within an A–B–C framework. The "antecedent" events (A) which precede behavior (B) control behavior because they set the conditions under which it will provide some consequences (C). Some consequences will cause the rate of behavior to rise (the behavior will be said to be reinforced). Some consequences will cause the behavior *not* to be reinforced. The antecedent conditions are, in a sense, the rules determining which behaviors will receive which consequences. Both antecedent factors and the behaviors are functionally linked to and dependent upon the consequences. For example, when we drive our automobiles to a crossing and see a green light, we go through the crossing. The green light (A) informs us which behavior (B) is appropriate, and we are reinforced (C) for our decision to "go" by continuing uninterrupted on our trip (also, of course, by not being hit from behind, and a number of other possible consequences). If we come to a red light (A), this is the cue to "stop" (B). We stop, for if we do not, there are consequences (C) such as getting a ticket, possibly being hit by another automobile, and other aversive consequences.

Much behavior that is operant might become so automatic that we could say it is "stimulus-response." In the above case, what we originally learned through an A–B–C sequence (how to act at a traffic light) might very well become automatic, and we respond as if it were a stimulus-response. However, more often than we may consciously realize, our behavior is not an automatic, reflexive response. In the instance of the traffic light, if we were driving in a busy city at noon through an intersection crowded with traffic and with a policeman standing nearby, we would almost certainly stop at a red light. However, if we were to come to a red light in the outskirts of the city at midnight and there was no one in sight, the probability would be much higher that we would go through the red light. We might or might not violate the law, but there would be almost no aversive consequences (except for those that come from our consciences).

In the operant model, we talk not about reflexive, determined behavior but about the *probabilities* of behavior. The probabilities of behavior are determined partly by the antecedent factors but more likely by the consequences of behavior. These conditions which affect the probabilities of behavior occurring are called "contingency relations." A contingency relation is the relationship of behavior to any of the antecedent factors and/or to any of the consequences. It is these contingency relations that are the central focus of any operant behavioral analysis and therapeutic interventions. It is not behavior itself we study, nor is it the antecedent conditions themselves or the consequences themselves, but the interrelationship of the three. The operant model is a fluid, ever-changing relationship.

The operant point of view concentrates upon the environments of the individual. Behavior is seen as a function of the environment, as a response to environmental demands. The extreme behaviorist view is that ultimately all behavior is under external control. In this orientation the therapeutic task is to change the environment; the assumption is that the individual's behavior will change in response to the demands of the changed external environment. For example, in the Toronto Science Museum, all the no-smoking areas are carpeted whereas the floors in the smoking areas are not. The "external control" works; in many visits to the museum, I have never seen anyone smoking in a carpeted area. This seems to be a more effective way of "controlling" behavior than merely posting "no smoking" signs and depending upon people's "will power" or individual consciences. The principles of operant conditioning are utilized to increase the frequency of some behaviors and decrease the frequency of other behaviors, by rearranging environmental contingencies and the environmental conditions that control the rate or frequency of behaviors. This is an extremely socially oriented view. Whether the behavior is desired or undesired and whether the rate or frequency is to be increased or decreased are ultimately matters of social definition.

In comparing the change procedures used in the operant and classical approaches, we are admittedly engaging in a somewhat arbitrary differentiation. Just as some of the respondent techniques overlap or are used in combination with the operant techniques, so some of the operant procedures overlap with some of the "self-control" procedures described later in this chapter. We cannot overemphasize that the distinctions made in this book are for teaching, heuristic purposes. In actual practice there is a growing tendency for the lines between these behavioral approaches— and the divisions between the so-called behavioral and dynamic procedures, as well—to become blurred. We shall, however, present an outline of the operant procedures, procedures that focus upon helping an individual to change his behavior by manipulating environmental factors.[1] We shall begin our discussion of the A–B–C operant scheme with a discussion of consequences, since both the antecedent factors (A) and the behavior (B) are ultimately governed or controlled by the consequences (C).

The Consequences of Behavior

REINFORCEMENT OR PUNISHMENT

Generally, we can differentiate between consequences which *occur* after a behavior is emitted and consequences

[1] Since we cannot here present more than an elementary outline of the basic principles of operant conditioning, we strongly suggest that the interested reader consult an introductory textbook—for example, Reese (1978) or Sundel and Sundel (1975). For a brief overview of operant psychology, see "The Operant Model," Chapter 2, in Schwartz and Goldiamond (1975).

which are *removed* after a behavior is emitted (White, 1971). When a behavior occurs, a consequence is produced or presented. If the rate of that behavior goes up, then that consequence was a positive reinforcer and the entire procedure is called *positive reinforcement*. If somebody is speaking directly to you, you nod your head at significant points that the speaker makes. If the nodding of your head results in his continuing to talk, then your nodding of the head is a positive reinforcer. The entire procedure—his behavior (talking) followed by the positive reinforcer (your nod), followed by the rise in the rate of the behavior (his talking)—is called positive reinforcement.

It is important to recognize that the element of "intention" is not important in this conceptualization. For example, if a child jumps up and down in a classroom, the teacher yells "stop it," and the child continues to jump, we can say that the teacher's shouting (or the attention she pays to the child) is a positive reinforcer because it resulted in continuance of the child's behavior even though the behavior is undesirable from the viewpoint of the teacher. In the case of the speaker and the listener, the reinforced behavior was desirable; in the case of the child and the teacher it was undesirable (a value judgment), but both are instances of positive reinforcement. The term "positive" merely means that something has been presented rather than removed; positive does not signify desirable or "good." Positive reinforcement is the addition or presentation of a reinforcer following a behavior which tends to maintain or raise the rate of that behavior (White, 1971).

"Negative reinforcement," on the other hand, is what happens when a response results in the removal or discontinuance of some aversive stimulus. For example, a teenage daughter may clean her room in order to avoid her mother's nagging (an aversive stimulus) which does not occur if the daughter cleans her room. Therefore, the daughter cleans her room (her behavior is negatively reinforced) in order to discourage her mother's nagging. Many of our laws are based on this principle. We often obey laws to avoid unpleasant consequences rather than to gain positive consequences. We stop for a red light so that we will not receive a traffic ticket.

Two additional types of negative reinforcement may occur. One is called "escape" behavior, when an individual leaves a situation to avoid something aversive. The other is "avoidance" behavior, where an individual manages to postpone or evade something aversive. Paying taxes is an example.

Both types of reinforcement maintain or strengthen behavior, which is why they are called reinforcement. A consequence is defined as a reinforcer only "in terms of its effect upon behavior," as determined either by observation or some other empirical test, not by speculation as to an individual's inner motivation (Reese, 1978).

There are some consequences of behavior which result in lowering the strength or rate of behavior. These consequences are called "punishment." When an aversive consequence follows the occurence of a behavior, this is "positive punishment." For example, if a child does a "naughty" act, a parent slaps the child, and the behavior (naughty act) drops in frequency, this is called positive punishment—positive not because it is a good way to handle the situation (obviously it is not) but because a stimulus (a slap) is presented rather than removed.

In "negative punishment," on the other hand, something the individual desires is taken away when he performs an undesirable act. If the child, for example, misbehaves, and the parent takes away a privilege, such as watching TV and the misbehavior drops, this is called "negative punishment." Both kinds of punishment have the effect of reducing behavior. This is why they are classified as punishment.[2]

---

[2] In popular usage, however, both forms are referred to as "punishment," and both are basically aversive procedures, although they may

The concept of negative reinforcement is frequently confused with the two kinds of punishment. Both positive and negative reinforcement result in the continuation or strengthening of behavior. Both positive and negative punishment lower or eliminate behavior. The confusion is understandable because the words have popular meanings that do not conform to their technical usage in the behavioral vocabulary.

In this model the individual generally tends to engage in behaviors which produce a pleasant or satisfying state of affairs for him and to avoid behaviors which produce an unsatisfying or stressful or aversive state of affairs (Thorndike, 1898). This is the "Law of Effect." (The reader may notice that there are similarities between the Law of Effect and Freud's "Pleasure Principle.")

EXTINCTION

Sometimes behavior that has previously been reinforced or punished ceases to have any consequence when it occurs. A mother may decide that she will ignore her child's demands for water after he is in bed. If the behavior has previously been reinforced (by giving him the water or by scolding him) the rate of his asking behavior may drop. If it has been previously punished (the child denied television privileges the next day if he asked for water), the rate of asking behavior may rise. Both types of occurences have been called "extinction." Note that extinction is not the withdrawal of reinforcement or of punishment. It is simply the absence of a consequence that once occurred.

Extinction is often misapplied. For example, mothers are

---

result in behavior control. We firmly believe that punishment is to be avoided whenever possible (with some exceptions to be noted) and that positive reinforcement procedures be used in attempting to change behavior.

often told that if they ignore a child's crying it will stop (be extinguished). It will, eventually, but at least at first, it will increase in frequency and may continue at a high rate until the child is exhausted—a most undesirable way to stop a baby's crying. Extinction is a complex process closely linked with and dependent upon the schedules of reinforcement and punishment under which the behavior was learned and was being maintained.

SCHEDULES

In the Pavlovian or classical conditioning model, a response generally occurs every time the stimulus occurs. In the operant model, there is recognition that a consequence (the operant equivalent of a response) may not occur every time the particular behavior occurs. There are patterns of responses called "schedules."

If a response does occur every time a behavior occurs (every time a child completes a chore he is praised) this behavior-response sequence is called a "continuous schedule of reinforcement" (CRF). If a response does not occur every time, it is an "intermittent schedule of reinforcement." (The child may not be paid after every errand he runs but rather after several errands, or after a certain period of time.) In intermittent reinforcement the consequence may occur after a fixed or variable number of responses or may occur only after a fixed or variable period of time passes. Furthermore, the consequences of behavior can vary depending upon the *rate* of behavior within a fixed period of time (Schwartz and Goldiamond, 1975). A schedule can be a simple schedule, or it can exist in various combinations with other schedules.

A general observation is that behaviors on continuous schedules of reinforcement tend to extinguish more quickly than those that are reinforced on intermittent schedules.

For example, if a child cries for a cookie and after the fifth cry (nagging behavior on the part of the child) the parent "gives in" and supplies a cookie ("inconsistency"), the child will thereafter continue to cry for a very long time whenever he wants a cookie. The general rule is that to teach a new behavior a continual schedule of reinforcement is more effective; to maintain a behavior, an intermittent schedule of reinforcement is used.

Knowledge of schedules is specifically applicable to certain clinical conditions, such as depression (see Chapter 6). The study of schedules in animals has been quite widely developed (Ferster and Skinner, 1957), but the early assumption that the analysis of animal schedules could be transferred to the behavior of humans has not proved valid. While the results can be generalized from animals to humans to some degree, we cannot make a one-to-one analogy because of such human factors as consciousness, decision making, values, ethics, and other "soft" variables.

The Antecedents of Behavior

STIMULUS DISCRIMINATION

A given form of behavior may occur under some conditions or variables that precede the behavior and may not occur in other conditions. For example, a child may yell for a cookie when his mother is in the room because he knows from his previous experience that he will get a cookie as a result. He may not yell for a cookie when his father is in the room because he knows that the father will not give him the cookie but will scold him for yelling. The mother has become a "discriminative stimulus" for the behavior of yelling, for yelling produces a cookie and this positively reinforces the yelling behavior. The father is a discriminative stimulus for yelling to produce a punishing response. If the child's sister is in the room, she may ignore him completely, neither reinforcing nor punishing the yelling behavior. The sister is a discriminative stimulus for "no consequence" (the child will receive neither cookie nor punishment). When the child learns to yell for the cookie in the presence of the mother and not to yell in the presence of the father (perhaps, instead, to ask nicely for it), he has learned to "discriminate."

Not all stimuli are discriminative stimuli; only those that produce certain kinds of consequences.

In the example above, the yelling behavior of the child can be said to be under the stimulus control of his mother, and the "ask nicely" behavior under the control of his father. This is a two-way process of control. The child learns that he can control the response of his mother—get her to give him a cookie—if he throws a temper tantrum. The mother learns that she can control the child's behavior—stop him from yelling—if she presents him with a cookie. It is important to emphasize that this is an observable contingency relationship. Furthermore, the child has learned this behavior. Because it is learned and unadaptive behavior, it can be unlearned, and more adaptive, more mutually pleasing (less aversive) behavior can be learned in its place.

In some instances effective therapy may necessitate teaching or heightening the client's ability to discriminate. For example, the child who sings in math class and does his math homework in music class has the appropriate behaviors, but they are under inappropriate stimulus control. Teaching the child discrimination would be teaching him to engage in the appropriate behavior in the appropriate situation.

Discrimination training is a basic procedure in helping people to establish "stimulus control." Stimulus control is establishing that certain behaviors occur only under certain conditions. For example, a student should do his homework in the school library and have a coke in the lounge. He should not drink coke in the library or expect to study successfully in a noisy lounge. When people engage in the proper behavior but under the wrong stimulus condition then there is a lack of discrimination, a "lack of stimulus control" (Schwartz and Goldiamond, 1975, p. 163).

STIMULUS GENERALIZATION

When behavior that is learned in one situation is repeated in another situation, we say that "generalization" has taken place. When the client who has learned to act or behave or talk in a given way with the therapist carries that behavior out to other kinds of situations, "stimulus generalization" has occurred.

"Response generalization" occurs when training in one behavior "spreads" to another behavior. For example, if a client's listening behavior has increased, then his talking, approach behavior, etc. may also increase.

The encouragement of generalization (or transfer of learning) is an important component of the behavioral therapies and, in fact, is a significant factor—and often a problem—in *all* kinds of therapies.

BEHAVIOR: A DYNAMIC DEFINITION

A core concept in behavioral analysis is that behavior can be viewed in several different ways. It may be classified by the way an observer may see it or by the way it would be recorded on some sort of a machine. Or the behavior may be viewed in terms of the consequences it produces (Skinner, 1953). These two are often not the same. The former is called the "topographic" definition of behavior and the latter, the "consequential" or "functional" definition. Behaviors that are topographically different may be functionally similar if they produce the same consequences. Thus a man driving an automobile may put his foot on the brake, grasp the hand brake, slow down, or turn the car off the road. These are topographically different acts but they are functionally similar if they all prevent the car from hitting something (Schwartz and Goldiamond, 1975).

Another example is that a person may run his eyes over some black and white symbols (letters) on a page, which is one kind of behavior. He may then run his fingers over some raised braille dots, which is another kind of behavior. The behaviors are topographically different. However, they are functionally similar in that both may be called "reading."

Behaviors may also be topographically similar but have different functions. One person may stutter because he has not learned proper speech and is incapable of pronouncing his words correctly. Another person may stutter because the stuttering is being reinforced by the attention he receives. A third may stutter because of some sort of "hostile" (conscious or not so conscious) motivation. These are topographically similar but functionally different.

What behaviorists are most interested in is the "function" or "consequence" of behavior, which in a sense constitutes its "meaning."

Behaviors that are functionally similar may be said to be "similar operants." When we talk about operant behavior we do not talk about one behavior at a time; if we did, it would take us forever to discuss a theoretical infinity of behaviors. We must view operant behaviors as *classes* of behavior. Thus we group topographically different behaviors which are functionally (consequentially) similar as essentially the same *operant* because of the consequences these behaviors produce. By considering classes of operant behavior in an individual, we can do a behavioral analysis—assessment, diagnosis, and intervention—with a comparatively limited number of variables. In addition, intervention into one set of operants may also generalize into other stimulus situations or other kinds of operant behaviors. It is because the behavioral approaches use functional rather than topographical definitions of behavior that the operant analysis of behavior is truly "dynamic" analysis (Schwartz and Goldiamond, 1975, p. 38).

A General Approach to Operant Treatment

Intervention based on operant principles can be grouped into five steps which we shall now list and elaborate in the next chapter after we present an outline for an initial interview:

1. Ascertaining with the client what he would like the final state of affairs (his terminal repertoire) to be. Examining terminal goals will clarify what is to be changed and will also lead to step 2.

2. Clarifying what will *not* be changed, what is going well for the client. In other words, what are his strengths? What are his assets that can be utilized in the therapy process? What are the factors maintaining both adaptive behavior and behaviors that are problematic, and what are the potential ranges of reinforcers that are available to help him reach his goals?

3. Formulating an intervention program: The step-by-step *procedures* to bring the client (with his strengths) to the achievement of his terminal goals. In this phase, the managerial details of the therapy, such as appointment times, fees, requirements for records, etc., are spelled out.

4. Detailing the goals of the therapy, the procedures to be used and the mutual expectations of client and therapist. The use of a contract, which may or may not be written, is one of the distinctive features of behavioral work (Sulzer, 1962), and its adaptation for use in all therapies has been

urged by consumer groups (Adams and Orgel, 1975). Stating the specific requirements also facilitates an ongoing evaluation of the therapy (Schwartz, 1975). The contract is based upon an explicit understanding between client and therapist that emerges from the initial interview or sets of interviews.

5. Carrying out the intervention, using specific procedures, evaluating progress, and then fading out the therapist, insuring continuity and generalization (permanence of changes) and making plans for follow-up.

As in any therapy, intervention is, of course, preceded by an evaluation and assessment phase, which may take one or more interviews. In this phase there is not only evaluation of the rates and frequencies of the individual's behaviors (desired and undesired) but also an examination of the controlling contingency relationships. In other words, the individual's situation is examined within the A–B–C framework. For example, a client may report that he feels very anxious at times, to the extent that he cannot function. During the taking of a history, and a description of his current life, we would focus on those situations and times when he was anxious, and upon those times when he was not (the "A" conditions). We would also investigate the consequences ("C") of being anxious as well as the consequences of not being anxious. The relationship of the anxiety, and the anxiety behaviors (Bs) to the conditions under which the anxiety takes place, and the consequences (Cs) whether the problematic behavior is being reinforced or maintained by the consequences, would be an example of the A–B–C or contingency view of problems, in contrast to those views that concentrate upon past history and inner drive states.

In attempting to help a client change behavior through a contingency analysis, or through the use of applied behavioral analysis procedures, the emphasis is primarily on observable contingency relations (the A–B–C factors), including the contingency of the individual's history of learning or conditioning ("observable" in the sense that it is accessible through verbal behavior).

Designing the program of intervention requires analyzing the current situation, selecting goals and priorities among these goals (within ethical limitations) in specific observable behavioral (and hence measurable) terms. Carrying out the program means recording the rate of behavior both before intervention (to obtain a baseline), establishing a recording system for evaluating progress (or lack of progress), ascertaining what motivators could be used to facilitate achievement of the goals, and selecting specific procedures and the specific contingency relations to be dealt with.

Suggested Outline for an Initial Interview Based on an A–B–C Theoretical Orientation

At this point, we now present an operant behavioral interview guide, to be used by practitioners to put the approach into operation. The following outline for an initial interview is based on an A–B–C, or operant conditioning, learning paradigm.[3]

STATEMENT OF PROBLEM

1. *Can you tell me what the problem is?* or *Can you tell me how I may help you?* or *What can I help you with?* The exact wording is less important than a question to facilitate the client's talking. It is of the utmost importance that the client tell the problem in his/her own words prior to any

---

[3] This outline is a revision of Schwartz and Goldiamond, 1975, p. 79–81.

attempted specification or reformulation in behavioral terms.[4] The client *must* be given the chance to verbalize problems and, of course, to express the affect accompanying the behavioral disorder. Very few clients come to an interview complaining of "a low rate of prosocial, adaptive behavior." Most come because they are unhappy, they "feel bad," or, perhaps, because someone sent them.

2. *How long has this been a problem?* A beginning formulation of the *history* of the problem and the history of the client.

3. *Is this a problem all the time? Are there some times when this is not a problem?* Further specification of the problems mentioned above, and a beginning specification of the *conditions* under which the problem is a problem. Attempt to get to the A–B–C, especially the "A".

4. *What happens when the problem occurs? What are the reactions of others?* An attempt to get at the *consequences* or the factors which may be reinforcing the "problematic" behavior. For example, if a woman states that she can't keep the house clean, try to determine husband's "role" in the situation (does he punish cleanliness or reinforce the problem by paying undue attention?) If a husband complains that he does not seem to have sexual desire for his wife any more, ask about her responses, the effect of this on her. Again, this is an attempt to understand the problem within an A–B–C framework, this time emphasizing the "C."

5. (If not volunteered by the client.) *Has this always been a problem? Was there any time in the past when it wasn't a problem?* If client says yes to the second question what is the difference in conditions (circumstances) now compared to then?

---

[4] While previous interview guides stressed the formulation of goals first, in an attempt to shape client verbal behavior toward specifiable goals (Schwartz and Goldiamond, 1975, p. 79) this author now feels this to be an error.

6. *Are there any other problems besides the one you have mentioned so far?* It may not be necessary to ask this question, for by this time the client is usually talking about his life situation.

HISTORY

7. *Can you tell me about yourself? Where were you born?* (Usually not necessary to ask if client has answered and discussed fully the previous questions. This will usually come out without probes.) What we are after here is a developmentally oriented history, focusing on naturalistic description rather than interpretive speculations. The emphasis is on the overt and the manifest. We go back in time far enough, and deep enough, to try to determine the effects of various environments on the growing child and adult. Again, the orientation is developmental rather than genetic or stage linked. For example, we want to know if parents are alive or dead (if dead, what was the cause of death?). Siblings; where are they; what are they doing; any therapy? Where client went to school.

If the topic has not been covered by this point in the interview—and it usually will have been covered—ask about client's job and job satisfaction/dissatisfaction, etc. How he spends his non-working time: His interests, hobbies, what he does for recreation.

8. *What is the state of your health?* When did you receive your last physical?[5] Any current or past illnesses, operations, or psychotherapy (if "yes" to psychotherapy, where, with whom, what precipitated, how long, under

---

[5] While it is an excellent idea for clients to receive a medical checkup to account for possible complicating physical factors, the psychotherapist, nonmedical as well as medical, is in a better position to suggest particular areas of concern for the doctor to examine *after* he has had the initial interview.

what conditions it ended, feelings about therapy, why did not go back to previous therapist.[6] If client is a woman, details on gynecological care, including date of last exam, menstrual history, what birth control device used, etc. Do you take any medication? (Note: *Any* drug, including aspirin, antihistamines, etc.) Amount and frequency. Extent of current and past use of tobacco, alcohol, marijuana, and mood-altering drugs.

EXPECTATIONS OF THERAPY

9. At some point in the interview, generally after we have a picture of the client, his problems, his history of therapy, etc., we then ask the following question: *"You are coming here for help. Assuming we work together and everything works out well, what would life be like for you?"* This above question usually has to be followed up by such probes as "Can you be more specific?" or "How would I be able to tell?" "What would I see if I were looking at you?"

This is an attempt to encourage clients to voice their therapy goals in positive terms. Most clients come to therapy fully prepared by their past experiences to tell what they don't want, and often to tell what miserable people they are.

We are trying to help the client to indicate behaviorally

---

[6] The purpose here is to help the client verbalize his feelings about the previous therapy experience. Whether or not he perceives it as a positive one or a negative one, in most cases these feelings will sooner or later have to be ventilated and discussed to allow the current therapy to go forward. While behavior therapists tend to downplay "resistance," it is a phenomenon that must be dealt with, and feelings toward previous therapists often increase "resistance" to current therapeutic efforts.

specific goals. This is often difficult to do. Some clients will answer "to be a better person," "to have a stronger ego," "to have a happier marriage." These are all fairly nonspecific goals. In the case of "have a happier marriage," when asked for details the client might answer "We'd go out more, we'd have a more active social life." This is a step in the right direction; the client is shaping his goals. The client might then be asked about current social life, and answer that "We don't go out at all," or "We go out only every two or three months." The client might answer that she'd like to go out at least once a week. Actually, at this stage during the initial interview, the setting of precise goals (e.g., go out three times a week) is less important than focusing on the problems to be explored within the A–B–C framework, and less in terms of personal shortcoming or disturbances in traits (e.g., "We'd be less introverted" might well be used as an explanation for a limited social life, but such an explanation lends itself poorly to specific interventions).

Another good probe is to ask, *"How would this be different from the way things are now?"*

Specification of goals is a process that may or may not be completed during the first interview or the first few interviews. Sometimes, of course, when a client finishes one set of goals, other problems may be uncovered, so goal setting might have to be continued. For example, if you help a school dropout to complete his high school equivalency exam, he might then want to go on to college or vocational training, so that there is another area to work on. A therapist might help an agoraphobic woman to overcome the fear that keeps her at home, only to find that when she *can* leave the house to go out socially with her husband, she really doesn't enjoy being with him. What started out as behavioral treatment of agoraphobia might well end up as a marital counseling case.

ASSESSMENT OF CURRENT STRENGTHS

10. *What things wouldn't you change?* or *What would you leave the way it is now?* This is an attempt to find out what the client has going for him, to point out to the client—often depressed and upset—that there *are* positives in the situation. (A caution: Reassuring an anxious client too quickly through verbal behavior may not only make him more anxious but perhaps make him feel that the therapist doesn't really understand how bad things are. People experiencing stress do not want to hear how wonderful and how strong they are when they feel that they are going to pieces inside.)

This set of questions leads to the next question.

11. *What would you say your strengths are?* Just as the client is not conditioned to think of positive results of therapy beyond getting rid of his misery, so he is fully prepared to tell how miserable he is but not what he has going for him. This question is an attempt to point out to the client what assets and strengths he and the therapist can build upon, can work with to change the client's life situation. Just as the implicit message in question 9 above is hopeful, that we can change the situation, so it is the message here that the client is not helpless but has some assets, some things to work with.

12. *Is there anything else?* Anything that we left out, or didn't cover? Anything that you'd like to add to what we've talked about? The purpose of this catchall question is to jog the client's memory, or to go back to add information, perhaps that he was not comfortable to bring up during the session, to correct erroneous impressions and so forth. Of course, during the course of any therapy additional information will be obtained, additional problems may emerge, and the order of importance or salience of the problems may change.

13. *I've asked you a lot of questions. Are there any questions you'd like to ask me?* Generally this question is met with surprise, sometimes with silence and often with an initial "no," for the dominant tendency in therapy seems to be that the therapist should be a blank, a "mirror" on which the client should project his feelings. We feel that a client has the right—if not the obligation—to find out more about the person to whom he has told so much. In a sense, the client is hiring the therapist. The therapist must sometimes facilitate clients' questioning with a prompt, for often they will respond with a surprised "What do you mean?" They might then ask questions about where the therapist studied, how long, or personal questions such as "Are you married?" "Do you have children?" and so forth. Sometimes they will use this set of questions to voice some anxiety about themselves and their future, such as "Have you ever treated a case like mine before?"

After the initial interview, the usual procedure is for the therapist to give the client some feedback as to his view of the problem, a preliminary statement as to whether or not the therapist thinks the problem is one that may best be treated through "behavioral" means. It may not be possible to make this judgment after merely one interview. If additional interviews are necessary for diagnostic assessment, this should be made clear.

As soon as possible in the process, the client and therapist agree on the goals of the therapy and the mechanics, such as hours of meeting, fees, mutual expectations, and so forth. These details of the process of therapy are included in the *contract*. If client and therapist are unable to agree immediately upon a contract, then they may contract to make a contract. In chapter 6 we shall illustrate examples of initial interviews, therapeutic contracts and the process (condensed) of the conduct of a case.

Summary

The predominant behavioral orientation in the United States is the operant conditioning approach of B. F. Skinner. In this view, phenomena are viewed within an A–B–C framework. The antecedent events (A) set the rules or conditions under which the behavior (B) is consequented (C), i.e., either reinforced (raised in rate or frequency), punished (decreased in frequency), or extinguished (neither reinforced nor punished). In the A–B–C model we speak of the probability of behavior, determined partly by antecedent factors but primarily by the consequences of the behavior. Therapy based upon this model consists of the analysis of the interrelationships of these factors (called contingency relationships) which then provides the basis for interventions. Behavior, as well as affects and cognitions, is seen as a function of these contingency relationships.

Each of these contingencies is related to a technology for intervention. Some antecedent conditions specify whether the behavior will be reinforced, punished, or extinguished. There are methods related to consequences: Reinforcement procedures (which raise the rate of behavior) and punishment and extinction, which usually lower the rates of behavior. Learning to connect the appropriate behavior (B) and consequences (C) to the appropriate antecedents (A) is called "discrimination."

We presented an outline for an initial interview, focusing on a statement of the current problems, conditions where the problem is a problem and conditions where it is not a problem, review of past history, specification of outcome expectations and requirements, delineations of strengths and assets on which to base intervention, and summary questions and suggestions for feedback.

Chapter 4

Applications of Operant Conditioning: Self-Control

Operant procedures focus on essentially the following therapeutic tasks:

1. Some behaviors are not in an individual's repertoire and need to be learned by him.
2. Some behaviors occur but need to be increased in frequency.
3. Some behaviors occur but under the wrong situations and need to be emitted in the right situations.
4. Some behaviors exist but must be either reduced in frequency or eliminated altogether.
5. When a behavior is learned, strengthened, weakened, or eliminated altogether, there remains the problem of maintaining the treatment effects and/or generalizing (transferring) these effects into other situations.

Teaching New Behaviors

SHAPING

When the therapist and the client agree on what the "new behavior" should be in its final form, they can then examine the client's present behavior patterns to see if any components of the desired final behavior are currently in his repertoire. The therapist then helps the client to reinforce those behaviors that are part of the desired final response (differential reinforcement) and does not reinforce (extinguish) those behaviors or parts of behaviors that do not resemble the final behavior. This "shaping" procedure is usually done in very small and often slow steps toward the final goal. For example, with one client we arrived at a terminal goal of "independence." One component (subgoal) of "independence," in specific terms for this man, was driving an automobile. The client had no driving experience in his current relevant repertoire. He could, however, read and he could take public transportation. These behaviors were steps in achieving the final subgoal—driving a car. The first program steps were to take a bus to the motor vehicle bureau, fill out an application for a learner's permit, and read the driving manual. The next steps were to call a driving school, take one lesson, then two lessons, and so on until the final step was taking the driving test. This led to another set of steps toward obtaining a car, and so forth.

Step-by-step shaping is also called the "method of successive approximations." The focus is on reinforcing "approximations" closer and closer to the final goal. This method is a basic element in most operant training programs but has particular usefulness in the areas of overlap between education and therapy—for example, in teaching self-care skills and behaviors (such as toilet training, self-dressing) to the mentally handicapped (and others), training stutterers to become fluent speakers, improving student behaviors in schools, and teaching social skills to skill-deficient ("shy") people. In the last category, shaping may be part of the process for helping a socially ill-at-ease young man approach a young woman and ask her for a date. If he is a student, we might begin having him approach grandmotherly women in the university cafeteria, then younger and younger women (perhaps from middle-aged married women to unmarried middle-aged women to married younger women to unmarried younger women) and then reinforce those approach behaviors such as conversation, etc. Part of the shaping might be to have the young man strike up a conversation with a young woman, extend the conversation, ask her for her lecture notes, then engage her in conversation, then invite her to have a cup of coffee, then ask her out for a date.

CHAINING

Most behavior takes place not in isolation but as part of a string of behaviors, called a chain. The completion of one part of a chain is a step toward the next part of the chain. For example, driving an automobile is a complex set of events, which are chained. Putting the key in the lock is reinforced by hearing the lock open. The lock turning then becomes the discriminative stimulus (cue) for the next behavior of opening the door. Opening the door, which is the reinforcement for the previous behavior, becomes the cue for entering the car, then sitting down, then closing the door, then inserting the key, then turning the key, and so forth until we actually drive away in the automobile. Learning to drive involves learning each step of a very complex chain, and learning them in the order necessary to complete the task of driving the automobile.

The examination of behavioral chains is useful in many educational situations, such as teaching mentally handicapped children, but it is also very important in such clinical conditions as marital counseling, where the therapist is concerned not so much with one part of behavior as with a pattern of behavior, such as the frequent arguments between partners. Here one event is the first part of a behavioral chain that leads to the second event, usually with disastrous results. One therapeutic technique is to help the couple intervene and alter the parts of the chains so that they lead to different end results. For example, a man comes home from work and, when his wife opens the door, he says, "Hello, how are you?" She immediately responds, "The refrigerator broke, Johnny hit Jimmy and broke his tooth, and the kitchen sink overflowed." The husband might then turn away from his wife, take a beer from the refrigerator, slam the door, turn on TV, and fume silently throughout dinner and for the rest of the evening. His wife may then feel hurt, rejected, and angry at his lack of support. Neither of them would be aware of why he or she was so angry with the other. Examining the chain of events might very well show that the husband is indeed sympathetic and supportive, but that he perceived his wife's greeting as an assault and her lack of personal interest as a rejection. If the wife were to change her initial behavior to a warm greeting and postpone the complaints to a later time, such as after dinner, this would interrupt the destructive chain of events and set up a different chain where each got what he or she wanted: Warmth, understanding, and support.

PROMPTING AND FADING

We may also wish to help clients place behavior under more appropriate discriminative stimulus control by using a prompting or a fading procedure. A "prompt" directs the person's attention to the behavior required. It may be a verbal hint or a sign or a light or any other form of signal. For example, a therapist attempting to teach a child some new activity, such as an orthopedic exercise, may start by guiding the child's arms and legs through the entire sequence of motions. Gradually the therapist guides him less and less, first for only part of the actions, then not on the legs, and then partly on the arms and then not on the arms at all but with verbal prompts only. Finally she eliminates the verbal prompts as the child learns the activity (Sundel and Sundel, 1975, p. 102).

As a behavior is learned, the "prompts" are gradually removed until the individual is doing the behavior without them. The procedure of removing the prompts is called "fading." Fading is used to ensure that new behaviors remain part of the individual's behavioral repertoire.

Increasing the Frequency of Behavior

POSITIVE REINFORCEMENT

The most frequently used and certainly the most ethically desirable methods of behavioral intervention are based on the principle of positive reinforcement. In the counseling situation, positive reinforcement procedures can be used to help patients increase the rates of desirable behavior without the use of punishment procedures for eliminating behavior that is undesirable. One prime principle, stated by Wolpe, is to reinforce behavior that is incompatible with the undesirable behavior, on the theory that one cannot engage in behavior that is desired and at the same time engage in behavior that is undesired. Actively exercising is incompatible with passively lying in bed.

Positive reinforcement is used, planfully and not so planfully, throughout most counseling situations. The responses of the therapist—nodding his head or saying "uh-huh"—are often powerful positive reinforcers that sometimes maintain the verbal behavior of the client.

We have noted that the term "reinforcement," like many other words in the behavioral vocabulary, has a specific technical meaning in addition to its "common sense" meaning. A reinforcement is not the same as a "reward" although sometimes things an individual considers rewards can also be reinforcers. A positive reinforcer is an event (the consequence) that follows a behavior (or behavior sequence) which results in the rate or frequency of that behavior either being maintained or increased. It need not always be something "good" or something the person likes. For example, ice cream (a reward for most of us) *may* function as a positive reinforcer if a child (or an adult) will work for it, and if the presentation of ice cream will result in a rise in the rate or frequency of behavior. However, as in the example given earlier, if a teacher yells at a child, this seemingly aversive act (meant to be a punishment) might result not in the child's stopping the undesirable behavior of jumping up and down but in his increasing it, because of the attention it brings him. In this case, the teacher's reaction has served as a "positive reinforcer."

Too many therapists interpret this term incorrectly. They feel that if they do or say "something nice" in response to a client's action that they want to encourage him to repeat, this will be or act as a "positive reinforcer." Unfortunately, this is not so. Just as the goals of behavioral intervention should be spelled out in specific terms, so the procedure of "positive reinforcement" should not be left to what the therapist thinks the client would like but should be based on information (observation, if possible) about the *effects* of the consequence on the client's behavior. The ultimate empirical question is "Does it raise (or maintain) the rate of behavior?" If it does, then it is a "positive reinforcer." Any use of positive reinforcement as a technique or procedure of behavior change should involve an analysis of a number of factors, including the use of the problem assessment procedures.

It is possible to use a number of kinds and forms of reinforcers. Sometimes a problem situation is so serious, as with autistic children who are badly deteriorated or regressed, that the primary, unconditioned, unlearned reinforcers, such as food and water, are the only ones these children can respond to. They cannot immediately respond to learned reinforcers such as smiles or human companionship, and certainly not to items such as coins, etc.

Secondary reinforcers have to be learned. They include praise, higher grades, money, social approval, and the like. Not all of these are reinforcing to everyone, for not everything a person may consider "pleasant" or a "reward" will have the specific effects on behavior that are central to the definition of a reinforcer.

An important secondary reinforcer is money. Most of us will work for—in fact, we *have* to work for—this conditioned reinforcer called "money." Money is also a "generalized reinforcer," for it can be used in a number of situations, and by most people. Generalized reinforcers such as money are effective in maintaining behavior, not because they are valuable in themselves, but because they can be exchanged for an almost infinite variety of other things people want. These "things" are called "backup reinforcers"; it is because a reinforcer such as money has so many "backup reinforcers" that it is so successful in maintaining behavior. Money is rarely coveted for its sake alone except by pathological misers. One particular "generalized reinforcer," the "token," can be exchanged for backup reinforcers. We shall discuss the "token economy" later in this chapter.

Positive reinforcers must possess certain characteristics. The consequence, which is the positive reinforcer, should follow only (or primarily) upon the performance of the desired behavior. It should be *contingent* upon the behavior (Reese, 1978), something that the client does not have free access to, and something he will want to work for. Further, the reinforcer should be given immediately after the behavior, so that the client is aware of *what* behavior is being reinforced. (We shall discuss below alternate ways of handling the "immediacy of reinforcer" problem.) If there is a delay the reinforcement may follow (in time) some *other* behavior, and the client would not know what is being reinforced. These rules also apply for punishment behavior. The child who is told "just wait till your father comes home!" and then is spanked five hours later often doesn't have the foggiest idea of *why* he is being spanked.

The amount of the reinforcer is crucial. Too much and the client will be satiated; too little and he will get discouraged and figure that it isn't worth the effort to acquire the reinforcement. The reinforcement should be consistent; if the client is flooded with reinforcement when he does the behavior once, he will be confused if he does not receive the same amount the next time he does it. For example, one student teacher, in a misapplication of the principles, promised a silent student a candy bar each time the student raised her hand and asked a question. From a previous rate of zero, the student asked twelve questions the first day, and even more the second day. The flabbergasted student teacher, seeing her own spending money disappear, raised the behavioral requirement drastically, giving one candy bar for every seven questions. The disappointed, and angry, student immediately stopped raising her hand and asking questions.

There can be many ways to potentiate an event to be a reinforcer. One way is to let the client "sample" the list of reinforcers (called a "reinforcement menu"). (The procedure of reinforcer sampling is discussed by Homme, 1969, and by Ayllon and Azrin, 1968.) Also relevant are modeling procedures (see Chapter 5), where a client may see someone else enjoy the reinforcer. Still another way is not to allow yourself the reinforcer until you do something—let us say—you are avoiding. One example of this procedure—called the Premack Principle—is to allow yourself to watch TV (a high-probability behavior) *only* after you have studied (a low-probability behavior).

There is a distinction between the *learning* of behavior and the *maintenance* of behavior. In learning, as we have stated above, initially each act should be reinforced. As the behavior becomes part of the repertoire, the reinforcement can then be switched to an intermittent schedule to maintain the behavior. There should not be sudden shifts in "reinforcer density," for these shifts are very likely to confuse and bewilder the client. If there are shifts, these should be explained to the client.

The behavioral literature illustrating the use of positive reinforcement procedures is enormous.[1] These procedures are being used with respondent as well as operant techniques and are also an integral part of the self-control, modeling, and cognitive-behavioral approaches to be discussed later in this book.

THE TOKEN ECONOMY

As we stated above, a token is a generalized reinforcer which, like money, may be later exchanged for items that a person wants (called "backup reinforcers"). A token economy is a system of behavior management or of behavior reinforcement which simply states that certain behaviors are required and that upon doing these behaviors the individual will be given tokens. Ideally, the required behaviors and the standards as to whether or not the requirements are being met are determined jointly by the therapist and client.

The use of tokens makes it possible to reinforce immedi-

---

[1] Numerous illustrations may be found in Gambrill (1977), in Leitenberg (1976), and in almost every issue of such journals as *Behavior Therapy* and *The Journal of Applied Behavior Analysis*, as well as psychology and psychiatry journals considered to be nonbehavioral. The concepts, as well as the practice, are also increasingly noted in social work journals. For a more comprehensive "entry" into the vast literature of behavior therapy, see the Appendix.

ately, without delay, at any time in order to maintain performance. (Performance is usually not affected by a delay in the obtaining of the backup reinforcer.) They can be used to shape sequences of behavior without interruption. Tokens lessen the probability of satiation or overdeprivation. They also provide uniform reinforcement for different individuals with different tastes, for people can select different backup reinforcers (one child might trade in his tokens for candy, another for balloons, a third for pencils). The tokens can be saved (and sometimes hoarded, unfortunately). They can be durable (and sometimes subject to counterfeiting).

The token economy is the most widely known and the most widely used of the operant procedures. Unfortunately, it is also the most widely misused of all of the operant procedures. When properly used, can be positive and constructive motivational tools. The token economy may also be called a "motivational system," as there is a very positive message that the problematic behavior can be changed, and we are going to help you change it.

In mental hospitals, for example, patients are reinforced with tokens for cleaning up their rooms, making their beds, socializing, kitchen work, self-care activities, and almost all of the daily events of living. Certain privileges, such as passes, may "cost" a certain number of tokens. These tokens may also buy cigarettes, toiletries, and a number of other items (the "reinforcement menu"). With mentally handicapped children, for example, tokens may be awarded for reading, writing, and a number of activities and exchanged for toys, candy, and other things that will "motivate" these children to learn.

Setting up, carrying out, and the eventual fading out of the token economy are complicated tasks, requiring thorough knowledge of the procedures and a great deal of thought, planning, and trial-and-error experimentation. The behaviors to be changed have to be spelled out in specific terms ("sweep under your bed" instead of "be a good child"). The reinforcers, both currently and potentially available, have to be identified. The "reinforcement menu" must also be identified. Whenever possible it is highly desirable to have the person applying the token economy and the person to whom it is applied decide the items jointly. This can be done with very young children, with the mentally handicapped, and with the mentally ill. The procedure of "reinforcer sampling" can help to identify which reinforcers will "work" and which will not work. Then the tokens have to be established as conditioned reinforcers. If token economies are used aversively as a way of guaranteeing compliance, they will often be sabotaged and resisted by the people whose behavior one is trying to change. There are instances of prisons and correctional institutions which have used token economies as ways of repression and control (Rest, 1973).

In addition to the problems of spelling out the behaviors, the reinforcers to maintain the behaviors, and the methods of accounting, there are problems in applying the token economies (see Kazdin and Bootzin, 1972, 1973; and Kazdin, 1977). First of all, staff must receive additional training. There is often staff resistance to applying the new procedures, especially if the staff has had a long history of keeping people in line through the use of aversive procedures. In institutions the staff begins to pay attention to and reinforce positive behaviors rather than focus on eliminating "bad" behaviors (usually with aversive, repressive measures). "The 'norm' becomes 'health,' and it is 'health' that gets the token" (Schwartz and Goldiamond, 1975, p. 50).

A great number of people, particularly parents, have difficulty in applying the token economies because they see them as bribery and believe that the child should behave through "inner motivation." It is the goal of the token economies to reinforce externally only until the token economy can be phased out and the behavior maintained by "intrinsic" rather than "extrinsic" reinforcers.

Another problem with the token economy is that often the results do not generalize once the person is out of the institution or once the token economy is not in effect. There are problems both of stimulus generalization (application of the same behavior in other situations) and response generalization (change "spreading" to different behaviors).

Often the clients will resent a token economy, for a number of reasons. They may try to get either the reinforcers or the tokens without carrying out the behavior. This resistance may be justified if the token economy has been applied without consulting them first.

The token economy has been applied in a number of settings with a wide variety of clients (see Schwartz and Goldiamond, 1975, pp. 49–53; Kazdin, 1977; Agras, 1978 and Ayllon and Azrin, 1968) such as psychotic patients in institutions to outpatients, juvenile delinquents, married couples, mentally retarded and handicapped children, soldiers, autistic children, students in classrooms at all levels from preschool to college, and a host of other types of clients, settings, and problem situations.

Two reports published almost simultaneously describe similar negative effects of the token economy in hospital settings. Biklen (1976) reported a situation where students applied a token economy, designed by one of their professors, in a state hospital. This token economy resulted in a not-so-subtle form of social control. The students' enthusiasm and spontaneity were interpreted as a kind of charity and indirectly reinforced the idea that it was "not the environment, the hospital, the society, the situation that they had trouble coping with, that constituted the problem" (ibid, p. 57), but the patients themselves who were basically at fault.

Biklen's comments were backed up in a report by Zeldow (1976), who also investigated a token economy. The program he investigated was "established to combat patient passivity with planned activity, to encourage the kinds of behaviors necessary to obtain satisfaction in the community, and to keep patients working toward discharge through a better method of rehabilitation" (ibid., p. 319), as well as to improve staff morale. Zeldow found that the program did provide "badly needed extrinsic motivation to those patients already institutionalized" (ibid.)

However, he also found that the patients saw the token economy as infantilization, thought it often was too difficult to earn points, and believed that there was unequal treatment from the staff. Above all, the token economy relieved staff of the necessity of handling conflict. Zeldow found the staff rigid, arbitrary, and insensitive in applying the token economy. He concluded that the token economy was too good a control system, overemphasizing the extrinsic and the external. Many patients did perform the target behaviors but with no change in their symptoms or emotions which precipitated admission into the state hospital.

Zeldow's most serious complaint was that the token economy tended to circumvent the patient government. Many of the patients' complaints related to the token system were actually complaints against staff and personnel. These were never discussed directly; instead the patient government meetings were spent on the technicalities of the token economy. The interpersonal relations between staff and patients were downplayed in favor of a bureaucratic relationship.

The experiences reported by Biklen and Zeldow are familiar to many behavior therapists. It is not uncommon for families with adolescent children to ask a therapist for permission to set up a token economy to "straighten this kid out." Almost invariably what the parents want the therapist to do is to set up a system which will make their teenager "behave," that is, guarantee conforming behavior. Of course, this is usually not what the teenager wants. He may formally acquiesce, but he often has no intention whatsoever of following rules set up by the parents and the therapist, "rules" which he sees as authoritarian. It goes without saying that these token economies will fail. The result will be a system that will control rather than heal or change the patient for the better.

The token economy does, however, provide a neutral ground which enables two individuals—say, a teacher and a pupil, or a parent and a child—to relate to each other in a different manner. The token economy is a way in which each person can change his behavior and still save face. In a sense, the use of a token economy "cools off" the situation, enabling people to relate to each other differently.

One further comment on token economies. There are many instances in which token economies were established as a demonstration, with no plans for the token economy to become a permanent part of the institution (Malott, 1974). The token economy then either is discontinued or deteriorates into a repressive measure more than an aid to therapy.

In our opinion the best use of the token economies is not as a method of behavior change by itself but as part of a more comprehensive system of therapy.

CONTINGENCY CONTRACTING

In the token economy, there is a specification of mutual expectations. Both parties agree to fulfill certain behavioral requirements in exchange for certain consequences. These statements of mutually agreed-upon expectations may also be called "behavioral contracts." The "contracts," which may be oral or written agreements, can also be used in their own right (Schwartz and Goldiamond, 1975, pp. 53–55) in various clinical situations such as with parents and children (Reese, 1978, 873–78), very young children (Christopherson et al., 1972), with delinquents (Levitt, et al., 1978; Stuart, 1971, Stuart and Lott, 1972), and with prisoners (Rest, 1973).

One of the most promising areas is in the treatment of marital discord (Stuart, 1969). A very good way to break the cycle of arguments and mutual recriminations is to help the couple make their expectations of each other clear, specific, behavioral, positive, and realistic (Stuart, 1969, 1976). The therapist then asks each partner to specify what he or she will do in return for these behaviors. Then a contract is set up in which each states a commitment to carry out the provisions of the contract. The contracting may often be for matters that seem peripheral if not irrelevant to the main problem areas. However, this can be an advantage, for once the couple can agree upon these issues they may have reestablished communication and a way of negotiating with each other so they can then proceed to issues that are more central to their problems.

For example, a highly disturbed woman who had been hospitalized several times was seen with her husband who had not been hospitalized, although his behavior and his expectations of her were often quite bizarre. Among the many complaints her husband voiced was that she was sexually cold, would not engage in fellatio, and did not keep the house clean. Her reply was that he was inconsiderate to her and even brutal at times and that she did not feel like having sex with him when he treated her that way. On the rare occasions when they did communicate, such as on a Sunday when they both were free of other pressures, they did get along and the sexual interaction was pleasant. The wife also complained that she often had to use public transportation to get to work, which took her at least an hour, but that when he drove her it took only fifteen minutes. Sometimes he would not let her know until the last possible minute whether he was going to drive her, and he would use last-minute cancellation of the ride as a way to punish her by making her late for work. She would then retaliate—for example, by not ironing the shirt he wanted to wear to work.

The first part of the behavioral contracting, to which both agreed, was the he was to drive her to work every day, and she was to iron his shirt every day. If one member did not fulfill his or her part, the other was to remind the other of this omission before refusing to do his/her share. A ride to work and an ironed shirt certainly were not the factors that brought this couple into therapy, and they were most certainly not the most central and pressing issues in the relationship. However, precisely because they were peripheral *but important,* and the subject of many negative interactions, they were a good place to begin contracting with this couple. The contracting and the therapeutic work proceeded to a number of other housekeeping chores. As the couple learned that they could deal with each other around these "peripheral" issues without destroying each other, the therapy moved on to more central issues of love, commitment, power, etc.

Behavioral contracting, like the token economies, is a direct but deceptively simple technique that actually can be quite complex. The therapist should use them with care, and if he does not have a background in behavioral psychology he may want to consult with someone. Stuart and Lott (1972) point out that the use of contracting with delinquents is fraught with difficulties and that, in the final analysis, it may not be the contracts themselves that are the cause of change but the *process* of contracting, the changing of communication patterns between the people who make the contract. Similarly, Jacobson and Margolin (1979) stated that in treating marital couples the contracting was of less utility than training the couple in problem solving. We feel that their comments have utility for other classes and types of clients (see chapter 5 for a discussion of "problem solving").

Stimulus Control: Putting the Right Behavior in the Right Situation

Occasionally behaviors are acceptable in themselves but occur in the wrong situation—that is, under the wrong stimulus control. We mentioned above the young man who sings in math class but does math homework in music class and the student who socializes in the library and attempts to study in the lounge. The appropriate behaviors are certainly there, but they are not performed in the proper circumstances.

While both antecedents (A) and behavior (B) are ultimately under the control of the consequences (C), helping the client to change the antecedent conditions (the stimulus-control factors) often is an effective way to teach or reinforce behavior. Profound changes can occur by putting behavior under the appropriate stimulus control. For example, for a student, the library table (or a specific table at home, not in the bedroom and not facing the TV set) is established as the appropriate *place* to study. He is to work at the table, and there are procedures to insure that he continues (for example, if his mind wanders, he is to get up and go into the lounge, where he may then socialize). Time at each activity may be graphed by the student so that he can have immediate feedback. Study behavior will be reinforced when the line of the graph of studying behavior goes up.

We also want to help train the individual to generalize behavior from one set of stimuli to another. If the behavior is learned in the classroom and/or in the therapeutic office, we want to help him to transfer that behavior into new situations.

When we work with one behavior, other behaviors may change through response generalization. If we help a client to change his eating patterns, there may also be changes in exercise, dressing, self-care, and other physical fitness kinds of behaviors.

Stimulus control procedures are central to "self-control," where we work with individuals to help them analyze conditions and to set up their own contingencies to control behavior. They can be used not only to make behavior appropriate to the situation but to raise or lower the frequency of a behavior. For example, rather than scold a child who jumps up and down in class (thus reinforcing this undesirable behavior), the teacher might tell him that he could jump up and down as much as he liked, *outside* the classroom, away from her (and his classmates') reinforcing attention. The probability is that this disruptive behavior in class would drop in frequency (unless, of course, the child *liked* being away from class).

Another example is a young man who was consistently sulking and engaging in other problematic behavior with his wife. His therapist suggested that he could sulk all he wanted but should do so at a special "sulking stool" in the garage. The sulking behavior soon dropped in frequency (Goldiamond, 1965). A therapist dealing with a client who wishes to stop smoking might suggest that he can smoke as much as he likes as long as he wears a special smoking jacket, or smokes in a particular place. He may eliminate ashtrays from some rooms and put them only in restricted places, such as the living room (Novar, 1976).

There are discriminative stimuli (cues) that indicate whether certain behaviors will be either reinforced or punished, or not consequented at all (extinction). These "cues" or "rules" can be used to bring the behavior under appropriate stimulus control. This is often done in treating such conditions as obesity. Many obese people tend to eat in a number of settings; while watching TV, reading, working at their desks, and doing other things. In addition to reducing the amount they eat, we attempt to bring eating under strict stimulus control. For example, eating is to be a "pure" procedure; the client should not eat while watching TV, reading, etc. Furthermore, he is encouraged to eat only at one specific spot (preferably not where food is prepared) and to use distinctive reminders or cues such as a placemat (Stuart and Davis, 1972; Mahoney and Mahoney, 1976).

Stimulus control procedures are extremely useful in childrearing. Smith and Smith (1976) emphasize the importance of parents making clear their behavioral expectations of children—that is, establishing the "rules" they will use to control the behavior of their children. Many parent-child problems are related to vague and indistinct rules. Having clear, realistic rules which are not aversive provides security for the child because he knows what behavior is expected and what will be the consequences of both doing the behavior and not doing the behavior. The parent should be consistent in applying these procedures, but once again, we caution the reader not to substitute rigidity for flexibility. The rules should never become the ultimate standard but should serve as a guide to parent-child relations.

Sometimes we can help the individual weaken or eliminate behaviors that he does not wish to occur. Basically the procedure is to help remove the cues for the behavior he wants to lessen in frequency and to provide stronger cues for behaviors that he wishes to increase. Incidentally, the cues need not be a physical place but often can be an individual. For example, a therapist is a cue or stimulus situation for talking about one's personal problems. It might be very desirable to eliminate the cues for talking about personal problems with one's nosy neighbors and to strengthen the therapist as a cue for talking about one's problems.

Attempts to change behavior through stimulus control are most effective when combined with positive reinforcement of the desired behavior. There are a number of ways to establish stimulus control, including the use of verbal instructions (put the big toy in the box before the little ones), by setting an example (mother might unfold napkin, then deliberately take fork in right hand, etc. to show table manners), or by fading (mother might first give detailed instructions on putting dirty clothes into hamper, then only say "clothes in hamper," then "are your dirty clothes put away?" then "ready for breakfast?").

Eventually, the management of stimulus control should be switched from the therapist to the client himself. Once the client learns the principles of self-control, he himself can ultimately control the stimulus conditions.

Reducing or Eliminating Behaviors

In the earlier days of the behavior therapies, much of the emphasis was placed on eliminating and reducing undesirable behaviors, particularly behaviors that were defined as "excessive," such as children talking out loud in the classroom or, more important, addictions to alcohol, drugs, food, etc. Critics of these early behavior therapies have justifiably stated that eliminating undesirable behaviors alone was not sufficient; the individual had to learn new behaviors to take the place of those that were eliminated.

Unfortunately, many of the procedures used to eliminate behaviors are aversive. However, to reduce excessive behavior or eliminate it completely, it is usually best to use a combination of procedures. For example, if one uses a punishment procedure to eliminate behavior, it should be coupled with a procedure designed to reinforce or help the individual attain the desired behavior, as is described in the next section.

REINFORCEMENT OF INCOMPATIBLE BEHAVIOR

An ideal way to help a client eliminate or reduce behavior is to reinforce behavior that is basically incompatible with the undesired behavior. In an early study, Stuart (1967a), working with a depressed religious woman, had her translate sections of the Bible when she was depressed, for she could not be depressed and revel in the glory of God at the same time. Reinforcing the behavior of being on time is incompatible with being late, just as behaviors that keep oneself neat eliminate behaviors that result in a sloppy appearance.

With particular reference to children, many parents regard "good" behavior as behavior that is to be expected and ignore it when it happens, but they are quick to punish undesired behavior. A better procedure would be to reinforce behavior that will eliminate the undesirable behavior. For example, to eliminate behavior such as coming to the table with dirty hands, they might reinforce coming to the table with clean hands. Rather than punish the dirty-hand behavior they should always praise (and reinforce) clean hands.

EXTINCTION

Behavior is often maintained by its consequences. If a behavior has previously been reinforced—for example, by the teacher's giving special attention to a child who acts up in class—one way to eliminate it might be not to pay any attention to it at all. Ignoring a behavior that has previously been reinforced (or punished) is putting the behavior on "extinction." This procedure is effective only if it is followed 100 percent of the time. Behavior must be completely ignored. If one responds to behavior every fifth or tenth or fifteenth time, one is reinforcing on an intermittent schedule, and behavior reinforced intermittently is very resistant to extinction, because of the *inconsistency*.

Extinction is basically an aversive procedure. The immediate response is generally that the individual tends to increase the behavior. Thus the parents who apply extinction by ignoring a child's temper tantrums will find that the temper tantrums, at first, will increase. This is understandable, for the behavior has worked in the past for the child, and he or she merely increases the tempo. From the viewpoint of the child, being ignored when in the past he was reinforced is extremely aversive.

Once again, extinction by itself merely eliminates an undesired behavior and does not strengthen a desired behavior. Extinction is more effective when combined with positive reinforcement.

Behavior usually does not extinguish on a straight line. There may be outbursts of behavior long after it is thought to be extinguished. For example, a person who has not smoked for years may suddenly have a desire for a cigarette, unrelated to any known stress. In such cases, people generally think that the previous therapy has failed. The phenomenon of extinction should be explained very carefully to clients, anticipating that there may be bursts of behaviors in the future. It is true that this may result in "self-fulfilling prophesy" but we have found that when individuals come in depressed after having "binged," explaining the phenomenon of extinction and that this is not a permanent change of behavior often reassures them and enables them to reinstate desired behavior.

PUNISHMENT

Punishment, in the operant sense, is a response following the occurrence of a behavior that tends to lower the rate of that behavior. "Positive punishment," most familiar as spanking and corporal punishment, is not recommended as a way of reducing behavior because it constitutes aggression by the punisher. Aggression produces emotional responses such as counteraggression and, more important, avoidance behavior and escape behavior in the person who is being punished. This is one of the technical difficulties of applying punishment; the punisher must have control over a great number of the contingencies. In addition, punishment must occur on a fairly heavy schedule to have a marked effect. Behavior that is not consistently punished may be reinforced.

The primary objections are ethical ones. Punishment procedures can be all too easily abused, as the literature testifies (Chaiklin, 1973). Too many of us, as individuals, are conditioned to use aversive more than positive procedures in attempting to control or change behavior. The aversive procedures are immediately reinforcing to the punishers. The parent who spanks his child relieves a little of his own tension. However, the punishment procedures tend not to be used by a great number of behavior therapists.

Whenever possible, therapists should use positive reinforcement. However, there are times when the patient's condition is so serious that it cannot be changed by any procedure other than punishment. Lovaas and his associates (1973), for example, use aversive procedures in dealing with extremely deteriorated, often low I.Q. children who engage in self-destructive and self-mutilating behaviors. However, Lovaas has abandoned his early use of electric shock for milder aversives such as shouting and slapping, always on a carefully planned basis. In addition, he combines his punishment procedures with positive reinforcement. A child who is punished is immediately given the opportunity to engage in the desired behavior, for which he is highly reinforced. In a moving film of Lovaas's early work[2] a young child named Karen was exhibiting bizarre behavior in response to requests to identify the color of a crayon. Lovaas, in the film, slapped Karen on the thigh and said

[2]Lovaas, O. I., Birnbarauer, J., and Schaefer, H. H., *Reinforcement Therapy*, 45 Minutes, 16 mm. Black and White, sound, 1966. Produced by Smith, Kline, and French Laboratories, available from the American Medical Association Film Library, 535 North Dearborn Street, Chicago, Illinois 60610.

"You tell." Karen's bizarre behavior immediately stopped, she gave the correct color of the crayon, the therapist reinforced Karen both verbally ("very good") and physically (she hugged Karen), and the remainder of the session proved to be a positive learning experience for the child.

Aversive procedures are therapies of last resort. They should never be used without ethical and legal safeguards, including review by committees for the protection of human rights, the appointment of legal advocates for the client, and the close involvement and always the permission of the family of the involved patient—in short, informed consent, with the client's free access to other opinions.

While we are not attempting to justify the use of aversive procedures, it is unfortunate that research in this area has been discouraged by a combination of public prejudice and justifiable reactions to their misuse by therapists who irresponsibly treat clients as experimental subjects rather than suffering human beings. However, as we have stated earlier, for some clients the verbal, evocative therapies are inappropriate or ineffective. Baer, whose own work is based overwhelmingly on the use of positive principles, notes that by not using aversive procedures to eliminate very destructive behaviors we may be condeming these people to live out the remainder of their lives in a "small hell" or a "state of recurrent punishment" (Baer, 1970). "Can we now refuse that they endure a small number of painful episodes over a short span of sessions, hopefully designed to let them live the rest of their lives awake and untied?" (ibid., p. 246). He points out that we need to investigate not only in what situations punishment may be helpful in eliminating these serious conditions but also what combinations might be used to shorten the therapy and to make it more effective. He particularly advocates the combination of punishment and other procedures with the procedures of positive reinforcement (Baer, 1970, discussed in Schwartz and Goldiamond, 1975, p. 254).

It is our opinion that these punishment procedures should be considered only by therapists who are attached to institutions where there are adequate safeguards for the rights of the human subjects. We do, however, include them in this volume, in part for completeness, in part to inform those readers who are not familiar with the manner in which most behavior therapy is practiced in the United States today and therefore erroneously equate behavior therapy or "behavior modification" with the use of aversive or punishment procedures. As we have stressed throughout this book, the overwhelming majority of behavior therapists use procedures based on the principles of positive reinforcement, not only for ethical reasons but for the technical reason that they have generally proved to be more effective.

RESPONSE COST

Response cost is an aversive procedure in which a reinforcer is removed from the individual when he engages in an undesired behavior. A commonplace example of this is paying a speeding ticket or a fine for an overdue library book (Reese, 1978). Response costs have often been used in combination with token economies but may also involve the loss of behavioral privileges such as watching television, play time, and recess.

Response cost is most effective when combined with positive reinforcement procedures, but, as pointed out by Reese (1978), it has often been used in an aversive sense. For example, a client may be asked to deposit money at the beginning of a treatment prodedure for, let us say, obesity. He would pay a fine (lose some of the money) if he didn't succeed in reducing to his dieting goal but he would get the money back if he *did* succeed in reaching his goal. To avoid giving the therapist a vested interest in the client's failure, the money forfeited is usually sent to a charity. To increase the response cost, a client may designate an organization that he abhors.

TIME OUT

The procedure called "time out from positive reinforcement" is often used with misbehaving children, who might be asked to stand in a corner or go to a "quiet room" or corner, where the child is left alone or isolated. It has been used extensively in institutions, particularly institutions for the treatment of seriously disturbed children. It is most effective when applied for very short periods and in combination with other procedures. It is imperative that the reason a person is removed be specified in advance and known by both parties involved. Merely sending a child out of the room for five minutes because he has "misbehaved" is strictly a punishment procedure (in the layman's sense of the word) and a misuse of the time-out procedure.

Time-out procedures can be very effectively used by parents. For example, in one situation two brothers, close in age, fought continually over television. The idea of decision making and problem solving (see below) was explained to these brothers with the caution that if decisions were not made by a certain time without squabbling, each was to have a time out of three minutes away from the television set. This time-out procedure, especially when it came at the beginning of a television program, when squabbling was most likely to occur, was admittedly aversive but worked very quickly to shape prosocial, adaptive behavior.

OTHER PROCEDURES

There are a number of procedures that are fairly technical but which we shall here describe briefly for completeness; we caution the reader not to use them without consultation.

One way to lower a behavior is to supply a high amount of the reinforcer desired. This is a procedure called "satiation," where the individual gets a desired response to the point where he literally gets fed up with it and stops the behavior. Illustrative is the oft-cited case of the psychiatric patient who stole towels from the other patients and hoarded them in her room (Ayllon, 1963). The therapist did not try to stop the behavior by punishment or prohibition. Instead, he had the ward staff give her towels on almost any occasion. After three weeks, and the accumulation of over 600 towels, the woman herself began to remove the towels. She stopped her hoarding, and there was no "symptom substitution."

An extreme procedure designed to reduce behavior is "restraint," including physical restraint in the home as well as incarceration in an institution. Needless to say, this is a drastic punishment procedure. If restraint is to be used at all, it must be used with the same caution and safeguards for individual dignity and human rights that are to be used with all aversive procedures.

Another procedure is to reinforce any behavior *other* than the behavior the therapist is trying to help a client eliminate. This has been called "differential reinforcement of other behavior" and "omission training" (Grant, 1964). This is a complicated procedure; the reinforcement is delivered when certain behavior is not performed. A complete and clear discussion may be found in Reese (1978).

Sometimes one wishes a behavior to be reduced in frequency rather than eliminated. The behavior may be speaking out in class, compulsively checking the gas stove for leaks, or obsessive hand washing. One procedure is called "DRL" (differential reinforcement of a low rate of behavior). This again is a complicated matter; a clear discussion may be found in Reese, 1978.

In our opinion, the best way to lower the rate of a behavior is to reinforce behavior that is incompatible. If one *has* to use aversive procedures, they should always be combined with procedures of positive reinforcement to raise the level of the desired behavior. In any event, any procedures that use a combination of methods will generally be more effective than approaches that use merely one method.

Maintaining Behavior Change

While the use of behavioral approaches often produces behavior change within an amazingly short time, once the intervention is stopped the new behavior will sometimes drop away and the old behavior reappear. This may be true of many kinds of therapeutic interventions, but it seems especially critical with the behavior therapies. First, because the behavioral approach is so specific, changes in behavior seem to be more easily noticed. Secondly, behaviorists have made many claims of the effectiveness of their methods in treating "behavior and conduct disorders" that have not been substantiated over the long run. Referring to weight control programs, for example, recent commentators (Stunkard and Penick, 1979) have stated that in order to judge effectiveness the program must be evaluated for a period of at least two years. The literature is full of successful short-term interventions where the individuals later regained the lost weight.

The problem of maintaining behavioral gains involves generalization and transfer. As we stated above, in "stimulus generalization," behavior learned under one set of environmental conditions should then be carried out in other situations. For example, it is obvious that behavior learned in an institution, such as a correctional school, often does not persist once the individual is released from the institution. Similarly, the gains achieved through effective token economies in institutes for juvenile delinquents often disappear when the individual is returned to the natural environment. The marital couple who learn to speak sweetly to each other in the therapist's office may not carry this behavior over into their own home.

In "response generalization," the effects of a change in one behavior carry over into other behaviors. If we work with the married couple to enable them to communicate better verbally, this behavior should gradually expand into other behaviors such as being considerate of each other, their sex life, care of the children, etc. But often this gain is restricted to one behavior and does not generalize to others.

There are a number of methods of achieving generalization. If behavior is being reinforced on a heavy schedule of reinforcement, then the reinforcement should be made more intermittent or less frequent. For example, working with a child who is habitually late for school, reinforcement should be given for each day that he is on time. After he is on time for a number of days, the teacher might begin to praise every other day, then every third day, and ultimately compliment the child on being on time *all* week. If possible, the reinforcement should be taken over by the natural environment of the individual. At first, both the parent and the teacher would reinforce the late child for being on time. Gradually, the parent would drop out, leaving the reinforcement to the teacher. Gradually, the teacher would fade out, the reinforcement being the child's pleasure at being in line with the other children when the early bell rang, getting to his desk with the other children instead of dragging in late, etc. The lack of attention from the other children would be supplanted by the group approaval, "being with the other kids."

It is best, above all, if one can actually treat an individual in his natural environment. Treating a person in the home—for example, in a parent-child relationship—gives the behavior a better chance of generalizing and becoming permanent than working with them exclusively in the office (Miller, 1975; Miller and Miller, 1977). The therapeutic value of home interventions has long been known to social workers and other therapists.

If one cannot work in the natural environment, then one may work to help a client "reprogram the natural environment" by involving "significant others," such as a spouse, in the treatment (Schwartz, 1965). For example, a husband might be helped to cooperate in the weight loss program of his wife. He might be urged to do such things as clear the table after meals, throwing away scraps of food that his overweight wife might eat, for "it's a sin to throw it away!" One may also work with children, grandparents, even neighbors. Some clients cooperate in reprogramming their natural environment by setting up support systems. Certainly the use of groups is helpful here.

It is possible to devise a specific maintenance program where the influence of the therapist is "faded out" and the influence of the natural environment and/or significant others is "faded in." Of course, the new activities in themselves may be so reinforcing that they carry over to new behavior; that is, the effects of the new behavior may be so reinforcing and pleasing to the individual that he continues it, especially if the behavior which it replaced is extremely aversive and punishing. However, this does not often happen in practice. Certainly the effects of sobriety—not having hangovers and saving money, among others—are better than the effects of drinking. However, the one positive aspect of drinking—the release or dulling of pain (similar to drug addiction)—may be immediately reinforcing to the drinker.

If a parent and a child both learn new ways of relating to each other, these may be so pleasant that they continue. If a child has learned that when she is in bed by eight o'clock she is reinforced not only by certain reward systems but more particularly by the good feeling she has with her mother (and vice versa), the new habit of being in bed by eight o'clock may be highly self-reinforcing.

We mentioned previously that some behaviors may be "self-reinforcing." This is a controversial topic among behaviorists. Self-reinforcement means the individual himself sets up the conditions for maintaining the behavior. Unlike a number of previous investigators, we believe that the main thrust of behavior intervention with most individuals should be a form of "self-control." The more the individual client can be helped to assume the responsibility for effecting and maintaining the change, the more successful will be the change program, the more the change program will generalize and persist, and the less it will regress or fade out.

Self-Control

One behavioral development is to focus on working with the individual to examine his environment and the contingencies which control his behavior, including his own subjective response. His feelings are often the first indication that something is wrong with his contingency relationships (Schwartz and Goldiamond, 1975). The individual, with the therapist's help and guidance, analyzes the contingency relationships controlling his behavior and then—on the basis of this analysis—himself changes the contingencies, which in turn change his behavior. We can say that such a person is engaging in "self-control." For example, one client (an accountant) smoked excessively and felt he could not stop. When he did an A–B–C analysis of his smoking behavior, he learned that whenever he had a problem with the figures he was working on, or he felt a little bored or tired, that these circumstances were cues for lighting up a cigarette. He decided on some possible alternative behaviors, such as getting up for some water or some coffee, taking a walk, stretching, and so forth. He was able to cut his rate of cigarette smoking almost in half within a few days.

The exact nature of self-control has long been a subject of

debate among behavior therapists, but it is generally agreed that clients do engage in self-initiated or self-maintained changes in behavior.

Both behaviorists and nonbehaviorists agree that there is a "self," although they most certainly differ as to what constitutes the "self" (Stuart, 1977). Behaviorists would not engage in the kind of reification that a Rogerian might engage in when he talks about the "distance" between the "ideal self" and the "actual self." The theoretical differences centering around "self-control" concern the relative importance of "external" and "internal" factors. The early behaviorists tended to deny the importance or sometimes even the existence of internal factors, insisting that behavior could best be changed by a careful variation in the external environments.

The recent upsurge of interest in "self-control" measures, including use of the "unobservable" concept of the "self," includes a return to the examination of variables "inside" the individual; the "internal" or "black box" set of variables. Radical behaviorists say that it is not necessary to turn once again to these vague, untestable ideas, especially when the "external" environments have not been sufficiently examined and researched.

The "internal-external" controversy can be clarified if we look at the ways "self-control" has been defined.

One definition states that self-control occurs "when an organism or an individual, in the relative absence of immediate external constraints, engages in behavior whose previous probability has been less than that of alternatively available behaviors" (Thoresen and Mahoney, 1974). The important element of this definition is that an *individual* chooses to engage in a particular behavior when there are *other* behaviors immediately available.

Self-control is also said to exist when there are two or more behavioral alternatives whose consequences are conflicting or mutually exclusive *and* where the actions are not met by immediate reinforcement. An example would be the individual who approaches a candy dish but, instead of reaching for the candy (the taste and pleasure of which are immediately reinforcing), performs some other behavior such as turning away from the candy dish or perhaps reaching for a piece of celery. The trait psychologist would say that the person is engaging in "self-control" as a personality variable. The operant psychologist would say that the person's behavior is being maintained by the eventual *external* consequence—for example, of overweight and its possible social and medical consequences (e.g., diabetes) rather than by any "internal" force, such as "will power."

This is indeed an attenuated argument, especially when one considers addictive and habituating behaviors. The long-term effects of smoking are well known and are dire, especially death from lung cancer. The individual who does not smoke (assuming he was previously a smoker) is engaging in "self-control" according to the operant psychologist because of the long-term consequences of lung cancer. However, the immediate reinforcing consequences of smoking are so great that many people continue to smoke and hence do not exercise "self-control." In fact, it has been shown that many people who are shown slides or pictures of diseased lungs become so nervous that they immediately reach for a cigarette. The instant relief from anxiety (the immediate consequences of smoking) is much more compelling than the possible long-term effects of lung cancer (besides, not every smoker gets it, etc.).

Some theorists have called self-control a continuum in which both the external environment and the internal environment are involved; change must occur in both. Often it is difficult to differentiate between what is external and what is internal (Thoreson and Mahoney, 1974). Overt behaviors are always accompanied by covert processes, such as feelings, affects, imagery, subvocal verbalizations, and, also, physiological concomitants. This is vividly illustrated when somebody gives us some bad news or tells us something we don't want to hear. We may consciously suppress any overt manifestation but there are obviously internal or covert processes such as our "stomach flipping" which we feel but are not visible to the outside observer. There is, in most cases, an interaction between the external and observable and the internal and the unobservable. This is the true meaning of self-control being on a continuum.

One of the chief advantages of self-control procedures over other methods of behavior change is that by helping the client to analyze and diagnose his particular interactions with his contingencies the therapist may equip him with a set of procedures that he can use in similar situations in the future. In essence, working with a client in a self-control approach means helping him to increase his behavioral repertoire, not only in a remedial sense (to change the current situation) and to generalize the gains made in the therapist's office, but in a preventive sense, equipping him with "tools" or abilities to handle similar emergencies or problem situations in the future.

The traditional therapist might interject that "awareness" seems to be a necessary part of the self-control procedures. This point is valid and moves contemporary "behavioral" practice closer to the mainstream of psychotherapy. In one of the clearest presentations of the principles of "self-control," Watson and Tharp (1977) ask the reader to select certain of his own behaviors to be changed and then outline the steps for analysis of the conditions controlling the behavior, list potential reinforcers, give suggestions for alternate methodologies, and so forth. This is an effective way to introduce the student to the possibilities of changing aspects of one's own behavior—not just "behavioral" items like weight loss, but also self-concept and interpersonal relations, among others. It is also an effective introduction to some of the basic principles of behaviorism and behavior therapy.

Often the first task of a behavior therapist is to help the

client become aware of the contingency conditions that are controlling and affecting his behavior. We refer not only to external controlling conditions but certain internal and covert processes. It is also most important to understand how these events have occurred in his past, by examining his history of conditioning and learning. History is an important contingency and, as we have repeatedly stated, a concept central to many views of human behavior, including the behavioral.

In self-control analysis we focus constantly on the *specifics* of the situation rather than on global, nonspecific, mentalistic, or unobservable constructs. (We are, of course, referring to the behavioral analysis within the functional definition rather than the topographical definitions of behavior.)

In self-control, the client often deliberately carries out procedures that will alleviate the external situation. Modifying the environment can be an act of self-control; the act of modification itself can be a kind of controlling response. The control can be achieved arranging the antecedent conditions (stimulus control), by changing the outcome (the reinforcing or punishing consequence of the behavior) or by engaging in "symbolic covert control" (Bandura, 1969). "Symbolic self-control" refers to self-statements, self-instructions, images, and other. (Cognitive procedures are described in the next chapter.)

Self-control can be discussed under two sometimes overlapping categories: Environmental planning and behavioral programming (Thoreson and Mahoney, 1974, p. 77 ff.).

ENVIRONMENTAL PLANNING

Environmental planning, very generally, focuses on events prior to the occurrence of the behavior, the antecedent conditions. These "antecedent conditions" can be modified by the procedures of stimulus control. For example, a student might deliberately arrange his desk at home as the only place to study, his kitchen table as the sole place to write letters and checks, his living room chair as the place to read newspapers and non-school magazines, and so forth. A dieter could make the table in the dining room the *only* place he'll eat; all other places—for example, standing at the refrigerator—are "off limits" for eating.

Another arrangement of antecedent conditions is to pre-program the controlling responses, or the consequences of behavior, to help the individual avoid undesired behaviors, as in behavioral contracting. One contract might be to reward himself with some expensive item *only* if he achieves the task.

Another environmental planning procedure is for the individual to expose himself very gradually to a stimulus which may have some sort of aversive effect. This has been called a "self-regulated stimulus exposure" and is a form of systematic desensitization, with the pace of the exposure and the other factors involved, planned and carried out by the client himself. A client who fears heights, for example, might gradually go higher and higher in an elevator.

A third environmental planning technique is the area of "self-instructions," manipulation or change of the discriminative stimuli, the "cues" that control behavior. One dieter put a big "STOP!" sign on his refrigerator. Another placed her scale in front of the refrigerator so that she had to step on it every time she opened the door to reach for food. Another placed a mirror near her refrigerator, so that she could not avoid looking at herself every time she approached the door.[3]

Other kinds of "self-instructions" will be discussed in Chapter 5.

---

[3] Just before finishing writing for the day, this author will post a list—a directive—telling him exactly where to start the next day, often even writing out the first two or three sentences. This is an adaptation of a procedure used by the late Ernest Hemingway. He would never stop

BEHAVIORAL PROGRAMMING

A second major division of self-control procedures is behavioral programming that focuses on the consequences of behavior. Procedures consist primarily of (1) self-observation to become aware of the consequences; (2) self-reward; and (3) self-punishment, both overt and covert.

Self-observation is not only the gathering of information about oneself but is often, in its own right, a method of behavior change. Certainly the individual who keeps records on when, and under what conditions, he smokes may be quick to realize that he does so when he is depressed, under tension, or bored. He sees that when things are going well he can go for a long time without smoking. He soon learns to discriminate the conditions under which he smokes and abstains. Part of this self-observation, of course, is a growing awareness of his own bodily and emotional responses. Often the "felt sensation" of tenseness or depression is the first indicator that something is off in his life, that something is off in his relationship to his contingencies.

There are a number of ways of recording behavioral data, including charts and diagrams (Thoresen and Mahoney, 1974). There is also a growing technology which includes such items as counters, worn on the wrist much like golf counters. Devices that can be used to note frequencies are valuable adjuncts to behavior change (as long as the main purpose is helping the patient and the secondary payoff the data for research). Only the imagination limits the possibilities and range of recording devices. One researcher, during a fad where women wore belts made of beads, had a client switch a bead from one side of her waist to the other every

---

writing for the day when in the middle of a difficult passage or where he was stumped. He would try, whenever possible, to break off writing in the middle of a scene or a passage that was going well, that he could pick up again easily the next day.

time the woman made an assertive statement (Richey, personal communication).

While there are many advantages to self-observation, the data collected must be treated with caution. The individual who collects data about himself is hardly unbiased. Usually there is no external reliability check. Even when the individual sets out to collect complete and objective data, he/she may unconsciously slant the facts. Part of this may be a compliance factor, where the subject is giving the therapist what he/she thinks the experimenter wants. Part of the reality is also that collecting data on oneself has a reactive effect (McFall, 1970). The collection of data *does* affect the rate of behavior; smoking of cigarettes has been known to go down, rates of sexual intercourse up, all in the direction of what the desired behavioral change might be. The alert therapist might even *use* this reactivity response deliberately to try to reduce an undesired behavior through self-observation and self-recording procedures.

"Positive self-reward," giving oneself something good (reinforcing) immediately after one engages in the desired behavior, is another self-control procedure. For example, an hour of TV watching may be the reward for two hours of studying or a new dress the reward for losing ten pounds.

A "negative self-reward" is removal of an aversive situation but only after a specific behavior is performed or a certain goal is achieved. One example might be to remove a poster of a pig after you have been successful on the diet.

"Positive self-punishment" would be the removal of an available reinforcer after you perform a specific undesired or negative response. One example is to give a dollar to charity for every one hundred calories you eat over a certain amount.

"Negative self-punishment" occurs when a freely available aversive stimulus is presented after the performance of specific negative responses. This might be inhaling a noxious odor after smoking (Thoreson and Mahoney, 1974).

Our strong belief is that therapists should utilize the self-control procedures of self-observation, self-reward, and reinforcement in preference to self-administered aversive procedures. With aversive procedures, since the individual applies the procedures himself, he can either *avoid* applying them ("I'll just skip it this time") or apply them *extra hard* because of perceived (or possibly real) failure to meet some criterion, failure to "stick to it," or "lack of will power." Individuals faced with failure, such as dieters who "cheat," often are very harsh on themselves and excessively intrapunitive. For this and other reasons, we again recommend the use of the constructive, positive procedures in self-control rather than the aversive or punishment self-control procedures.

Some Additional Comments

The research on self-control procedures, as reported in the literature, reveals several shortcomings. The first is a bias in subject selection. Certainly these procedures, like most therapeutic procedures, which require some degree of awareness, are most easily applied to and by the so-called YAVIS patient.[4]

We have also referred to an expectation effect sometimes called the "demand characteristics of the situation." The client will sometimes respond with what he feels is expected of him. This need not necessarily be a negative, but it can distort reporting and performance of behaviors. Meeting the demand characteristics of the situation is referred to by the more traditional therapists as "transference." Part of this effect may be due not to the procedures

---

[4] YAVIS is an acronym used in psychotherapy research to stand for the client who is *Y*oung, *A*ttractive, *V*erbal, *I*ntelligent, and *S*uccessful (i.e., has enough money to pay the therapist).

or even to the behavior of the individual but to suggestion, and nonspecifics such as the placebo effects.

Summary

The therapeutic tasks in operant treatment may be conceptualized as teaching new behaviors, increasing behaviors already in the client's repertoire but occurring too infrequently, putting behavior already in the repertoire but occurring inappropriately into the right situation, reducing or eliminating a behavior, and, lastly, maintaining behavioral changes. For teaching new behaviors, some of the procedures are *shaping,* where that part of the behavior already in the repertoire is reinforced and undesired parts are extinguished until the behavior more and more resembles and finally is identified with the end behavior desired; *chaining,* where behaviors already in the repertoire are linked together in steps toward a final behavior (or state of affairs); *prompting* and *fading,* where cues are presented (prompted) and/or then removed (faded) to apply stimulus control or to strengthen behavior.

To raise the frequency of desired behaviors, in addition to the techniques above, we use *positive reinforcement,* where consequences are delivered (including the verbal approval of the therapist) that result in an increase in the rate of behavior. The *token economy* is a form of positive reinforcement where desired behaviors are rewarded with tokens which can then be turned in for desired items. (Tokens, like money, are called *generalized reinforcers,* for they may be used for many purposes. The items for which the tokens are exchanged are called *backup reinforcers.*) Another positive reinforcement technique is called *contingency contracting,* where both parties agree to certain behavioral requirements in exchange for certain consequences. Other reinforcement procedures are *negative reinforcement,* an aversive procedure where behavior is kept high by the removal of an aversive stimulus when the individual engages in a desired behavior.

Another therapeutic task is putting the behavior in the right situation, or *stimulus control.* These procedures usually employ *cues, prompting, fading,* and *programming.*

To eliminate behavior, the most desired and nonaversive approach is to *reinforce behavior incompatible (competing) with the undesired behavior.* In addition, there are a number of aversive procedures, such as *extinction* (neither reinforcing nor punishing behavior), *punishment* (any response which lowers behavior). Punishment has many negative consequences, including the disputed idea that punishment merely suppresses and does not eliminate behavior), *response cost* (where a reinforcer is removed when the individual engages in a behavior), *time out* (where the individual himself is removed from the opportunity to engage in reinforcing activities, e.g. the "quiet room"), and other procedures.

Maintaining behaviors is a major problem in the behavioral therapies, as in all therapies. Generally, this involves *generalization* and *transfer of learning.* When a client repeats behavior learned in one situation in another situation, we say that *stimulus generalization* has occurred. When change in one behavior "spreads" to another behavior, we say that *response generalization* has occurred. Generalization and transfer of learning may be facilitated by adjusting *schedules of reinforcement, transfer of control to the natural environment,* and *self control,* in which the individual himself assumes the burden of maintenance by learning to analyze the contingency interrelationships, plan the change program, and evaluate its effectiveness.

Self-control involves a combination of *environmental planning,* where the individual concentrates on arranging the stimulus control of antecedent conditions, and *behavioral programming,* where the individual himself plans and applies the consequences, which are *self-observation* (monitoring the course of therapy, to become aware of the consequences, often with graphs and charts), and *self-reward* and *self-punishment* procedures (which are adaptations of the operant procedures, but self-administered). Again, the most effective procedures are nonaversive, self-applied, self-reinforcement procedures.

Chapter 5

Modeling and Cognitive-Behavioral Approaches

Learning Through Vicarious Means

There are times when neither the classical stimulus-response model nor the operant-conditioning (A–B–C) model can adequately account for behavior. This is the case, for example, with the acquisition of new behavior, particularly verbal behavior (speech or language). There are also times when a person learns new behavior for which he is neither reinforced nor punished (i.e., is not subject to direct behavioral consequences). For example, if one of a group of school children is punished by the teacher, his immediate neighbors may quickly change their behavior. Similarly, school children exposed to movies showing acting out or aggressive behaviors will tend to behave more aggressively (Bandura, 1969).

While one may teach by shaping and reinforcing new behavior or by telling someone what to do, a person may also teach by having the learner pattern his behavior after what the teacher does in a process called "modeling" or "imitation." This is sometimes called a vicarious approach. For example, a person may learn to use chopsticks by looking at the other diners in a Japanese restaurant and imitating them. If he followed what his neighbors were doing, he would be learning vicariously (Kanfer and Phillips, 1970, pp. 188–189).

Modeling accounts for a great deal of our learning. It is especially applicable in situations where the individual learns a behavior for which he is not immediately reinforced. In fact, actually doing the behavior may take place many months after he has learned it. One example might be the emergency procedures which flight attendants are taught. They might put the procedures into practice much later or, perhaps, not at all.

As we know, the more immediate the reinforcement, the more effective the learning. However, there are times when behavior is not immediately reinforced, yet the learning takes place. For example, many of the behaviors that new parents exhibit towards their children are actually behaviors that they themselves learned through their own parent's modeling, by observing (and remembering, often not consciously) how their parents behaved.

Here we come to an interesting distinction between learning and performance. According to Patterson (1969), a consequential (A–B–C) relationship may not be necessary for learning to occur. However, performance is more likely to occur if the behavior has consequences for the person, if it is reinforced. For example, a child in nursery school might observe the proper way to hang up his coat. He might not do so unless hanging up his coat was necessary to participate in class, and the teacher reinforced him verbally for the behavior. The literature is fairly consistent in showing that while learning may be accounted for by an "internal" or vicarious model, and performance may sometimes be maintained without reinforcement, procedures that combine both the modeling approach of learning and reinforcement of performance are more effective in establishing new behavior permanently than the use of either modeling or reinforcement alone (Baer and Sherman, 1964).

How Modeling Works

Modeling is a very complex process, involving a number of procedures and possible theoretical explanations. We are only beginning to become aware of some of them (Bandura, 1969, 1971; Rosenthal and Bandura, 1978). We can say that modeling has a number of effects upon an observer. The first is that modeling can be used deliberately to teach new patterns of behavior (and, in the process, help the individual to unlearn old, dysfunctional patterns). New ways to combine old behaviors can be modeled, as well as ways to learn and integrate new kinds of behaviors (Bandura, 1969, 1971).

By observing a model, one can also grasp the entire pattern of responding, as well as the component parts, especially if the observer can question the model and the model can provide instructive feedback. A third effect is that the model can facilitate new and/or more adaptive responses by providing a cue, by "priming" these new behaviors (Bandura, 1969). The presence of the scoutmaster might provide the cue for Boy Scouts to engage in certain behaviors while setting up tents for a camping weekend.

Observing a model can strengthen or weaken the inhibition of behavior. For example, one might want to reverse the inhibition of a response (such as a phobia) or to strengthen an inhibition (such as antidrinking behavior). As Bandura makes quite clear, the increase of inhibitory effects is used quite rarely. Rather than focus on the dysfunctional behaviors, the preferred strategy is to focus on increasing the positive, prosocial, adaptive behaviors of the individual (Skinner, 1953). Modeling is more effective when used to facilitate responses than when perceived as a negative or coercive pressure (Rosenthal and Bandura, 1978). Later in this chapter we shall discuss the cognitive change effects attributed to modeling.

Modeling has a great deal of potential for use not only in teaching but in psychotherapy. The procedures can be used either by themselves or in combination with any number of other procedures, both behavioral and nonbehavioral. Many of the items discussed above, such as learning through observation, which includes the setting of cognitive standards for self-evaluation, have been a part of psychotherapeutic interventions for a long time. "Whether called modeling, imitation, vicarious reinforcement, or observational learning, there is a teachable skill that may be used to alter a behavior and that has been shown to be effective in experiments conducted in a laboratory and clinic" (Ullman, 1969, p. 177).

There are a great many similarities between what the behaviorists call "modeling" and what the psychodynamic theorists call "identification" or "imitation." However, one essential difference is that behavioral modeling is highly procedural, a deliberate portrayal of the behavior to be imitated. The teacher (or therapist) will act as a role model,[1] deliberately using complex techniques, including lessening and strengthening prompts and cues as needed.

The therapist, as a model, serves as discriminative stimulus or cue for his client. He indicates to the client, either through behavior, through speech, or through covert attitudes handed to the client, that if the client behaves in a particular way there will be specific consequences. If he behaves in another way, different consequences will result. Of course, having a teacher serve as a discriminative stimulus, setting the occasion for the desired behavior, is a deliberate part of the educational process. To the extent that psychotherapy is an educational process, these same procedures may be included and may be condoned to the extent that they are democratically decided upon and that they

---

[1] The use of therapists as "role models" is noted in the literature of all therapies. The most deliberate use in social work is the work of McBroom (1970) in her "Socialization" orientation.

also fit the best needs of the patient (rather than the best needs of the therapist).[2]

One definition of modeling states: "A model is any stimulus array so organized that an observer can extract and act upon the main information conveyed by environmental events without needing to first perform overtly" (Rosenthal and Bandura, 1978, p. 622).

Certainly "transference" may be seen as falling within this definition. If the patient has related to the therapist in such a way that we can say there is a transference, then the therapist—in some way or another, either actually or through symbolic processes—has undoubtedly modeled behavior, attitudes, speech, opinions, etc., which the client is imitating. The behaviorist would state that the more overt and deliberate this process—modeling as opposed to transference—the better and the more facilitative of client change. This is based on the assumption, of course, that the direction of the changes was in line with the patient's wishes and best interests. If this direction were strictly therapist determined, then the therapy would be authoritarian and probably would eventually be sabotaged by the client.

While the therapeutic use of modeling involves deliberately setting up the conditions wherein one person observes and reproduces the behavior of another, modeling is more than the imitative, motoric reproduction of behavior. As we stated above, it is often combined with a reinforcement, shaping procedure. For example, in teaching speech to an autistic child, the therapist may form the letter "m" as the first sound in "mother." When the child imitates "m" and

[2] This view is the opposite of "nondirective psychotherapy" but a closer examination will show that nondirective psychotherapy is not only *not* possible (see the research of Rogers and Truax) but may even be undesirable. In the idealized form of nondirective therapy, the therapist showing "unconditional positive regard" may even be abdicating his responsibility to serve as a cue or a prompt (as a model) to the patient.

no other sound, he will be reinforced either with food (a primary unconditioned reinforcer) or with a pat or a hug (secondary, learned reinforcers). This is modeling with a reinforced, guided performance. These procedures are good for teaching behaviors that are absent from the repertoire of the individual; they are often used to teach other behavior and social skills as well.

Applications of Modeling

THE TEACHING OF SOCIAL SKILLS

Verbal behavior, assertion, social competencies and skills and other behaviors can best be taught through demonstration, modeling, and behavioral rehearsal or role playing (see below), where the learner observes someone engaging in the behavior, repeats it, and is then reinforced for his actions. These procedures breach the theoretical gap, if any, between learning and performance.

In using modeling procedures to teach social skills or other behaviors, the learning task should be structured into an orderly sequence of small steps, utilizing the shaping procedure. The steps themselves may then be modeled. For example, in teaching youngsters how to look for a job, one would first demonstrate the appropriate dress and job-seeking behavior. These large tasks could be broken down into steps such as approaching the employer, filling out the form, conducting oneself during an interview, etc. This can be taught in a group through a behavioral rehearsal.

In teaching generalizable rules of social conduct, it is important that the therapist continually check the client's understanding of what is being taught. We have stressed that modeling is not simple motoric reproduction of behavior. Checking the client's understanding allows the therapist to give feedback and to correct errors. In the area of informed mecical consent, for example, a patient may state that he agrees to a procedure, signing a statement that he understands the procedures, risks, etc. The patient may even be able to repeat what the doctor has said and the physician may feel confident that he understands. However, research on communication has found by interviewing such clients even minutes later that they often have not the slightest idea of what is going on, what they have been told, or what they agreed to. In a state of emotional arousal one is often not able to assimilate and integrate information.

THE USE OF MODELING IN GROUPS

Modeling procedures can be extremely effective when used in groups. Within a group there are several possible models for each group member to observe and to emulate: The leader, fellow group members, and guests deliberately brought in to display certain characteristics. In addition, "symbolic" models such as audio or videotapes and films may also be used to demonstrate certain behaviors. The members may also be encouraged to engage in covert modeling, where they imagine first a model and then themselves engaging in certain behaviors. One example might be to imagine a model approaching rodents and then to imagine oneself approaching and handling the rodents (Cautela, et al., 1974).

Sheldon Rose and his associates at the University of Wisconsin, who pioneered the application of behavioral procedures to groups, note that modeling may be combined with a number of other behavioral methods such as role playing in a group, and homework assignments in a real-life situation (*in vivo* modeling) (Rose, 1973, 1977). In addition, the group members may observe a model engaging in a behavior and then be asked to role-play the behavior in the session and to carry out assignments performing the behavior outside the group. The use of all of these procedures is enriched by corrective feedback from the leader as well as from other group members.

Modeling may be used both with clinical therapy groups and with non-therapy groups, utilizing respondent, operant, and cognitive procedures as well as nonbehavioral methods.

We shall elaborate further upon the use of behavioral methods with groups in Chapter 7.

The Social Learning Orientation

The person most closely associated with the development of the modeling or "social learning" approach is Albert Bandura of Stanford University. Bandura, beginning with his masterful *Principles of Behavior Modification* (1969), has examined the use of modeling in a number of clinical and learning situations and has investigated such factors as the characteristics of the model and the conditions of the modeling that are most likely to facilitate learning and change.[3]

Bandura's work has been criticized by some behaviorists as going too far inside the organism, of needing to refer once again to "internal" or "black box" or "inferred" characteristics—that is, to unobservable and therefore unmeasurable variables.[4]

---

[3] We cannot do justice to Bandura's contributions by summarizing his work here and by summarizing the research results. We refer the reader to a recent summary of this research which may be found in Rosenthal and Bandura (1978).

[4] This author feels that some of these criticisms are not justified. Whenever possible, Bandura and other cognitive behaviorists try to focus and give emphasis to these external observable variables.

However, Bandura and his followers have not stated that the external variables are unimportant; instead, they have said that the radical behaviorists' view, concentrating strictly upon external variables, does not fully explain learning or performance. Furthermore, radical behaviorists do not fully utilize such nonspecific, "nonbehavioral" variables as relationship factors to effect change in clients.

Bandura hypothesizes a fourth major effect of modeling, derived from his earlier work (1969, 1971). This fourth effect is that an observer may acquire standards for self-regulation (Bandura, 1978b, and Rosenthal and Bandura, 1978). By watching others one can acquire appropriate and useful criteria for evaluating oneself. A common clinical problem is that individuals often set goals for themselves that are too high. Observing a model may provide more realistic standards for self-evaluation, self-reward, etc. The model's choice of standards (which can be varied experimentally in the clinical and laboratory situation) can be useful in helping clients to establish realistic criteria for themselves.

Bandura has expanded his conceptualizations of the effects of modeling into a comprehensive theory that further accentuates the importance of "internal" factors and, because of this, widens the gap between him and the extreme environmentalists. We shall present Bandura's new theory (called "Self-Efficacy") later in this chapter. Next, though, we shall discuss one of the newest and most controversial developments within the "behavioral" orientation, and that is the increasing interest in cognitive factors and variables.

Cognition and the Behavior Therapies

The increased interest in cognition and cognitive activities, which has recently characterized much of psychology, has also involved the behavioral approaches (Mahoney,

1977c).[5] Both the early Watsonian behaviorists and the later Skinnerian behaviorists shared an extreme environmentalist view, stressing the "external" and ignoring or giving mere lip service to "internal" factors. This view was understandable for, as we have seen, the emphasis of the behavioral approaches on the environmental (i.e., the "measurable") not only reflected certain social conditions (see Chapter 2) but was also a reaction to the introspectionism of the psychotherapeutic professions—and the academies. Nevertheless, as reflected in Bandura's social learning approach, with its inventive use of modeling theoretically based on "mediating" factors, there has been increasing awareness of the limitations of the radical behavioral view—combined with reluctance to abandon a database, research-oriented approach for the quicksands of introspectionism, with all the accompanying philosophical problems and unresolved methodological issues.

While the external-internal dichotomy is to some extent artificial, the fears of the behaviorists were understandable. Even the most ardent behaviorist recognized that there were nonspecific, unexplainable, and even "internal" and "unobservable" factors in operation. In an early paper, Klein et al. (1969) observed the clinic of Wolpe and Lazarus for a week and, while they praised the success of the procedures (chiefly systematic desensitization), they noted that there were nonspecific factors at work, such as suggestion, therapist influence, clients trying to please their therapist—in short, the same vague variables that the behaviorists had been operating against. Correctly or incorrectly, Klein and her associates concluded that "relationship" was responsible for a large part of the therapeutic efficacy of the most effective of the behavioral therapies at that time.

[5] This is due to a number of factors, which we shall not go into here. The reader may find a historical overview and a discussion of the general philosophical issues in Michael Mahoney's excellent book, *Cognition and Behavior Modification* (1974).

Many of the operant procedures involved cognitive factors. This is particularly true when one considers the issues of "self-control" (see Chapter 4 above). Skinner (1953) devoted a whole chapter to the topic of "self-control" in *Science and Human Behavior*. While there was some research on self-control, operant investigators viewed it as the manipulation of external factors and continued to overlook the importance of the "internal" factors; yet it seems (especially from hindsight) that the introduction of self-control procedures and research was the harbinger of an inevitable increase of interest in the nonspecific factors and a more considered use of relationship along with the manipulation of environmental contingencies and/or the utilization of stimulus-response bonds.

In short, there was an increasing emphasis on cognitive factors—not only how (or why) the client behaves in a particular way, but what he thinks (and eventually, of course, how he feels). Of course, these factors of human functioning cannot be so neatly dissected from each other as the academicians and theorists would have it!

Bandura (1969, p. 45ff.) stated that the social learning approach involved "reciprocal influence," the environment influencing behavior and the individual interacting with and influencing the environment. Expand this mutual influence to interchange of internal and external factors, and the result is a departure from extreme environmentalism. Furthermore, this meant that the individual was viewed not merely as the passive recipient of environmental forces (the "empty organism" referred to by some writers) but as an active participant in affecting his/her own life.

There was a similar rediscovery of "private events," the so-called covert processes. Homme (1965) talked of "covert operants" (or "coverants"), private events which he believed were governed by the same laws of conditioning and contingency relationships that governed external events. Similarly, Cautela (1967) formulated procedures of "covert sensitization," which he expanded to include other procedures such as covert punishment and covert reinforcement (see Chapter 2 above). The work of Homme and Cautela was based on the assumptions (oversimplifying greatly) that the coverants, and the processes in Cautela's procedures, were merely chains of covert stimuli and responses. They tended to ignore or overlook the existence of what we now call cognitive factors and the recent developments in ego psychology, such as the growing interest in "independent ego energies," the "executive functions of the ego," etc.[6] The work of Homme, Cautela, and others reflected the interest of some behaviorists in what went on "under the skin." Needless to say, their work met with a great deal of criticism, both methodological and philosophical. Some saw it as a return to vague, "mentalistic" explanations. Actually, we can see now that their investigations presaged the progression toward the inclusion of cognitive factors within the domain of interest of behaviorists.

When behavioral therapists began to experience success in certain areas, such as treatment of the phobias or of the mentally handicapped, it was almost inevitable that they would pay attention to a broader range of phenomena. The exclusively behavioral explanations that could satisfactorily account for these allegedly "simpler" conditions would not be sufficient when applied to more complex phenomena. Thus, the recent upsurge of interest in cognitive factors and the recent reexamination of theories from other fields, such as systems theory, cognitive dissonance, attri-

---

[6] Homme's work might also be placed in the earlier chapters because of its reliance on the respondent and operant principles of conditioning. Similarly, we placed Cautela's work in Chapter 2, for we feel that the majority of his procedures could be better classified and discussed among the aversion therapies. The placement is somewhat arbitrary, for both Homme's and Cautela's work—as well as the work of Wolpe and others—could justifiably be placed in this chapter on the cognitive behavioral approaches, expecially considering the role of "imagery" so prominent in all of these procedures.

bution theory, and others (see Mahoney, 1974), might have been predicted when behavior investigators and therapists began to leave the experimental laboratory for the clinic and the consulting room.

While it is difficult to present a brief, orderly summary of these many developments, we shall utilize a somewhat chronological theme as a general framework. This framework (adapted from Mahoney and Arnkoff, 1978) classifies these therapies into three major divisions: (1) those featuring some form of "cognitive restructuring," (2) the "coping skills therapies," and (3) the "problem-solving therapies," including the "personal science" approach of Mahoney, a pioneer in extending the cognitive approaches to behaviorism and in furthering the rapproachment of the various helping professions. We shall then briefly summarize the more recent contributions of Arnold Lazarus, whose "Multi-modal Therapy" represents a promising attempt to develop a "school-free" approach to helping. We shall also discuss Bandura's "Theory of Personal Efficacy."

Cognitive Restructuring

THE RATIONAL-EMOTIVE THERAPY OF ALBERT ELLIS

Albert Ellis is one of the most influential figures in contemporary American psychology. Ellis, after becoming disenchanted with the practice of psychoanalysis and psychoanalytic psychotherapy, began to practice a method of therapy which later developed into a scheme he called "Rational-Emotive Therapy."[7] Briefly, Ellis states that peo-

---

[7] Adequate and complete accounts can be found elsewhere, for Ellis is a prolific writer (see Ellis [1977a, 1977b]; Ellis and Grieger [1977]; and Whiteley [1977]).

ples' problems are the results of misconceptions and mis-perceptions of reality, that basically peoples' problems are due not so much to what they *feel* as to what they *think* and *believe*. These misconceptions and irrational ideas can be directly challenged and then corrected in therapeutic work.

In Ellis's view, there is something that happens out there—a stimulus event of any sort—which he calls an acti-vating event (A). This activating event has consequences (C) for the individual, due not so much to the nature of the activating event itself as to the often irrational belief system (B) of the individual. The individual may think that "A" causes "C" but it is actually "B" that causes "C". The individual's interpretation (B) of the activating event is what provides the consequences for him. Part of the thera-peutic work is to dispute (D) this interpretation so as to facilitate new effects (E).

Ellis, in one of his later writings, states that these irratio-nal beliefs reflect one of three false ideologies: (1) "*I* must do well and must win approval for my performance or else I rate as a rotten person." (2) "*You* must act kindly and con-siderately and justly toward me, or else you amount to a louse." And (3) "The *conditions* under which I live must remain good and easy, so that I get practically everything I want without too much effort and discomfort, or else the world turns damnable and life hardly seems worth living" (Ellis, 1977a, p. 11). People who find support for these irrational beliefs find life "awful" and tend to "awfulize"!

Ellis also believes that we all suffer from the "tyranny of the shoulds" (Horney, 1950). The minute we say "should" we are in essence laying an aversive trip upon ourselves. Much of Ellis's therapy consists of rational, straightfor-ward, intellectual discussion and confrontation, challenging and redirecting the client's beliefs. While at first this may seem more promising with the highly educated, intelligent client, Ellis and his disciples have worked with a large number of conditions and situations including the mentally retarded and the psychotic. Paradoxically, the rational-emotive approach also works with clients who use "intellectualization" as a defense. Rather than play into this defense, RET tends to use it and to defeat it.

Ellis's work was discovered by behaviorists at just about the time they were beginning to realize the limitations of some of their methods. Behaviorists found that one actually could affect cognitions (and feeling) by changing behavior. They found, for example, that they could help people with problems such as weight control, phobias, and depression, but that changes would not persist unless the therapists also worked with the clients' cognitions and perceptions—in particular, their cognition of the meaning of events and their therapeutic expectations.

Ellis's work has influenced such behaviorists as Meichenbaum and Mahoney in their search for more effective therapeutic procedures. His therapy, especially the disputing and relabeling of experiences, cause-and-effect reasoning, and differential self-structuring, does involve several kinds of cognitive restructuring, including "detecting your irrationalities, debating against them, discriminating between logical and illogical thinking, and semantic defining and redefining that helps you to stop overgeneralizing and stick closer to reality" (Ellis, 1977a, pp. 21–22). Despite the occasional faddism of Ellis's work, his work has had a profound effect on the practice of therapy in this country. Certainly, his concepts have enriched behavioral change procedures, especially among those whose work is discussed in this chapter. Furthermore, Rational-Emotive Therapy, and the variations and permutations of this approach, has stimulated a multitude of research efforts. In a recent listing, Ellis described some of the hypotheses confirming (and questioning) Rational-Emotive Therapy. The bibliography for this publication lists 987 references (Ellis, 1977b)![8]

COGNITIVE RESTRUCTURING THROUGH SELF-INSTRUCTION

Meichenbaum (1973) found in his doctoral work with schizophrenics that some patients who had been trained to engage in "healthy talk" continued to use the instructions past the original experimentation. This generalization of training helped the patients to deal more effectively with other situations in their everyday lives. Meichenbaum expanded his work from hospitalized schizophrenics to children. Using hidden microphones, he found that impulsive children tended to use much self-stimulating private talk; that is, they spoke to themselves in a highly stimulating manner. Nonreflective children tended to use more self-guiding talk. Impulsive children obviously had less control or less "self-control" of their behavior (Meichenbaum and Cameron, 1974). Very young children will engage in self-talk while doing a chore or playing, but tend to give up this practice as they mature. Many adults, when learning a new behavior, will also engage in a kind of self-dialogue, repeating to themselves the various steps of that behavior. For example, a person learning to drive a car might say: "I insert the key, I turn the key and at the same time put my left foot on the clutch, my right foot gently on the gas, my right

---

[8] This bibliography was published after the lead article in an entire issue of *The Counseling Psychologist* devoted entirely to a presentation by Ellis, critical comments by several authors, and a rebuttal by Ellis (see Whitely [1977]). In that issue, one author commented that the thirty-two hypotheses Ellis presented were "[not] a model or theory at all [but] a collection of loosely related and poorly elucidated propositions" (Mahoney, 1977a, p. 45). Mahoney elsewhere questioned the relevance of much of the evidence supporting Rational-Emotive Therapy (Mahoney and Arnkoff, 1978, pp. 704–705).

hand on the gear shift, etc.'' Sometimes this talk is out loud, but more often it is verbalized on the subvocal level. The self-talk, even at a subvocal level, tends to drop out as the new procedure is learned. Similarly, overt self-talk tends to drop out and become more subvocal as the child develops and grows up.

There is evidence that in schizophrenia, the nature of a person's behavior and perception can be changed by giving him instructions, altering the kind of self-talk he engages in. The evidence indicates that changing the self-talk of schizophrenics by either method results in improved functioning.

Meichenbaum combined modeling and operant procedures with self-instruction. In one experiment, he had the therapist model certain behaviors while talking out loud with self-guiding verbalizations. For example, "What do I have to do? I have to draw the line. I have to finish the task," etc. (Meichenbaum, 1977). Then the child repeated the instructions, first out loud and then in a whisper, then the model performed the task without verbalization, with the child repeating the act, first repeating the verbalization and then, after he learned the task, dropping out the overt verbalization and then the internal verbalization (Meichenbaum, 1977, esp. Ch. 2).

The self-instruction procedures of Meichenbaum can be combined with the reinforcement procedures of the operant approach and even with some of the procedures of the behavior therapy or Pavlovian approaches. Meichenbaum has stated that it is not enough for a behavior to be simply modeled; the child must go through the behavior rehearsal in self-instruction (Meichenbaum, 1977, p. 33). Meichenbaum's work has great utility in working with both seriously and moderately disturbed children as well as implications for the education of the "nondisturbed" or "normal" child. He and his colleagues are continuing their research on the efficacy of self-instruction methods with children, used alone as well as with other procedures. He has also used these procedures in working with a number of clinical and social situations and also to enhance creativity training for adults. Some "set-inducing" self-statements are: What to do? (answer) "Be creative, be unique, break away from the obvious," "be free wheeling," "quantity helps breed quality." What not to do? "Get rid of internal blocks. Defer judgments. Don't worry about what others think."

Meichenbaum has also developed a set of procedures designed to help clients increase their coping abilities. He calls these procedures "stress innoculation" (Meichenbaum, 1977). While both cognitive restructuring and stress innoculation are, in a sense, coping procedures, like other aspects of Meichenbaum's work, they not only have therapeutic and remedial value but also have prophylactic effects in that they equip the client with a technique—indeed, a "world view" or a philosophy—that will help him in future situations in addition to the immediately problematical.

THE COGNITIVE THERAPY OF AARON BECK

Aaron Beck, a Philadelphia psychiatrist trained in psychodynamic treatment approaches, began in the sixties to explore alternate methodologies, especially several of the behavioral therapies. No doubt his close geographical proximity to Joseph Wolpe, plus his disenchantment with some of the more traditional procedures, facilitated this exploration. Beck has worked primarily in the area of depression (Beck *et al.*, 1978, 1979). In his work, Beck became more and more impressed with the role people's false beliefs and misconceptions played in their illnesses: "The individual's problems are derived largely from certain distortions of reality based on erroneous premises and assumptions" (Beck, 1976, p. 3). Independently, he reached some of the same conclusions as Albert Ellis. While in his early works he attempted to tie his work to that of the more traditional behavior therapists (Beck, 1970) his later writings have tended toward the development of a system of therapy in its own right.

Beck states that the main job of the therapist is to help the client "unravel" his distorted thinking and learn more realistic ways to approach his problem. He helps his clients to build upon past successes in formulating some of the steps in cognitive therapy, utilizing the "method of successive approximations."

Beck's work in many ways utilizes his psychodynamic background, for he states that the results of cognitive therapy are most "readily observable by the patient through introspection" (Beck, 1976, p. 4). However, it differs from that of the prebehavioral introspectionists in that he provides a number of specific procedures by which the client can unlearn his distortions. The cognitive therapist helps the client to correct misperceptions based on incorrect inferences from incorrect information. Beck states that many distortions are a result of the developmental processes and that in treatment "the therapist helps the patient to identify his warped thinking and to learn more realistic ways to formulate his experiences" (Beck, 1976, p. 20).

Beck perceives his system of Cognitive Therapy as a middle ground between the behavioral and psychodynamic approaches. He criticizes psychotherapists who deny that there are conscious thoughts intervening between a stimulus and a person acting on the stimulus. By "tapping the internal communication," he claims, one can examine these thoughts and help the client to correct them through "cognitive restructuring."

Beck introduces the novel idea of "automatic thoughts." These, he explains, are thoughts on a subvocal level that may even occur at the same time that a patient is free-associating on the psychoanalytic couch. These internal thoughts can serve as signal to the individual. By self-monitoring and self-instruction a client can learn to change the nature of these automatic thoughts. For example, a client might be expressing some very hostile feelings to his therapist but, at the same time, might be experiencing a train of thought that he (the client) is "bad" and wrong for criticizing the therapist (Beck, 1976, pp. 30–31). The therapist helps the client to become aware of the two lines of thinking, which are a central expression of his conflict(s).

Beck cites Karen Horney (1950) who referred to the overactive process of self-monitoring as "the tyranny of the 'shoulds' "(Beck, 1976, p. 39). These "shoulds," which guide how the person responds in certain situations, are often based on misperceptions but serve as "rules" for behavior. Changing these rules comprises the chief work of cognitive therapy (Beck, 1976, p. 42).

Beck most certainly does not ignore behavior and emotion. However, he believes that changes in both can be facilitated through examination of the person's conscious awareness and the internal messages of the "automatic thoughts." In practice, Beck combines his cognitive approach with some specific behavioral procedures, as we shall see in the next chapter on depression.

Beck hypothesizes that depression, euphoria, anxiety, and other formal diagnostic categories of emotional disorders have certain ideational contexts and meaning (Beck, 1976, p. 81). For example, depression has a central theme of "loss" to the individual. Hypomania is an inflated evaluation of the individual. Anxiety neurosis consists of "a danger to the (person) of a general nature," while a phobia is a "danger connected with specific but avoidable situations." He views the paranoid states as "unjustified intrusion" on the individual. Beck sees a hysteric as a "sensory imaginer" who imagines the illness and then takes the sensory experience as corroborative evidence of having the illness (Beck, 1976, pp. 88–89). An obsession is "a remote risk experienced as a warning" (ibid., p. 87), while a compulsion serves as a "self-command to perform a specific act to ward off danger" (Beck, 1976, p. 84).

This brief overview does not do justice to the richness of Beck's conceptualization of the ideational content of each of these emotional disorders. He also extends his views to include psychosomatic medicine (Beck, 1976, pp. 186–212).

Viewing each of the disturbances within a cognitive frame of reference enabled Beck to formulate a direct therapeutic approach to these problems. He specifically advocates the use of cognitive reorganization and relabeling, defining Cognitive Therapy in a broad sense as "all the approaches that alleviate psychological distress through the medium of correcting faulty conceptions and self-signals" (Beck, 1976, p. 214). He further states that we approach a person's emotions through cognitions and that by correcting erroneous beliefs we can decrease and eliminate inappropriate emotional response, both behavioral and emotional. He emphasizes that the behavioral procedures can be quite helpful in encouraging differential ways of coping with the outside world but must be combined with cognitive restructuring procedures, particularly the examination of perceptions, thoughts, and fantasies.

Cognitive Therapy places an obligation upon the client. First, the client has to be aware or helped to become aware of what he is thinking. Secondly, with the therapist's help, he has to recognize which thoughts are inaccurate. Finally, he must consciously work to "substitute accurate for inaccurate judgments." The client also needs feedback regarding the appropriateness of changes in thinking and in behavior that follow changes in his thinking (Beck, 1976, p. 271).

Beck's work in Cognitive Therapy anticipates the "Problem-Solving Approaches" (discussed later in this chapter) in which the therapist very deliberately teaches the client certain procedures such as "recognizing maladaptive ideation," in particular "maladaptive thoughts." Here Beck's work is very close to the work of Ellis. Another technique is "distancing and decentering." Beck defines distancing as "the process of regarding thoughts objectively" (ibid., p. 243) involving the ability to make the distinction between

"I believe" and "I know." These confusions in thinking are often characteristic of a number of disturbances, in particular anxiety, depression, and certain paranoid states. The therapeutic procedure is to convince the patient that he is not the focus of all events, a process which Beck calls "decentering," for example, not all negative events are aimed directly at him (ibid., p. 244).

COMMENTS ON "COGNITIVE RESTRUCTURING"

There are similarities as well as differences among these three approaches of cognitive restructuring. The differences may be a matter of the personal style of the therapists. Ellis's Rational-Emotive Therapy is characterized by a great deal of confrontation to eliminate maladaptive behavior patterns and a focus on what Ellis calls "core irrational ideas." Mahoney and Arnkoff (1978) have described Meichenbaum as more concerned with "idiosyncratic thought patterns" and concentrating on constructive skill development. Beck's techniques emphasize a therapeutic interaction (perhaps reflecting his traditional training) and working to help the client recognize the distortions of his thinking and reformulate his views.

All three approaches are concerned with changing the patient's perception of the "event out there" and the message he gives himself. The changing of perceptions may be viewed as discrimination training, leading to the individual giving himself self-assurance. This is a logical first step toward the next group of therapies, the "Coping Skills Therapies."

The Coping Skills Therapies

Mahoney and Arnkoff (1978) have described "Coping Therapies" as a midpoint between cognitive restructuring and the problem-solving approaches, with the emphasis on developing skills that will help the individual deal with a number of situations. There is use of the self-instructional procedures discussed above and a number of other procedures as well. Actually, any procedure, including cognitive restructuring, muscle relaxation, and the behavioral attempts at coping directly with a problem, may be called a coping skill procedure. Cognitive-behavioral coping skills therapies differ in that they focus not only on increasing the behavioral repertoire, as in social skill training (see Chapter 3), but also on examining the person's belief system and his emotional reactions with the aim of changing the way he addresses himself (his self-messages). Sometimes the therapist must challenge the assumptions underlying a client's actions, as do both Ellis and Beck, before attempting to teach social skills.

In short, while we feel that this differentiation is somewhat arbitrary, we shall briefly describe a few of the coping skills that *do* specifically entail the changing of cognitions.

COVERT MODELING

In covert modeling, a procedure associated with Cautela (Cautela, 1971, Cautela et al., 1974), the client imagines someone else doing an act; in overt modeling, the client actually observes someone engaging in the act. In the latter procedure, the imitation would be of another person; in the former, the client imagines doing it himself! In a test of approach procedures to a feared rodent, Cautela et al. (1974) found no differences between groups practicing overt and covert modeling. In both groups more members approached a rodent than in a control group. The practical as well as the theoretical advantages of using oneself as a model, not needing the service of another person with whom the client may or may not identify, are obvious.

We have previously discussed Cautela's work as a covert

conditioning procedure but we also include his work under the cognitive therapies as being similar to that of the vicarious learning and other processes associated with Bandura (1969, 1971).

ACTIVE SYSTEMATIC DESENSITIZATION

Active systematic desensitization is a variation of systematic desensitization first described by Goldfried (1971) and elaborated by Goldfried and Davidson (1976, pp. 126–128). The change that Goldfried recommends is that in the process of systematic desensitization, instead of terminating any images that cause anxiety, the images are maintained and the person is taught to cope with the anxiety. He would engage in a behavior to counter the anxiety, such as answering an examination question. He then will learn to relax in the presence of the anxiety. Goldfried believes that this strategy is a more usable skill, with much greater carryover, than Wolpe's procedures, and there seems to be some evidence to back up this claim. Actively retaining the image in view of the anxiety it causes is very close to the extinction procedures of Stampfl and Levis (1967, 1968) and very similar to the technique of "Anxiety Management Training."

ANXIETY MANAGEMENT TRAINING

In "Anxiety Management Training," as developed by Suinn and Richardson (1971), clients are asked to visualize an event which stirs up anxiety. Then they are taught to respond to these anxiety-provoking scenes with new responses that are incompatible with the anxiety, such as deep muscle relaxation or by visualizing scenes that terminate the anxiety. Unlike the systematic desensitization procedures of Wolpe, anxiety management training does not necessarily require the use of a hierarchy. Clients are encouraged to experience the anxiety as completely as possible so that they will learn to recognize feelings of discomfort in themselves as discriminative stimuli for anxiety and learn to cope with these feelings. For this reason, in their original work Suinn and Richardson asked subjects to imagine feeling anxious in areas other than the one that was the main cause of their concern (a procedure most unlike Wolpe's) on the theoretical basis that anxiety resulting from one situation is functionally similar to anxiety from other causes, and that the "inhibitory" procedures will generalize from one anxiety-producing situation to another.

The first part of the procedures is a training in awareness to heighten the individual's awareness of his own cognitions. In short, if the subjects feel anxiety, regardless of the cause, then they are to self-instruct themselves to use the anti-anxiety procedures that they have learned. The awareness training that characterizes the first part of these procedures helps to diminish the anxiety response even more rapidly.

THOUGHT STOPPING

A procedure somewhat similar to the self-administered anxiety-management technique is the thought-stopping technique described by Wolpe (1969, 1973). This procedure was first applied to obsessional thoughts, although it may also be used in the treatment of other kinds of unpleasant thoughts and ruminations. During the procedure, the client is asked to close his eyes and to focus on the obsessional thought. At some point, when the client indicates that the thought will not leave his mind, the therapist suddenly and loudly yells "STOP!" The client is usually startled and generally reports that the obsessional thought was indeed interrupted by this rather dramatic intervention. The client is encouraged to try the procedure himself, yelling "STOP!" subvocally to himself. The procedure really does work, although often only in the short run. The thoughts may return, at which time the procedure may be repeated.

This author has used this procedure successfully, with two adaptations. The client is asked, before focusing on the obsessive thought, to imagine something pleasant for him, like being at the beach or walking on the grass. He is then told: "I am going to do something and after I do this something you are to shift your mind to the pleasant scene." When I yell "Stop" the first time the client is often too startled to shift his mind. However, the second time we go through this, he is usually able to shift.

In another variation, the suggestion is made that the subvocal voice, at least at the beginning, might be the therapist's voice and then later the client can shift to his own. The justification for this is that the therapist is giving the client permission *not* to think the obsessive thought.

Mahoney (1971), in an adaptation of this procedure, advised a client to wear a heavy rubber band around his wrist and to snap it to interrupt the obsessive thought. While many clients reject this alternative, this author found it to be very successful with a client who was obsessed with thoughts of death. The pain of the rubber band did interrupt these thoughts. (Analytically oriented readers might observe that the pain of the band might have been a kind of punishment. They may be correct!)

Thought stopping is not without its critics. Matthews and Shaw (1977) found it ineffective with anxious (as contrasted with obsessing) patients. Teasdale and Rezin (1978) did not think the procedure useful with a depressive. They report that the procedure did banish the thoughts from the "front of her mind" but that they piled up in the "back of her mind." Teasdale and Rezin interpreted these results to mean that there must be a further step, to investigate the meaning of the obsessing thoughts. This observation may or may not be true, depending upon the details of the particular case situation.

STRESS INOCULATION

A coping skills therapy similar to Anxiety Management Training is the Stress Inoculation Program of Meichenbaum (1974, 1977). Meichenbaum also views relaxation training as "an active coping skill" (Meichenbaum 1977, p. 146). Meichenbaum, quoting Epstein (1967), posits that when one strengthens a patient's defenses or coping skills, mastery will result, and that this "mastery" in effect provides an "inoculation" against the possible sources of anxiety. He views his stress inoculation procedure as the behavioral equivalent of medical immunization (Meichenbaum, 1977, p. 150).

Meichenbaum conceives of this procedure as consisting of three phases: The first phase is *educational* in that the client is taught a rationale, an understanding of his responses to the anxiety-provoking situation. (As with the "self-control" procedures described in Chapter 4, there is an assumption that the more the client knows about what is happening to him the better equipped he will be to learn procedures to counteract the anxiety.) The second phase is *rehearsal*. Here the task is to help the client acquire specific coping procedures. These are of two classes; the first class is *direct action,* such as collecting information about the feared object and "escape routes" (imagined ways the client could evade the feared object), and learning relaxation, tension reduction, and other procedures for directly counteracting the anxiety. The second class is what Meichenbaum calls *cognitive coping,* such as corrective self-talk. The client learns to monitor his self-statements and become aware of his "internal dialogue," to change the nature of the statements he makes to himself. He is to use the feelings of anxiety as a cue to use the "therapy package." The cognitive coping skills consist of a number of "coping self-statements" (i.e., a kind of "pep talk"). For example, in "preparing for a stressor," the client might say to himself: "What is it you have to do? You can develop a plan to deal with it. Just think about what you do." In "confronting and handling a stressor" he may say to himself "You can handle it. You can convince yourself to do it." In "coping with a stressor" he is taught to say, "When fear comes, just pause, label your fear from 0 to 10, and watch it change. Don't try to eliminate fear totally; just keep it manageable."

He then engages in "reinforcing self-statements" such as "It worked; you did it, wait until you tell your therapist about this. It's getting better every time you do it," and so forth. (All of the above taken from Meichenbaum, 1977, p. 155.)

Meichenbaum's third phase is *application training* where the client first tests out these procedures in a group of threatening situations other than the target anxiety situation. These rehearsals build up his "resistance" (hence, the "Inoculation").

Meichenbaum draws comparison between self-statements as in these procedures and the "positive thinking" of Norman Vincent Peale and W. Clement Stone. Certainly both Meichenbaum and Norman Vincent Peale realize the therapeutic efficacy of positive self-talk. However, Meichenbaum emphasizes that "the use of a formula or 'psychological litany' tends often to become mere ritual and repetition and does not really resolve the client's problems" (Meichenbaum, 1977, p. 159). He states that the self-talk of Norman Vincent Peale is far too general and not tailored to a client's individual problems. Just making the positive statements without coping skills training and without a chance to *act* on the thoughts is not enough to remedy a person's problematic situations (Meichenbaum, 1977, pp. 161–162).

The Problem-Solving Therapies

Problem-solving approaches use both simple and complex operant and respondent procedures as well as modeling and cognitive methods. Kanfer stated that "the goal of self-control methods is to train individuals to become better problem-solvers and behavior analysts" (Kanfer, 1977, p. 5).

"Problem solving" has long been part of many of the helping disciplines (Perlman, 1957). In their article on "Problem Solving and Behavior Modification" D'Zurilla and Goldfried (1971)[9] extended the concept to behavioral approaches.

Essentially, problem solving within the behavior modification framework refers to the ability of the individual to cope with problems, defined as "a specific situation or set of related situations to which a person must respond in order to function effectively in his environment" (D'Zurilla and Goldfried, 1971, p. 107). The resolution of problematic situations is viewed as increasing the number of alternatives by which the person can respond to or deal with the situation. The entire problem-solving process is, simply, for an individual to examine the situation, to examine the alternative ways of handling or resolving the problem, and to choose the best (and most practical) action from among the options available. Whatever action is taken should not only resolve the problem but should lessen negative conse-

[9] D'Zurilla and Goldfried later expanded their discussion of problem solving to include cognitive processes (D'Zurilla and Goldfried, 1973) and a more recent discussion of the application can be found in Goldfried and Davison (1976).

quences at the same time it heightens the positive consequences (ibid., pp. 108–109).

The problem-solving approach in the behavioral orientation is aimed at heightening the client's effectiveness in
coping and developing "self-control." (These goals are, of
course, identical with the goals of many "nonbehavioral"
therapies.)

Viewing the problem-solving approach within a social
learning framework, D'Zurilla and Goldfried have specified
a set of procedures and an orientation utilizing behavioral
techniques within five "general stages": General orientation (i.e., "set" in attitudinal factors); problem definition or
formulation; generation of alternatives; decision making
(i.e., evaluation of selection); and verification.

Under "general orientation," part of the work with a client is to impress upon him the realization that problems do
not necessarily represent pathology or deviance but occur
in everyone's life and are to be expected. Some problems
are easier to recognize than others, but the important factor
is the individual's reaction to the problem including his affective response. The affective response should be used as
a cue to alert the individual to the situation that preceded or
set it off (D'Zurilla and Goldfried, 1971, p. 113). The general identification of specific kinds of behaviors within an
A–B–C framework is the first step in problem orientation.

The next step is "problem definition and formulation."
The individual is to try to analyze the problem in specific
terms, breaking it down into its various subcomponents, so
that he can ferret out the information needed to set his
goals. Part of this process, in common with other behavioral procedures, is the translation of goals into specific
terms with empirical referents. Making this translation often necessitates reevaluation of exactly what information is
relevant and what information is irrelevant.

The next step is the "generalization of alternatives."

Here the individual considers a number of possible solutions. Assessing these alternatives should facilitate the determination of which will be the best to use in dealing with this particular problem situation.

After the individual has thought of a number of possible solutions, he then has to choose one he wishes to try ("decision making.") Generally, the more specific the procedure, the more it will lend itself to being tried out and evaluated. It is hoped that more than one alternative can be identified. In fact, if only one solution is possible, then decision making is not necessary and is redundant (Goldfried and Davison, 1976). The more alternatives formulated, the better the chance of finding one that will be successful in resolving the problem and in suggesting a strategy for implementation.

We cannot know all of the consequences of the alternatives in advance. Certainly one should consider the possible alternatives but only up to a certain point, not to excess. (This might be a problem in dealing with the obsessive patient who might very well form too great a number of different behavioral alternatives and not act on *any* of them. Needless to say, this problem-solving approach can be used to treat an obsession, but the therapist must monitor the procedure quite carefully.) As part of the specification of alternatives, we also want to specify criteria against which we can judge the comparative effectiveness of the alternatives chosen or the effectiveness of the one alternative we choose.

At some point the individual has to engage in a behavior—in other words, attempt a solution to the problem. This is the stage of verification. In carrying out this behavior, the individual again must observe its consequences, noting how close to his expected outcome the real outcome was. If there is a close enough correspondence, the matter is no longer problematic and the problem has been solved.

Problem solving as a general approach, especially when it involves internal, cognitive factors as well as external factors, has great potential for use with any of the "behavioral" techniques in this book or even with a number of other theoretical helping processes (Perlman, 1957). Gambrill claims that problem solving is useful for treating children as well as adults, depression, distressed marriages, drinking problems, the mentally handicapped (as having a preventive functioning), psychotics, and a number of other conditions (Gambrill, 1977).

Goldfried and Davison (1976) state that problem solving is particularly useful with the so-called dependent client, not only in teaching new problem-solving skills and solutions but in increasing the amount of self-generated behavior. It helps "the client to think for himself" (ibid., p. 207). It is also excellent as a carry-over procedure which the client can use on his own after he has discontinued seeing a therapist. It enhances utilization of his own behavioral and other resources and thus facilitates "generalization." Problem solving can be combined, if needed, with certain desensitization processes, especially *in vivo* desensitization. It may very well be that the individual who learns to utilize problem-solving approaches might also be helped to change the nature of the self-messages. They emphasize that with certain clients it may be necessary to program the increase of problem solving in very small steps. The client might also have to be helped in changing some of his perceptions (cognitions) of himself as a preliminary or concomitant phase of "problem solving."

One aspect of cognitive relabeling is the individual coming to see himself as competent rather than incompetent, and as able to formulate and carry out alternatives. Again, to become independent, to heighten his own "self-control." The problem-solving approach of D'Zurilla and Goldfried was influential in its own right, but also foreshadowed (and possibly facilitated) the development of a number of behavioral approaches including the contributions made by Michael Mahoney.

THE "PERSONAL SCIENCE" APPROACH OF MICHAEL J. MAHONEY

A prolific writer, Mahoney has been extremely important in influencing, in anticipating, and, in fact, helping to bring about changes in the "behavioral therapies."

Mahoney has recently devised an approach which he calls "personal science." It involves enhancing the coping skills of a client in order to help him learn to function more autonomously. In essence, it is an extension of the operant self-control procedures and, in addition, incorporates some cognitive therapeutic principles along with a problem-solving orientation. In the most recent statement of this approach (Mahoney, 1977b), he states that it is called "personal science" because it applies empirical skills of problem solving to the solving of intimate personal problems. The therapist is viewed as a "technical consultant or coach" (Mahoney, 1977b, p. 353) who helps the client in the "development of relevant coping skills." Mahoney views the therapy as an "apprenticeship" in learning the skills and sees the client as an active participant in the therapy.[10]

Mahoney's approach consists of seven steps, as follows:

1. *S*pecify the general problem area;
2. *C*ollect data;
3. *I*dentify patterns or sources;
4. *E*xamine options;

---

[10] This is an elaboration of a view of the client as cotherapist seen in earlier behavioral works (Schwartz and Goldiamond, 1975).

5. *N*arrow and experiment;
6. *C*ompare data;
7. *E*xtend or revise or replace.

(The first letter of each of the seven steps spells out the acronym "SCIENCE".) Each of these seven steps is explained in detail. For example, to "specify problems"; who is labeling the problems? In what areas (e.g., vocational, medical)? What is the degree of urgency, and what are both the short-term and long-term goals?

The second stage is to "collect data" (taking a history and making an assessment of the current contingency situation) including the usual material on medical status and affective states, but with an emphasis upon cognitive status (personal perceptions of the problem and assessment of whatever problem-relevant skills are already in the repertoire of the individual). Included is a history of the problem and its development.

In the third step, "identify patterns or sources," Mahoney tries to divide the problem to determine what aspects are due to the physical environment (e.g., living conditions, physical status, or money) what portion may be attributed to cognitive factors and/or skill deficiencies, or to irrational belief systems.

The fourth step is to "examine" the options, which is analogous to the problem-solving approach of "considering alternatives." This includes an overview of the potential goals in all areas and a survey of the potential means of achieving these goals. This analysis brings the therapist and the client into programming reward or punishment systems, and includes breaking the problem down into small steps (the method of successive approximations). Mahoney also emphasizes imitation and behavioral rehearsal, both in the therapy session and in homework assignments.

The fifth step, "to narrow and experiment," is an extension of the problem solving "eliminate unfeasible options" and includes the idea of cost efficiency, to select what is really the most feasible, to rehearse and revise. It leads to the sixth step, to "compare" data. After the client has tried out the various responses, he is to assess changes in the frequency, intensity or magnitude, duration and patterning of responses (Mahoney, 1977b, p. 355).

The last step, "extend, revise, or replace," is to continue with the program if there are signs of progress; to revise if there is no progress, or to find other means to achieve the end, eliminate those procedures which are not working and put in procedures which are working.

Mahoney makes it clear that he is not recommending a rigid formula to be followed blindly. He stresses the creativity of both the therapist and the client in providing his own programming. In fact, the client in this scheme is given a great deal of responsibility; the essential goal of the therapy is to enhance the individual's abilities.

Mahoney, to a very great degree, has synthesized many of the better tried and proven aspects not only of the behavioral approaches but of the new cognitive and problem-solving features. Future models of therapy that attempt a rapprochement of the various approaches will be influenced by Mahoney's synthesis. However, it has been pointed out by some critics that the method, while promising, has not been around long enough to evaluate (Rimm and Masters, 1979).

Mahoney makes an interesting comment in stating why he advocates the strategy of the "personal scientist." In his words, he views "psychotherapy (and, indeed, life itself) as a process rather than a product, a journey rather than a destination. Absolute lists and perfect adjustment are unattainable goals. The client who naively believes that one morning he will wake up to find himself 'cured' (normal, healthy, etc.) may be in for some very rude clinical awakenings. . . . it is one of the best signs of clinical progress when a client comes to recognize that his adjustment and coping skills can always be improved—but never perfected" (Mahoney, 1977b, pp. 361–362.)

THE "MULTI-MODAL THERAPY" OF ARNOLD A. LAZARUS

Arnold A. Lazarus, a psychologist originally from South Africa, was an early collaborator of Joseph Wolpe in works on behavior therapies. Lazarus began to differ with Wolpe not only on the theoretical basis of some of the behavior therapy procedures such as systematic desensitization of phobias, but upon their efficacy. He soon expanded his therapeutic interventions to include numerous other procedures in addition to systematic desensitization and other methods described in his joint publications with Wolpe (1966). Lazarus espoused what he then called "technical eclecticism" (Lazarus, 1967). In a provocative paper he urged therapists to remain open-minded and not to reject other techniques merely because they were from differing theoretical orientations. His concept of technical eclecticism was a plea for the therapist to be a technician rather than a scientist or a theoretician, stating that there often would be discrepancies between theoretical orientations and the procedures allied with these theoretical orientations. He quoted London's profound statement made in 1964 that "however interesting, plausible, and appealing a theory may be, it is techniques, not theories, that are actually used on people. Study of the effects of psychotherapy, therefore, is always the study of the effectiveness of techniques" (London, 1964, quoted in Lazarus, 1967).

This paper set off a flood of a debate that continued in *Psychological Reports* for the next three or four years. Lazarus illustrated his position with a very provocative article on the treatment of depression (1968) which we shall discuss in Chapter 6. In approaching this problem of depression, he showed his increasing willingness to draw procedures from many sources regardless of their theoretical origins.

Lazarus attempts to steer a mid-course between the more theoretical and the excessively empirical approaches. He states, for example, that "psychoanalytic theory is unscientific and needlessly complex; behavioristic theory is often mechanistic and needlessly simplistic." He does advocate a "social learning theory," as exemplified in his own work, and he includes many procedures other than systematic desensitization. His views tend to be somewhat antitheoretical and even antiresearch but highly clinically oriented. He believes that any approach within ethical limits can be used provided that it has an empirical orientation or basis. In fact, he states that the greater the number of approaches used, the more effective will be the therapy.

Lazarus expanded his approach of a "technical eclecticism" to include a "broad spectrum behavioral" which he then developed into an approach described best by the term "personalistic psychotherapy" (Lazarus, 1971, p. XI). His "technical eclecticism" grew into the approach which he now calls "treatment of the BASIC ID" (Lazarus, 1973). BASIC ID is an acronym which stands for *B*ehavior, *A*ffects, *S*ensation, *I*magery, and *C*ognition. The ID stands for *I*nterpersonal and the use of *D*rugs. The treatment of the BASIC ID is actually a multi-modal approach which includes borrowings from many techniques and disciplines. The seven modalities are quite interdependent. A recent statement of the development of the "BASIC ID" may be found in Lazarus (1976).

An example of multi-modal therapy given in Lazarus' initial article (1973) was of a rather disturbed young woman diagnosed as a chronic schizophrenic. Summarizing greatly, she was overweight, apathetic, withdrawn and heavily medicated. Lazarus took a detailed history and prescribed a number of therapies. For example, under "*Be-*

havior'', for inappropriate withdrawal responses he recommended ''assertive training.'' He also recommended ''nonreinforcement'' for frequent crying, specific grooming instructions for her unkempt appearance, a low-calorie diet for her excessive eating, ''rehearsal techniques'' for eye contacts, etc.

Under ''*A*ffect,'' because the client was unable to express anger, he recommended role playing; he prescribed and put into practice relaxation training; he used ''positive imagery procedures and desensitization'' for her frequent anxiety. Because she had suicidal feelings, ''time projection techniques'' (essentially a procedure for getting the suicidal client to think about herself in the future) were used. (We shall discuss this technique in Chapter 6.)

Under ''*S*ensation,'' because she had stomach spasms, he recommended abdominal breathing; because of her inner tremors he recommended the ''focusing procedures'' (Gendlin, 1978).

Under ''*I*magery'', because she had distressing scenes of her sister's funeral he recommended desensitization. She often hallucinated her mother's angry voice shouting, ''You fool!'' so Lazarus used the ''empty chair'' Gestalt technique by having the client imagine her mother sitting in the ''empty chair.'' She would confront her, argue with her, release relevant emotions, and so forth.

Under ''*C*ognition'', because she exhibited irrational self-talk, he trained her to deliberately ''dispute herself'' and to make ''corrective talk''—an application of the work of Albert Ellis.

On ''*I*nterpersonal'' relations he recommended ''self-sufficiency, assertive training,'' and other techniques. She continued on medication (*D*rugs).

We have deliberately abbreviated the procedures in this original article; there were at least five more problems under each heading with an appropriate technique for each problem. Lazarus does admit that it may strike the reader as "fragmented" and possibly mechanistic, but he stated that in the course of therapy these numerous procedures flow into a meaningful intervention and that each therapeutic intervention is thoroughly backed by evidence and rooted in empiricism.

BANDURA'S "THEORY OF SELF-EFFICACY"

Paralleling the work of Lazarus, who has concentrated on the development of therapeutic procedures, is that of Albert Bandura, who has emphasized the construction of theory. Bandura has long been troubled by the inadequacies of the theoretical rationales, and consequent practice implications, underlying the behavior therapies. As we have noted, early in his career he recognized the importance of vicarious processes, especially in his important work on modeling, and was criticized for allegedly introducing internal variables (Locke, 1979). Bandura's more recent contributions, especially the "Theory of Personal Efficacy," have been called the "most complete, clinically useful, and theoretically sophisticated formulation of behavior therapy" (Franks and Wilson, 1978, p. 15).

Bandura views behavior as governed by three factors: Respondent conditioning (classical conditioning), operant procedures such as reinforcement and punishment, and symbolic processes, particularly the cognitive or cognitive-mediating processes. Bandura, in effect, states that while all three factors affect behavior, cognitive processes are a feature of *all* methods of psychological change and all therapeutic processes are characterized by cognitive change. To ignore the central place of cognitive processes is to misunderstand the phenomenon of therapy. However, while the cognitive processes are central to and mediate change, they are only one factor in therapy. Both behavioral and cognitive changes must be accompanied by a feeling of "mastery," achieved primarily through performance. In other words, a person may have some feelings as to whether or not he can cope with a problematic situation but he will never know until he actually *tries* to cope with the problematic situation.

According to Bandura, people learn to cope by observation (modeling) and by other means through which they "acquire" and "retain" new and adaptive coping behaviors. They also learn from analyzing contingencies and from experiencing consequences. (All of these processes may be either on a conscious or on a nonconscious level.) Bandura contends that the antecedent and the consequential stimuli (conditions that precede and follow behavior), including the thoughts and the feelings that accompany the behavior, are all experienced by the individual, and they affect the probability and the form of his engaging in specific behaviors in the future. A person perceives these factors not in isolation but as part of a pattern. This perception of these factors as interconnected parts of a pattern enables him to predict whether or not he can act appropriately in the problematic situation. In other words, Bandura elaborates on the operant analysis; in addition to whether the consequences (or the antecedant factors) by themselves actually increase or decrease the behavior is the important matter of whether or not the individuals *believe* that they do so (Bandura, 1977a, p. 192). Diabetic patients receive a great deal of instruction in self-care procedures for diet, exercise, and taking medication. On the basis of his past experience with these procedures, or on the basis of observing other diabetics, a patient may predict that he will be able to learn the necessary information and skills; in this case, he will probably be very attentive to the instructor in his self-care class. The patient who feels overwhelmed by these procedures, or feels that he will never be able to learn them, will not be as attentive to an instructor.

Bandura thus sees motivation to change, or not to

change, as a reflection of whether or not the individual perceives the future consequences of his behavior and of what his expectations are. The individual must set goals, and in the process he engages in "self-evaluative reactions" (Bandura, 1977a, p. 193), establishing standards against which he then judges the effectiveness of his behavior. He also makes a judgment of the future in terms of what he thinks will result if he changes his behavior. He also assesses the *effort* that may be required for these changes to occur. "Motivation" is the sum of all of these factors interacting with one another. If there are gaps between the standards an individual sets and his performance, the result will be self-dissatisfaction, and his "motivation" for future behavior in this area will drop. For example, the diabetic who feels that his illness will be under control if he learns all of the self-care behaviors and carries them out meticulously will be highly "motivated" to follow his doctor's orders. The patient who feels that no matter what he does it will not make him feel much better will not learn the procedures; he will *not* be "highly motivated." If the first patient's efforts do not result in the expected control, he may find it difficult to continue following the procedures; he may not want to keep trying.

Another way of stating Bandura's "Theory of Personal Efficacy" is that the individual has expectations of his own ability to change, or not to change, some aspect of his life. If his feelings of "self-efficacy" are high, then his expectations are high; he feels that he can accomplish the required change behaviors or procedures and will probably attempt to do so. If his feelings of "self-efficacy" are low, he will not be "motivated" to try to make changes.

Bandura differentiates "efficacy expectations" from "outcome expectations." By the former he means the person's estimate of his ability to engage in the behavior to make a change. The individual assesses his efficacy expectations *before* he engages in the behavior. By "outcome expectations" Bandura refers to the individual's estimate that his behavior, if he does perform it, will make a difference. Many theories of change, both behavioral and others, talk about the actions people take, and about their motivation in terms of what they think the outcomes would be.

These are two separate matters that are often collapsed into a misleading single concept of "motivation." Bandura argues that there are different problems, and different focuses of intervention, specific to each. A person may feel that a particular behavior would result in a particular outcome, but that he cannot do it; his "efficacy expectations" are low. On the other hand, he may feel he can perform the behaviors (his "efficacy" is high) but that doing so will make no difference (his "outcome expectations" are low). A "highly motivated" client would be a client who feels that he *can* engage in the behavior *and* that his engaging in the behavior will make a difference in the problem or life situation.

Bandura further breaks down "self-efficacy" into its component parts, thus setting up some possible areas for training and research. Efficacy expectations can differ in *magnitude,* from simple to complex tasks; in *generality,* either restricted to one specific instance or broadened to a wide range of problems; or in *strength,* for if expectations are strong, people will persist in their actions.

Furthermore, "personal efficacy" is based on four sources of information: Performance accomplishments, vicarious experience, verbal persuasion, and emotional arousal. Each source presents a possible range of intervention procedures. Expectations based on *performance accomplishments* mean that the individual's self-efficacy (expectations of success) have been verified by the outcome. That is, he has shown *mastery.* Success raises the feelings of efficacy; failure lowers them. However, if the individual has occasional failure or difficulty with a problem and then masters it, his sense of efficacy will be even higher than if he had initial success. A diabetic patient, on the basis of experience or observation, may feel that he can master a self-care regimen. If he tries and fails, but tries again and succeeds, he will feel even more confident of his abilities than if he had been initially successful. There can be generalization of this mastery based on accomplishments to other behaviors and to other situations. Bandura suggests that while mastery can be achieved successfully through symbolic processes, real-life encounters with problematic situations produce better results.

People can also learn through *vicarious experience,* by observing others and making inferences from these observations, but observation is generally not enough to effect real and lasting changes in one's sense of self-efficacy. Learning, especially learning through modeling (live or symbolic), must be followed by performance. The diabetic patient who sees others successfully carry out their self-care regimen may feel confident that he also will be able to do likewise. He will be "highly motivated" to try, but his confidence will not last unless he is actually successful in performing his self-care procedures.

Of the various types of *verbal persuasion,* suggestion has some limited effectiveness but must generally be backed up by performance; exhortion is generally not too successful. Self-instruction is valuable if combined with modeling and with a chance to accomplish the activity.

"Emotional arousal" (invoking intense feelings of a positive, non-anxiety nature) can help raise "self-efficacy expectations," especially through therapist feedback. However, false feedback, false attribution as to the source of the problems, and misleading feedback exaggerating the efficacy of the individual have few, if any, positive effects and these are generally very short-lived.

Bandura observes that "a distinction must be drawn between information contained in environmental events and information as processed and transformed by the individual" (Bandura, 1977a. p. 200). The patient with a mild case of diabetes may have seen others whose illness was more serious, with more severe complications. He may very well perceive that "diabetes is diabetes", that all cases are alike and therefore hopeless, and so he may not attempt to engage in self-care activities to bring his case under complete control. Correcting inaccurate "processing" can obviously affect the individual's "self-efficacy" and this, in turn, can either raise or lower the rate of behavior necessary to attain "outcome expectations." Franks and Wilson (1978) commend Bandura for formulating a theory that includes different processes such as cognitive factors while at the same time maintaining an emphasis on performance as the ultimate criterion of the effectiveness of therapy. They state that while many behavior therapists ignore cognitions, and many cognitive and dynamically oriented therapists tend to underestimate the importance of behavior, "Bandura's Theory of Self Efficacy . . . provides the necessary means of elucidating the interdependence between cognitive and behavioral changes and integrating the three regulatory systems of antecedant, consequent and mediational influences into one comprehensive framework" (Franks and Wilson, 1978, p. 16). In our opinion, Bandura's theory offers great promise for facilitating generalization of effects and for avoiding the short-lived nature of the effects of many of the other behavioral therapies. Of all of the recent theories, nonbehavioral as well as behavioral, Bandura's theory promises to be one of the most provocative in stimulating research and further theory development in psychotherapy.

Conclusion

In this chapter we have presented an overview of the more recent developments in the behavioral therapies. Just as the therapeutic innovations of Wolpe and the later innovations of Skinner and his followers represented a drastic change from the earlier psycho-dynamic and nonbehavioral therapies, so some have seen the ideas discussed in this chapter as a drastic change from the mainstream of behavior therapies. To say that there is controversy and dissension among the ranks of "behaviorists" is both obvious and rather gross understatement.

There does seem to be increasing acceptance of modeling among behavior therapists, however. The introduction of the cognitive methods has reflected conflicts and produced dissensions that easily match the factionalism in the early histories of the psychoanalytic movements. While it is not appropriate to review all the details of these disputes here (these are summarized in the excellent annual volume edited by Franks and Wilson, *Annual Review of Behavior Therapy*), typical of the interchanges is the Ledwidge article (1978) entitled "Cognitive Behavior Modification; A Step in the Wrong Direction?" Ledwidge not only cites what he perceives to be the lack of evidence to substantiate the claims of the cognitive-behavior modifiers but states that there are not extensive comparative studies of behavior therapy and cognitive behavior modification. Such comparative studies, of course, are rarely—if at all—available for *most* therapeutic approaches. Until these studies are made, he suggests that the new developments be called "cognitive therapy" rather than cognitive behavior modification, as these new methods attempt to change cognitions directly rather than to change behavior directly. "To continue to render the phrase meaningless . . . if this new verbal therapy proves no more effective than the traditional verbal methods that behavior modification was meant to replace, it will unjustifiably detract from the good reputation that behavior modification enjoys today" (Ledwidge, 1978, pp. 371–372). For a critique of Ledwidge's views, see Locke (1979) and Meichenbaum (1979) and Ledwidge's rejoinder (1979).

Typical of another line of arguments is the statement that cognitions are important, but they are actually themselves a behavior and are mediated either neurally or are, like emotions and feelings, a kind of autonomic response. As autonomic responses they are subject to the same laws of conditioning, both respondent and operant, as are the phenomenon that we call "behavior" (Wolpe, 1978). In this sense, "cognitions"—so the argument goes—have always been a part, but a secondary—albeit necessary—part of behavior therapy and behavior modification. The thrust of this line of argument is, essentially, an attempt to minimize the importance of treating cognitions as phenomena that are not subject to the laws of conditioning. Furthermore, the return to these nonvisible and hypothesized variables is a return to what Skinner calls "mentalistic" explanations, which resist further explorations. In short, while the current behavioral paradigms may or may not fully explain and/or predict (depending upon which "behaviorists" you are reading), the radical behavioral position is that to invoke these "mentalistic" explanations is to revive the methodological errors of the past. As one behaviorist stated to me, "It's unscientific" (as if "Science" dealt only with the objective, the observable, and the manipulatable!). (For a response to Wolpe's views, abridged here, see Beck and Mahoney, 1979; Ellis, 1979; and Lazarus, 1979.)

It is unfortunate that the introduction of cognitive variables and the growing awareness of the inadequacies of some behavioral procedures (to say nothing of the lack of theory) has produced such heated discussion instead of careful consideration of what is operating in the treatment (successful or unsuccessful) of troubled people. Some of the behavioral pioneers have responded to the cognitive developments as a repudiation of a "scientific" ethos in favor of an "artistic" one. In the opinion of this author, the recent emphasis on the cognitive factors, like the previous developments in the social learning and modeling approaches, are not destructive or antiscientific; they are to be expected and to be welcomed as a natural evolution in the behavioral helping orientations. As Skinner says, "If an idea has survived unchanged, it only shows how bad it was. It wasn't strong enough to produce a better idea" (Skinner, quoted in Evans, 1968, pp. 90–91).

The evolving interest in cognitions may be seen as the beginning of the end of "behaviorism" or it may be a natural step in the evolution of an experimentally oriented, objective view of helping which may eventually bear so little resemblance to the approaches of Watson, or Wolpe, or Skinner that it might no longer be appropriate to call it "behavioral."

We shall return to this theme when we discuss future developments in the last chapter. In the next chapter, as an example of the utility of the various behavioral orientations, and of developments and changes in the clinical applications, we shall discuss depression as a case in point.

Chapter 6

Differential Approaches to Behavioral Intervention: Depression as an Illustration

According to an NIMH report, depression now "rivals schizophrenia as the nation's no. 1 mental health problem" (Secunda et al., 1973, p. 3.) While it is difficult to ascertain the extent of the problem, some estimates state that 15 percent of all adults between eighteen and seventy-four "may suffer from significant depressive symptoms" (Secunda et al., 1973, p. 3.) Srole found approximately 23 percent of a representative sample of the population of Manhattan suffering from depressive symptoms (Srole et al., 1962.) The incidence may be even higher when one considers that certain depressions may be overlooked or misdiagnosed as physical illness, especially those without observable organic causation (Mendels, 1970.) These so-called hidden depressions or masked depressions (Lesse, 1974) are often disguised as backaches, headaches, and other physical illnesses. As behavior therapists expanded their focus from simpler behavioral problems and the tractable phobias to more complex clinical situations, it is not surprising that they would also rise to the challenge of treating depression.

WHAT IS DEPRESSION?

While the clinical description of depression has remained remarkably consistent over the years, there is disagreement within the literature on its etiology and treatment. It has been considered variously as a transient mood state, as a symptom, as a syndrome in itself, as a disease or an illness, as a reaction to stress, and as a combination of several or of all of these. Beck (1967) raises the following critical questions: "Is depression an exaggeration of a mood experienced by the normal, or is it qualitatively as well as quantitatively different from the normal mood? Is depression a well-defined clinical entity with a specific etiology and a predictable onset, course, and outcome, or is it a 'wastebasket' category of diverse disorders? Is depression a type of reaction (Meyerian concept) or is it a disease (Kraeplinian view)? Is depression caused primarily by psychological stress and conflict, or is it related primarily to biological derangement?" (Beck, 1967, pp. 3–4.)

One view is that depression is an exaggerated form of what otherwise would be a "normal" emotion. In this conception there is a continuum from normal states of "feeling blue" to serious states, differing in degree like body temperature. The "environmentalists" favor this hypothesis, associated with the psycho-biological school of Adolph Meyer (the "Meyerian" view). Counterposed to this "continuity hypothesis" (Beck, 1967) is the view of those who see depression as a "disease" with an etiology, course, and prescription for treatment. This is the view favored by the Kraeplinian or the somatogenic school.

Some people experience only the "lows" of depression; this is called "unipolar" depression. Others experience "bipolar" depression: Periods of extreme excitement, called mania, alternating with periods of depression. In its extreme form this is a serious emotional disorder called "manic-depressive psychosis." Manic-depressive psychosis has been extremely responsive to drug treatment with Lithium Carbonate. Because of the therapeutic efficacy of Lithium, behavior therapists have not been active in the treatment of manic-depressive psychosis.[1]

The depressions have also been categorized into neurotic depression versus psychotic depression. While some authorities say that psychotic and neurotic depressions are markedly different, the environmentalists (the gradualists) state that the distinctions are a matter of degree. One theory postulates that as the neurotic depression gets deeper, internal biochemical changes may occur and the neurotic depressive becomes psychotic. It is vitally important that a careful differential diagnosis between neurosis and psychosis be made.

Some draw a dichotomy between "endogenous" and "exogenous" depression the former meaning caused by internal factors and the latter caused by external factors. More recently exogenous has been increasingly used for "reactive" causative factors, particularly stress associated with these life changes and losses such as losing a spouse, unemployment, success and various other life changes.

The diagnosis of "endogenous depression" is often used by internists and general practitioners to describe the sudden onset of depression in middle-aged people who have had no previous history of depression and where there does not seem to be noticeable environmental stress. (Beck, 1967, p. 63.)

---

[1] Lithium seems to be a symptom-specific treatment of a mental disorder, which is something longed for since the days of Freud. Lithium, however, is not a benign drug. The administration of Lithium should always be under close medical supervision. The patient must be able to follow certain dietary restrictions.

THE BIOGENIC AMINE THEORY OF
DEPRESSION

Recent developments in the psychopharmacology of depression have tended to favor the so-called disease or Kraeplinian theory. Among these developments is the Biogenic Amine Hypothesis (sometimes called the Cathectolomine Hypothesis). Greatly oversimplifying, there are chemicals in the brain called neurotransmitters. A neurotransmitter is a "naturally occurring substance in the brain cell" and it is released by the brain cell when it fires or stimulates the next cell. The neurotransmitter moves on to the receptor cell, which in turn becomes a firing cell and the signal is transmitted down the line. It is hypothesized that these neurotransmitters play a significant role in various psychological conditions. The neurotransmitter involved with depression is the one called norepinephrine. (Dopamine and serotonin are the neurotransmitters thought to be more involved with schizophrenia.) There is evidence that in a depressed person, less norepinephrine is transmitted between cells. Some is reabsorbed by the firing cell by a "re-uptake mechanism" which causes the cells to terminate the action of the "released neurotransmitter" and thus limits the amount of norepinephrine transmitted.

Two classes of drugs have been used with varying degrees of success in treating depression. The tricyclics, such as Elavil and Tofranil, in essence, interfere with the re-uptake mechanism of the firing cell, thus leaving more of the norepinephrine to go on to the receptor cell. The second class of drugs is the MAO inhibitors such as Nardil, Parnate and Marplan. Norepinephrine is stored in small "granules." When the cell fires, the norepinephrine leaves the firing cell and crosses the space between cells, called the "synaptic cleft." Some of the neurotransmitter is inactivated by an enzyme known as COMT (Catechol-O-Methyl

Transferase). The neurotransmitter is further inactivated by the MAO (Monoamine Oxidase), which takes it back to the firing cell and stores it again. The MAO inhibitors counteract the MAO, thereby allowing more of the norepinephrine to cross the synaptic cleft to the receptor cell.

It is beyond the scope of this book to comment further upon these classes of drugs except to point out that there have been positive results obtained by their application (Quitkin et al, 1979), particularly in combination with psychotherapy (Weissman, 1979). It goes without saying that determination of whether or not a drug should be used should be done in cooperation with and under the supervision of a physician. We feel that therapists of all orientations, both behavioral and psychoanalytic, have tended to ignore the potential utility of drugs as a part of therapy with the seriously and the chronically depressed patient. In fact, in some cases the use of drugs may be a necessity for successful treatment (Kolata, 1979).

THE SYMPTOMATOLOGY OF DEPRESSION

People who are depressed generally display a number of common symptoms. The first is disturbance of *mood*. Depressed patients generally are sad, feel "blue," are unhappy, do not feel pleasure, often feel worthless, empty, and futile. Sometimes they can attribute their feelings to external events, but often they cannot. They often cry (Mendels, 1970).

There may also be disturbances of *thought processes:* Feelings of pessimism, guilt, unworthiness, poor self-image. They often lack motivation for and interest in work. Very frequently there is a decrease in their efficiency and concentration.

There are also changes in *behavior and appearance:* A

sad, dejected face, a low rate of speech; they seem "mirthless." Some depressives attempt to hide despair, many do not. There may also be a lack of care about personal appearance with visible sloppiness and poor grooming. There is slowing down of bodily movements and thinking and a reduction of spontaneous movement and expressive gestures—a "psychomotor retardation" that initially attracted the attention of behavior therapists and has been, as we shall see, the focus of much behavioral intervention in depression.

The depressive may be agitated rather than retarded in his movement and speech. Such a person will show constant physical activity, such as picking at the face, biting the lip, inability to rest. Much of this behavior, of course, reflects despair, but it also is meaningless behavior that does not elicit reinforcement from others and not relieve the depression.

Furthermore, there are often *somatic symptoms*. Food does not taste good, there is a loss of appetite and a loss of weight sometimes so severe as to resemble anorexia. (There are some few clients, incidentally, who respond to depression with "depressive-equivalent" behavior which may be overeating to the point of obesity.) Constipation is not uncommon.

Sleep disturbance is one of the most common problems, either some difficulty falling asleep, or restlessness during the night, or awakening after a few (one to four) hours of sleep with inability to go back to sleep. Nightmares are not uncommon. Some depressed people may sleep *too* much, escaping reality.

Many times depressed people complain of vague aches and pains of all systems of the body. With women, there may be disturbances and changes in the menstrual cycle, either a lengthier cycle with a lighter flow, or a complete amenorrhea. There often is a loss of libido in patients of both sexes, ranging from a moderate loss of interest in sex to a marked aversion (Mendels, 1970, pp. 7–11).

The depressed person often does not go to a psychiatrist first, but to a general practitioner, or an internist, or a gynecologist. It is easy to concentrate on a "physical" problem and to overlook a depression. Of course, there is always the question of whether the depression is a cause of the physical problem or a result. Klerman (1971) considers depression a "psychosomatic disease." He states that people who suffer depression and report such things as constipation and lack of pleasure in food are not imagining these things. However, a complete physical workup is especially essential in depressed patients, for in a small number of these patients the depression may be the first indicator of a more serious physical disease. Depression may be the first symptom of certain central nervous system diseases, such as Parkinson's disease or multiple sclerosis (particularly in the twenty-five to thirty-five year old group.) Depression may sometimes be the first indication of brain tumors which can be characterized by crying spells, emotional lability, and in some rare cases, small strokes. The gastrointestinal system is often the focus of patients' complaints; dyspepsia, anorexia, and nausea. There is some evidence to show that "about 10% of the patients with pancreatic carcinoma first present with depression" (Klerman, 1970, p. 30). Certainly depression is involved in cardiac disease, although again it is often difficult to separate the cause and effect. The same may be said of rheumatoid arthritis. Depression often may be a sequela of diseases such as viral pneumonia, hypertension, gastrointestinal disease, or any of a large number of other acute or chronic problems.

It is safe to say that the role of depression is frequently understated in considering a number of medical problems and conditions. Furthermore, depression is certainly heavily implicated in such conditions as obesity and anorexia nervosa, as well as a number of other problems. It may be,

of course, that depression is secondary rather than causative in a number of these conditions.

Depression, then, is an extremely complex phenomenon.
It is the unfortunate tendency of many psychotherapists—
nonbehavioral as well as behavioral—to oversimplify the
manifestations and problems of depression. Oversimplifica-
tion can be dangerous, especially when considering the
treatment of depression.

DEPRESSION AND SUICIDE

A real danger in depression is suicide. According to some
authorities, more than 80 percent of people who have successfully completed suicide gave indications of depression.
Suicide, of course, may be the final result of the depression
as well as of other psychiatric disorders, mainly alcoholism
and schizophrenia. Overdrinking may be called a "depressive-equivalent behavior."

While older people may be more depressed, we know
that many younger people also are seriously depressed. Suicide was the second highest cause of death in the eighteen
to twenty-four age bracket, with the ages twenty to twenty-
four especially dangerous (Weissman, 1974.)[2]

Suicide as a phenomenon tends to be underreported. Sui-
cides often tend to be classified as accidents for a number of
reasons, such as religious prohibitions, insurance pay-
ments, etc. Most people who attempt suicide, as well as
many people who successfully complete suicide, announce
their intentions in advance in a number of ways, either by
speaking of it directly, by giving away their belongings,
making a will, or a number of other actions. We shall not go

[2] For a complete review of the literature on childhood depression, see
Schulterbrandt and Raskin, 1977. For a critique of the concept of childhood depression, see Lefkowitz and Burton, 1978.

into this at the moment, but we shall discuss the complications of suicide in relation to behavioral treatments below.

DEPRESSION AND GENDER

Women are diagnosed as depressed more often than men. For example, the label "neurotic depression, unipolar type" appears in a ratio of six women to every man. There have been various explanations advanced for this disproportionate frequency. Some authorities state that it is because most physicians are men.

Another hypothesis is that women tend to talk about their feelings more openly and are more likely to go to physicians to talk about their depression than men, who are inhibited in handling their emotions. A third explanation is that more men attempt to try to resolve their problems of depression by alcoholism. Thus the higher rate of alcoholism among men may actually hide the incidence of depression, with higher rates of depression cited for women but lower rates of alcoholism.

Others have stated that women in our society are conditioned and reared in a "depressiogenic" role (Pauline Bart, quoted in Albin, 1976.) Whatever the etiological reasons, and whether or not there is actually a difference in depression between the genders, it seems obvious that there is a clinical difference. Most clinicians, in the course of their professional lifetimes, see more women whom they diagnose as depressed than men. Any therapist, behavioral or otherwise, should be aware of the cultural factors that may influence the more frequent diagnosis of depression in women.[3]

[3] The reader is referred to Weissman and Paykel's *The Depressed Woman* (1974) for a specific study of depression in women, as well as to Franks and Burtle (1974) for psychotherapy with depressed women.

Behavioral Approaches to the Treatment of Depression

For our purposes here, we shall concentrate upon adult depression (adult meaning from late adolescence on to the end of the life cycle.) To the best of our knowledge, most if not all of the behavioral interventions have been done primarily with adult depressions.

INTRODUCTION

Perhaps it is ironic that increasing research into the behavior therapies has shown that they have not proved to be highly successful in the areas previously hypothesized that they would be, such as the treatment of enuresis, stuttering, smoking, and obesity (Yates, 1975). Yet is is becoming increasingly clear that these behavior therapies are effective in other areas and that the behavioral approaches have great potential for facilitating the effectiveness of nonbehavioral approaches. One of the areas of possible rapprochement is in the treatment of the affective disorders, particularly depression.

While the study of depression-qua-depression is fairly recent in the behavioral literature, there have always been studies of "depressive-equivalent" behavior, such as alcoholism and obesity. Most of the behavioral work has been with "reactive" depressions, which tend to be associated with the orientation of the "environmentalists" or "gradualists" and hence were considered to be more open to be treated by behavioral means. Just as there is overlapping among the differing theories of depression, there has also been overlapping between respondent and operant approaches to depression. While the treatment of depression seems to have been of more interest to the operant conditioning school and to the cognitive behaviorists (particularly Beck et al., 1978, 1979), an examination of depression as viewed by each of the various orientations will illustrate the differences.

CONDITIONED RESPONSES, ANIMAL MODELS, AND DEPRESSION

Some of the early work in the behavior therapy treatment of depression was done by Wolpe, paralleling the research on animal models, primarily the work with primates by Harry Harlow and his associates in Wisconsin (Suomi and Harlow, 1977) and the important research on "learned helplessness" by Martin E.P. Seligman (1975).

The idea of depression as a conditioned emotional response that accompanies the anxiety that results from continued exposure to noxious or threatening stimuli permeates the work of Wolpe (1973.) Wolpe, following a medical model, speaks of the "melancholic triad" of depressive affect, inhibition of action, and inhibition of thinking (Wolpe, 1973.) Wolpe points out, in agreement with Freud, that depression is sometimes an expected response to serious loss or deprivation. He also differentiates between "normal" depression and "pathological" depression. Wolpe believes that psychotic depression, like most of the psychoses, is basically biological. Neurotic depression, though, can be "(1) an exaggeration and prolongation of the normal reaction to loss, (2) a consequence of severe and prolonged anxiety and (3) a consequence of failure to control interpersonal situations, such failure being due to the inhibiting effects of neurotic anxiety" (Wolpe, 1973, p. 236). Wolpe talks about the feeling of helplessness in the face of death or severe deprivation, anticipating the work of Seligman (see below). He states that if the depression lasts a long time, the individual is increasingly less able to react with coping behavior that will stop the depression. He speculates that there may be a biological (endogenous) insufficiency predisposing an individual to depression. However, he also holds that people who have experienced losses (and depression) in the past experience "a conditioned helplessness" which becomes an "inhibitory reaction of great strength" (Wolpe, 1973.)

Learned Helplessness

The "learned helplessness" model is associated with the name of Martin E. P. Seligman and his collaborator, Steven F. Maier.[4]

As an illustration, they showed that if a naive dog is exposed to an unpleasant stimulus, such as electric shock, it either will escape the shock or can be taught to escape the shock. However, if the dog is placed in a yoke or harness so that it cannot escape the shock, and continues to receive shocks, if, after a period of time, the harness is removed and the dog is reshocked, it will no longer try to escape. It will whimper, run around, moan, and finally give up to the point where the shock has to be terminated to spare the dog. Quite simply, the dog has learned from his previous exposure to an inescapable shock that no matter what it does, it cannot avoid the pain; there is no connection between whatever it does and the consequences. In other words, the response of the environment is independent of whatever action it engages in. The dog's attempts at escape will not be reinforced; on the contrary, the punishment will continue. A naive dog who has not been yoked will soon learn that its escape behavior will terminate the electric shock. The dog who has been yoked will give up. This condition is called "learned helplessness."

[4] While Seligman and his colleagues are prolific writers, early statements may be found in Miller and Seligman (1976.) A short but comprehensive view may also be found in Miller, Rosellini, and Seligman (1977).

Research with humans shows that they respond in similar fashion. If a person is exposed to overwhelmingly aversive conditions which he cannot control, his "motivation" when he is reexposed to shock or trauma is nil (Seligman, 1975, p. 22.) Thus there is a "motivational deficit" that characterizes learned helplessness. It is important to remember that it is not the trauma the individual experiences itself that triggers the "learned helplessness," but the *lack of control* the individual feels in relationship to that trauma. There is nothing he can do, so he thinks, to change the effects or to have control over the trauma; he is helpless (Seligman, 1975.)

An individual who is not motivated in the face of aversive stimuli often may not be motivated in the presence of non-aversive stimuli. His lack of motivation, evidenced by a lack of behavior and depressed affect, is a condition analogous to depression and functionally *is* depression. The idea that one simply cannot do anything about "conditions," so that it is not even worth trying, is common to many definitions of depression (Miller and Seligman, 1975.)

The learned helplessness model has produced a great deal of research. The connection between learned helplessness and the individual's perception of the lack of reinforcement in his environment provides a bridge to the operant model to be discussed below (Miller and Seligman, 1976).

The learned helplessness concept has been criticized constructively and has been connected to other theories in cognition (see Miller and Norman, 1979.)[5]

---

[5] In Miller et al. (1977), there is a connection made between learned helplessness and the "negative cognitive set" of depression (ibid., p. 112.) He makes a connection between the so-called paralysis of the will and the poor self-image in the cognitive theories of depression formulated by Beck (1972, 1976). There is even a relation to the Biogenic Amine theory of depression, as animals who experience "learned helplessness" also experience lowered levels of norepinephrine (Seligman, 1975, pp. 69–74). This is a controversial linkage, for the question of causation *or* effect has not yet been answered. Is lowered level of norepinephrine a *cause* or is it a *result* of depression (learned helplessness)?

WOLPE'S TREATMENT OF DEPRESSION

While the learned helplessness theory is compatible with both operant and cognitive theories, it can also be related to Wolpe's view of depression. Wolpe consistently refers to the "conditioning process" in depressed states. He feels that reactive depression often is associated with severe anxiety; the depression follows the anxiety. The person may feel depressed or anxious or both. In this view, depression is another form of emotional response ultimately secondary to anxiety, which is a conditioned response to noxious stimuli in the environment. Thus depression is a consequence of conditioned helplessness; the patient has probably been anxious for a long time. In the past, he may have engaged in certain activities which reduced his anxiety but now they fail to relieve the anxiety, and the patient falls back into passivity, into the depression of conditioned helplessness (Wolpe, 1973, p. 237). Wolpe states that while the depression will tend to dominate the anxiety, in most cases of reactive depression the client can be counterconditioned successfully. Systematic desensitization or assertive training or other techniques can be used to diminish and eliminate the anxiety. When the anxiety is overcome, the depression will cease (Wolpe, 1973).

Wolpe also feels that depression may occur in relationships where one person unduly dominates another. The person who is dominated reacts with certain "conditioned anxiety-response habits" when he thinks of asserting himself or acting against the dominant person. This feeling of "powerlessness" may result in chronic depression. He says that these depressions have often been misdiagnosed as "neurasthenia" or even "existential neuroses." He recommends assertive training for this kind of depression. Assertive training, as we discussed in Chapter 2, is a form of reciprocal inhibition through positive counterconditioning.

Wolpe believes that learning the sources of their depression usually makes individual attacks of depression easier for people to tolerate. The next stage in the strategy would be to decondition the unadaptive emotional habits that were the sources of depression (Wolpe, 1976.)

Wolpe has also stated that despite his early contention that psychoses are basically organic, recent work has shown that they can be amenable to deconditioning or counterconditioning interventions (Wolpe, 1973; 1976.) While Wolpe's main therapeutic paradigm or model is basically a counterconditioning or reciprocal inhibition model, he also recommends the "systematic rewarding" of the individual's efforts to break the depressive cycle, an approach similar to the operant conditioning approach to be discussed later in this chapter.[6]

---

[6] Harry F. Harlow and his associates at the University of Wisconsin have produced anaclitic depression (depression suffered by human infants following separation from mother) in monkey infants. Conditions that allegedly produce depression in humans —for example, early separations that predispose toward later depressions—produce similar effects in monkeys (Suomi and Harlow, 1977, p. 172). They have also found that analogies of therapies used with humans were useful in treating depressions in monkeys. Harlow assigned depressed monkeys to socially hyperactive monkeys who were considered "therapist monkeys." Exposing subjects to "therapist monkeys" for two hours a day, in various combinations and experimental permutations (which we shall not go into here) showed that the therapist monkeys were successful in reversing the effects of depression.

They have also attempted to replicate, in monkeys, conditions that produce depression in adults, particularly related to the condition of "helplessness." They have concluded that while there are analogies between depression in monkeys and depression in humans, their animal models have not provided as much information as have their studies on the "total isolation syndrome," i.e., anaclitic depression. They point out (correctly, in our view), that this is partially due to the lack of agreement on certain aspects of human depression (e.g., endogenous versus exogenous depression) (Suomi and Harlow, 1977, p. 135.)

Depression in monkeys as produced by Suomi and Harlow may be viewed within a respondent model as conditioned responses to harmful stimuli, in this case the effects of early deprivation, producing "learned helplessness." However, one reinterpretation compatible with Wolpe and Suomi's and Harlow's is that the depression may be due to a fault or a deficiency in the ecology of reinforcement. It is primarily the consideration of the ecology of reinforcements that differentiates the operant from the respondent model of depression.

OPERANT, OR CONSEQUENTIAL, MODELS OF DEPRESSION

Depression received important attention from Skinner in his seminal book, *Science and Human Behavior* (1953). He first referred to "depression" as a "general weakening of other forms of behavior" (1953, p. 165.) In his chapter on "psychotherapy," Skinner referred to the emotional responses around passive resistance and around boredom, to the effect of not having one's behavior consequented or rewarded by a payoff (in other words, an "extinction" effect.) He stated that depressions are emotional states that are a function of manipulable variables, and that among these variables is the important influence of the individual's particular "environmental history" (as well as his history of other factors) (Skinner, 1953, p. 363.) In particular, Skinner viewed depression as a conditioned emotional response which accompanies the nonreinforcement of previously reinforced behavior. In other words, depression is a concomitant of extinction (linked functionally to extinction).[7]

Extinction, or loss, is a disturbance of the behavior-consequence sequence. Depression as a disturbance in the behavior-consequence (reinforcement) contingencies was described, among others, by Ferster (1965). Ferster states that depression could be due to a number of factors; the person might continue to behave but there is less or no reinforcement for the behavior; if there are lower rates of behavior, there is less reinforcement. This formulation was proposed by Lazarus (1968), Ferster (1972, 1973), Seitz (1971), and by Liberman and Raskin (1971).

[7] This view of depression accompanying the extinction of previously reinforced behavior is a theme that runs throughout later behavioral approaches to depression. Agras sensitively points out that extinction is "a thesis similar to 'loss,'" stating that psychoanalytic theory "hypothesizes loss to be an event central to the etiology of depression" (Agras, 1978, pp. 45–46).

There are a number of additional behavioral explanations of depression. It may be that there is a thin schedule of reinforcement or a slow decrease or sudden absence of reinforcement. There is ample evidence to show that sudden and traumatic life events can interrupt a behavior-reinforcement sequence (Rahe, 1975). For example, the death of a husband may mean the cessation of reinforcement for a number of his wife's behaviors, such as her cooking. Moving to a new community (even if the move is a desirable one) may involve loss of satisfying daily contacts with neighbors and friends in the old neighborhood.

If there is a lack of behavior to elicit reinforcement, then there will be no reinforcement; depression may occur instead. This is why Lewinsohn et al. (1970) found in studying college students who were depressed. There were potential reinforcers in the environment, but the students were not engaging in the behavior that would elicit these reinforcements. His students lacked "social skills." Lewinsohn used time-limited treatment groups with specific behavioral objectives and homework assignments to treat this particular form of depression (see Lewinsohn et al., 1970; Lewinsohn, 1975; Lewinsohn et al., 1976).

Another factor may be a loss of the discriminative stimuli which control behavior. A woman who has lost her husband has lost not only a source of reinforcement (i.e., praise for her cooking) but also the discriminative stimuli that set the "conditions" or the "rules" governing the cooking behavior. In a depressed state, she would probably not cook at all, finding cooking and even shopping for food for herself alone as unrewarding.

Stimulus props are another class of variables in behavior that are involved in depression. These are environmental conditions that are present when the behavior is being learned but that if disrupted can upset the behavior. For example, a couple might be suddenly transferred from one country to another. The wife, an expert and proficient cook at home, may find herself unable to cope with shopping and cooking in unfamiliar surroundings.

Still another possible "cause" of depression is that a behavior is being met either with punishment or with aversive consequences. By definition, behavior that is punished will drop in frequency, thus producing depression. A mother who receives considerable praise and affection from her teenage son when she prepares his favorite chocolate cake may suddenly find that when he develops acne, her cake will be met with hostility because he feels that the chocolate cake caused the acne.

Another possibility is that the person may be engaging in behavior that elicits punishment from the environment. If a young man is cynical and sarcastic in conversations with his peers, they may very well ignore him or attack him in response to his sarcasm. He may, in response, stop talking. Any behavior that drops in frequency, such as behavior that is being punished, may be accompanied by a flattened affect, a loss of motivation, and a number of other signs which could be equivalent to the clinical conditions of "depression."

Costello (1972a) states that when a person is in depression, his lack of interest in the environment and his low rate of behavior may be due not so much to a lack of density of reinforcement but to a "loss of reinforcer effectiveness." This lack of "reinforcer effectiveness" may be due to certain internal changes (biochemical or neurophysiological) or there may be interruptions of a reinforcer which maintains a whole *chain* of behavior. In a chain of behavior *all* elements of the chain must be present; if one element is missing, then the reinforcers may no longer be effective even though they are still being elicited (Costello, 1972a, p. 241).

Costello states that this would explain the lack of interest, the loss of appetite, and the loss of sexual desire among depressed individuals. Costello's argument becomes quite technical at points, but he states that the evidence for a chain of behaviors is suggestive because in many ways there is often not an obvious link between a *specific* loss and a *general* feeling of depression as usually formulated in the view of depression as an extinction phenomenon. For example, an immigrant who has not maintained contact with the father he left may lose his appetite for food, sex, etc., when hearing of the death of his father (Costello, 1972a, p. 244). Costello's views were criticized by Lazarus (1972), who states that generally "depression is due to a loss and a lack" (again we notice the similarity to psychodynamic theories).[8]

Depression may also relate to schedules of reinforcement. Certain schedules of reinforcement have unique characteristics. The fixed-ratio schedules are schedules where reinforcements are delivered after a specified amount of work is done (a specific ratio of work to reinforcement). In a laboratory experiment, for example, a machine can be set to deliver reinforcers after a specified amount of work has been done, such as every third or fifth, or tenth, or thirteenth, or *any* number. Piece work, where one is paid after completing a specified number of units, e.g., "X" dollars for every ten pairs of shoes on which a worker has placed heels, is an example of a fixed-ratio schedule. One characteristic of a fixed-ratio schedule is that a person will tend to complete a unit and then relax for a while before he begins to work again. This period of "rest" is called a post-reinforcement pause. If a small amount of work is required (a small ratio), the post-reinforcement pause will usually be small. The larger the ratio of work required, the larger the post-reinforcement pause. A very large effort will result in a long post-reinforcement pause, during which an individual may engage in no behavior, may

---

[8] For this debate, see Costello, 1972a; Lazarus, 1972; and Costello, 1972b.

brood, or may be sad or bored by the inactivity. In other words, an extremely long post-reinforcement pause may resemble a depression. For example, a student who spent several years writing an extremely difficult dissertation did nothing for seven months after receiving the Ph.D. but watch western movies on television. This was a post-reinforcement pause, but severe enough to be equivalent to a depression. Similarly, many so-called "success depressions" may be post-reinforcement pauses, though other variables may be operative.

A schedule of reinforcement which required a high degree of effort, with correspondingly less frequency of reward, may produce a condition called "ratio strain" (the technical name is abulia). Ratio strain results in a marked lack of behavior, where the individual may even eventually give up. This may be particularly severe in a schedule of reinforcement called a "progressive ratio," where the demands or the ratio of behavior required is constantly increasing, placing more behavioral demands but without increasing the amount of reinforcement. For example, a client was on a scholarship requiring that each semester he had to achieve a higher academic average than the semester before. If the requirement was continually raised, then the individual may react to his situation as basically providing aversive consequences, may give up attempting to meet the requirements and may simultaneously feel depressed.

Depression may be inadvertently reinforced by the individuals around the patient. For example, if nobody pays attention to a woman when her behavior is "normal," but attention is given when she is behaving in a depressed manner, then people around her may be unwittingly reinforcing her depression. The consequences of depression (someone paying attention to her) are reinforcing to the woman. The consequences of "healthy" behavior (being ignored) are not reinforcing to the woman. Hence, depression may become an operant to receive attention. In this formulation, depression may be seen as a manipulative maneuver, although not necessarily on a conscious basis (Bonime, 1966; Stuart, 1967c).

Another operant view of depression is that there may be potential reinforcers in the environment but the individual cannot perceive or recognize them, thus does not engage in the behavior that would elicit reinforcements. There may very well be reinforcements available for, let us say, the isolated college student or the housewife burdened by child care and housework. The behavioral intervention might well be to heighten the discriminative ability of the client so that he/she will recognize activities and people who could provide reinforcers. Having discriminated these potential reinforcers, the individual then has to conduct himself in such a way as to elicit these reinforcers from the environment. He/she may either not be able to act to elicit the reinforcers, or may not know how to act (see our previous discussion of the work of Lewinsohn and his associates in the teaching of social skills, often through groups, to college students).

OPERANT TREATMENT APPROACHES TO DEPRESSION

Most of the behavioral treatments of depression are based upon an interpersonal conception of depression, viewing the individual within his total life (contingency) situation. Within this conception, depression is seen as related to a disruption of the behavior-consequence sequence and/or to lack of discimination or to other components of the operant model such as schedule effects, extinction, etc. Depression may also be maintained by the attention it elicits from "significant others" (a "secondary gain") (Liberman and Raskin, 1971, p. 522). This view of etiology parallels the psychodynamic view of "loss" but emphasizes much more the objective, functional, and observable relations between events in the environment and the individual, eliminating behavioral deficits or lowering behavioral excesses (McLean, 1976). In other terms, treatment attempts to help the client to elicit the amount of reinforcement potentially available in his environment, or to increase his prosocial adaptive behaviors (his social skills) (Lewinsohn, 1975). If his current behavior is being met with punishment or aversive consequences, then one approach is to help the individual either to learn to avoid the punishing consequences or to learn to engage in alternative behavior that will elicit positive reinforcements for him. Heightening his ability to identify potentially available reinforcers is also an approach. All of these approaches also eventually include working with the client to analyze *all* of his contingency relationships that may play a role in either the etiology or the treatment of depression.

Early behavioral intervention tended to focus on increasing the amount of behavior that the individual engages in. While this certainly may break the cycle of depression, the technique is effective only if the increased behavior is continually reinforced (Liberman and Raskin, 1971). In an early paper, Lazarus (1968) suggested combining positive reinforcement with "time projection" not only to help the client to engage in additional behaviors, but to encourage him to view himself at some point in the future, e.g., make plans. This is a sensitive and effective therapeutic procedure, especially useful for treating those depressed clients with suicidal ideation. Lazarus also suggests "affective expression," the deliberate therapeutic provocation of anger or amusement, or affection—any feelings that may help to break a depressive cycle (Lazarus, 1968, p. 88). This procedure is very similar to the psychodynamic approach of "catharsis." It is well known in psychodynamic literature that while catharsis may lead to a temporary relieving of the feeling of depression, its effects are generally short-lived. A behavioral reinterpretation may be that unless there is an analysis of and intervention into the total behavior-contingency relationships, the positive effects of this procedure—the expression of emotion—will be short-lived. Lazarus's early formulations have been expanded into a treatment framework in which he applies a series of procedures to depression, his "multi-modal therapy" (treatment of the BASIC ID, Lazarus, 1974).

Depressed patients also show cognitive manifestations, such as low self-esteem, feelings of failure, powerlessness, and so forth. Most behavior therapists have been as sensitive to these factors as to the feelings of sadness, apathy, boredom, fatigue, and lack of interest in food, sex, and other identified aspects of depression. However, most of the early treatment programs in depression isolated specific behaviors (either lack of prosocial behaviors which could be reinforced or an excess of aversive behaviors which were being punished) and then had clients engage in certain activities to remedy these behavioral deficits or excesses. If depression is viewed as an extinction trial (if the lack of reinforcement produces less behavior which in turn produces less reinforcement), then the obvious therapeutic strategy is to break the cycle by getting any sort of behavior going. The homemaker who scrubs a floor or vacuums when she feels "blue" has learned that such activity works toward lifting the depression. (There may even be some physiological reasons, as there is some evidence that an increase in activity increases the norepinephrine level in the body.) Lewinsohn and his associates helped the patients to increase their activity level through a variety of "Pleasant activities." "Pleasant activities," incidentally, are *not* synonymous with positive reinforcement. They are only "positively reinforcing activities" if the environment responds in a positively reinforcing way (a response that maintains or raises the rate or frequency of behavior.)

Most of the attention of early behavior therapists was

concentrated on increasing the amount of reinforcement, increasing the amount of prosocial adaptive behavior to elicit reinforcement, or decreasing aversive behaviors that elicit punishment or aversive consequences. In addition, there have been programmed attempts to increase the behavioral repertoire, to increase behavior that can elicit reinforcement, and to break the extinction cycle.

It is important to remember that levels of behavior can change suddenly from very low to quite high, and from all outward appearances a person may be happy and certainly not depressed. However, if you were to ask him how he feels, he may answer, "I feel terrible." He might further elaborate that "my life has no pleasure." Despite the fact that his behavior is at a high level and he seems to be "over" his depression, he still doesn't feel good; he may even admit to suicidal ideation. Thus, while the behavioral aspects of this depression have been eased, the client still *feels* depressed. It is often not enough merely to raise the level of behavior, or to dispel the immediate feelings of sadness. It is often necessary to help a client to change the nature of his thoughts and to change his self-statements—in short, to change his cognitions.

Cognitive-Behavioral Approaches to the Treatment of Depression

The leading figure in the treatment of depression through cognitive-behavioral means is the Philadelphia psychiatrist Aaron Beck. In Beck's own accounting (Beck, 1972), he started out to prove Freud's concept that depression is inverted hostility. According to Abraham (1911), there may be a reservoir of hostility toward loved ones. This hostility is unacceptable; therefore it is turned against the self. Certainly, reasoned Beck, if dreams are the "royal road to the unconscious," then he would examine this concept by examining dreams. In Beck's study of dreams, he did not find support for rage turned inward, but found that his patients were afraid of loss. They experienced sadness and were afraid that if they expressed hostility it would cost them the affection of people around them. Beck theorized that depression was not so much inverted hostility, but much more a fear of losing the love and support of significant people. The difference is subtle, but extremely meaningful.

Beck feels that this overwhelming sense of loss might even be considered "causative" of depression. The sense of loss permeates the patient's view of himself, his world, the future, the past, etc. The losses may be real, such as the loss of a parent or spouse, or loss of youth, or they may be imagined losses. After the loss, either real or imagined, the individual views his entire life experiences negatively, as a defeat or a deprivation. He further feels himself as deficient, inadequate, unworthy. He is self-blaming and has extremely critical, negative views about himself. He experiences sadness as an "inevitable consequence" of the sense of deprivation, pessimism, and self-criticism. He may become apathetic, he may give up, he will certainly experience a loss of spontaneity and, in extreme cases, consider suicide.

There are behavioral manifestations as well as somatic symptoms. There are the so-called vegetative signs: Loss of appetite, libido, etc., all of which Beck postulates as further explained by a "feedback model" with the patient continually interpreting his life experience in the negative way, especially his dysphoria, sense of loss, and the physical symptoms (Beck, 1976, pp. 128–131). Beck further found in a series of studies that depressed patients had a higher percentage of "masochistic dreams" than nondepressed patients. In these "masochistic dreams" they viewed themselves as losers. They would put money in a coke machine and not get a coke. They would call their psychotherapist and get an automatic answering unit. In tests of fantasy, he found that depressed patients identified with losers more significantly than did nondepressed (Beck, 1972).

Beck also found that depressed patients interpreted their experiences and the happenings in their lives as rejections, failures, and deprivation. They tended to overgeneralize and to exaggerate negative aspects of their behavior, all leading to lowered (retarded) rates of behavior. Beck hypothesized a "cognition-affect" chain where he states that both affect and cognition are lowered by decreased rates of behavior. A drop in behavior is typical of many depressives (loss of appetite, libido, sleep disturbances, and so on). This drop in behavior (according to behavioral theory) results in more lack of reinforcement, further evidence to the depressed individual that he is worthless. Hence the downward spiral is accelerated. In addition to this "downward spiral" (an extended period of extinction), Beck found serious disturbances in the thought patterns of his depressed patients. Beck found that his patients' thoughts were characterized by a set of "idiosyncratic patterns" which he called the "cognitive triad" (Beck, 1967). The first part of this cognitive triad was that most patients felt that life so far had been very bad to them. They had an extremely negative view of the past. The second part was that they had a very poor opinion of themselves; they had extremely negative self-images. Thirdly, and very important as a prognostic for suicide and self-destruction, they had a very nihilistic, negative view of the future. They did not think that things were going to be different for them; they did not think that they could change or influence their negative futures.

Beck's work does not necessarily contradict that of the earlier behavior therapists. He also aims to halt the downward spiral of extinction at the beginning, through behavioral means (for example, the graded task mastery, see below) and later by the addition of cognitive means.[9] Beck feels that intervention into depression necessitates intervention into the cognitive systems of his clients, *in addition* to the behavioral interventions of raising or lowering behaviors.

Briefly, Beck attempts to stop the downwardly spiraling extinction trial of depression, with its accompanying feelings of sadness, inadequacy and self-blame, by getting some behavior going. He will assist a client in "scheduling behavior," starting with tasks that can be easily done and for which the client can elicit some reinforcements from the environment. He will then proceed to more difficult and more personally meaningful activities (the "graded task mastery"). For example, he will then endeavor to have the client learn "mastery" and "pleasure" techniques (Beck et al., 1978, p. 82ff). To facilitate the "graded task mastery," he will have the client try to imagine the steps in the program, the possible difficulties and successes, a technique he calls "cognitive rehearsal" (Beck et al., 1978, pp. 89–90). Beck will also use assertiveness training and role playing for specific situations as well as more generalizable ones.

After the client has begun to engage in behavior, after the extinction trial begins to become reversed (or at least the depression does not get any worse), Beck suggests the more concentrated use of cognitive techniques, including rational disputation; becoming aware of and analyzing "automatic thoughts" (see chapter 5 above); reattribution techniques, designed to help the client minimize self-blame; a search for alternative behaviors and ways of thinking in preference to the patterns that caused the depression; and

[9] Beck has described his therapeutic approach to depression in three volumes: A volume on Cognitive Therapy in general (1976) and two editions of a treatment manual for depression (Beck et al., 1978; Beck et al., 1979). In these volumes, Beck and his colleagues spell out their therapeutic rationale in great and interesting detail, presenting a useful model for the treatment of depression.

other methods of cognitive therapy (Beck, 1976). Beck makes extensive use of the client's keeping records, including the recording of thoughts as well as of behavioral interchanges. Beck also stresses the recording of daily activities, with a goal of raising the levels of behavior, but behavior that is pleasurable, and ultimately reinforcing, to the client. He will sometimes use devices such as wrist counters for recording activity levels.

Beck's work has been seminal in encouraging comparative research into depression throughout the world. Taylor and Marshall (1977) have found strong evidence that a combined cognitive-behavioral approach is the most effective method of treating moderately depressed patients. Similarly, a comparison of cognitive therapy and pharmacological therapy with depressed outpatients showed a significant decrease in depressive symptomatology with both therapies, but those treated with cognitive therapy had lower dropout rates. Gains at termination were maintained, but 68 percent of pharmacotherapy patients reentered treatment while only 16 percent of psychotherapy patients did so (Rush et al., 1977).

The recent contributions of the cognitive-behavioral views, combined with some of the reformulations in psychodynamic thinking and the advances in pharmacotherapy, auger well for the continued development of cross-theoretical models for the treatment of depression. The National Institute of Mental Health is sponsoring a massive research project at a number of hospitals and clinics across the country to test the effectiveness of two brief therapies—cognitive-behavioral therapy and interpersonal therapy—both with and without a tricyclic antidepressant, as compared with two "control" conditions: The drug plus "clinical management" and a placebo with "clinical management" (clinical management being, essentially, no treatment). While the results of this study will not be in for almost a decade, the study itself is a reflection not only of the seriousness of the problem of depression but of the increasing number of alternative treatments now available, including the variations of the behavioral approaches.

Case Illustration of Different Behavioral Treatments of Depression

We shall now present a very condensed case summary illustrating how the same person might be treated by behaviorists of different orientations. The case might also serve to illustrate the developments in behavioral thinking and orientations, as discussed in chapters 2 to 5, and in this chapter.

Robert Billings is a 43-year-old, unmarried man who was referred for treatment of depression. He appeared promptly for the appointment immaculately dressed in dark, very conservative clothing. He was thin to the point of emaciation, with the sunken eyes and hollow look of a concentration camp survivor.

Robert had recently been hospitalized for depression, spending three weeks at a large private hospital near Chicago. He does not have very good recollection of the events preceding hospitalization, but he describes himself as "getting increasingly down" until finally he could not function at work and began to spend more and more time at home. He would get up early enough to get to work, but took an increasingly long time to leave the house. It became obvious to him that "something was wrong." He had felt very despondent, felt that he was alone, felt bleak about the future, and had considered suicide. A devout Catholic, he confessed to his priest, who suggested an appointment with a physician, who hospitalized him immediately.

Robert feels that the hospitalization was a mistake. He is terrified of going back into the hospital ("I'd kill myself first") although he was unable (or unwilling) to specify any particulars of the hospital stay. He was put on medication, received group therapy twice a week and had individual talks with a staff psychiatrist "a couple of times." He rejected the hospital's suggestion of electric shock treatment; he is also terrified by the prospect of shock. He was finally discharged, against medical advice, two weeks ago and refused the hospital's suggestion of outpatient therapy with the staff psychiatrist. He has read a lot in "psychology" and requested a "behaviorist" as behaviorism fits in with his own "scientific orientation."

Robert is a chemist with a local firm. Although he received his degree from a well-known university, and in the past considered himself a qualified researcher because of his good administrative ability and patience and attention to detail, he has been increasingly assigned to routine but necessary tasks in the firm, to the point where he now bitterly describes the work he did as "making soap" (a term of derision among chemists). Nevertheless, he would like to go back to work for this firm, for the salary is high, the fringe benefits are excellent, and the firm *is* doing some interesting experimental work he'd like to become involved with.

He lives alone in a small apartment. His parents are alive and well, living nearby. He telephones them once or twice a week and sees them perhaps once a month. They do not press him. He has never felt close to either parent. He describes his father, now retired, as dominating and critical: "Nothing I ever did was right."

He is the oldest of seven children; the youngest three still live at home with his parents; the oldest three are married and living in nearby Wisconsin. He does not see them very often.

He went through local schools in Chicago, had considered going into the priesthood but changed his mind to major in chemistry. He describes himself as a devout Roman Catholic, taking the sacraments every Sunday.

Robert has had only casual relationships with women,

never becoming serious about any one. He describes himself as awkward and ill at ease in their presence. There have been infrequent visits to prostitutes, and some casual sex with "women I've picked up," but he speaks of these with a heavy affect of guilt. He denies any homosexual experiences or desires. He does not have any close male friends, although there are some men at the firm that he used to talk baseball with. He used to go to sporting events occasionally but has not done so recently. He describes himself as "in a rut" and he would like "to develop some new interests."

He describes himself as having been tense "as far back as I can remember." There are a number of things that make him tense, including contact with people—especially women. He also becomes tense in the presence of people at work, especially people in authority to whom he cannot say "no" or stand up to. He also states "I'm not the kind of person who would force myself on people." He describes himself as "full of fears and tensions." In particular, the thought of rehospitalization "fills me with panic."

His physical health is good. No major illnesses nor operations, no previous therapy other than the hospitalization. He is not now taking any medication, stating that the medication at the hospital gave him dry mouth, dizziness, and other symptoms.

He is still on the payroll from the firm, and he will be given his old job back when he feels ready and when the company doctor feels he is well enough to work. Understandably, he has a great deal of anxiety and apprehension about being interviewed by the company doctor. He usually eats at home, but he often skips meals. He sleeps a lot. He does keep his apartment and himself clean. He sometimes has sleep problems. While once in a while he has trouble falling asleep, more often he sleeps restlessly or lightly, feeling tired when he awakes and throughout the day, even though he often spends twelve hours a day, or even more, in sleep and in napping. He states that he stays in bed "to escape from things." He describes himself as "lazy," as "passive, liking to watch things rather than take part." It is "easier to watch the world go by."

The above case vignette, although condensed and typical of only *some* depressives, will serve as a good example to illustrate the ways in which a case of depression *might* be handled by behavior therapists of different persuasions. We wish to emphasize that the case and the following discussions are for illustrative purposes only. It is our feeling that in practice the lines among the three major behavioral orientations have become so blurred that only the most doctrinaire adherents would utilize only one approach and ignore the potential contributions of the others. This is illustrated, for example, in Wolpe's discussion of the advantages of systemative reinforcement (Wolpe, 1973), in the operant discussion of the necessity for consideration of affects and cognitions (Schwartz, 1977), and in the recent work of the cognitive-behaviorists (Beck et al., 1978, 1979), which show their eclectic approach.

A RESPONDENT (WOLPEAN) BEHAVIOR THERAPY APPROACH

Wolpe's view is that neurotic depression (the above case is not a "psychotic depression") can be due to one of three distinct sets of circumstances: (1) An "exaggeration and prolongation of normal reaction to loss"; (2) reactive depression associated with severe anxiety; and (3) failure to control interpersonal situations (Wolpe, 1973, pp. 236–237).

With Bob Billings we may clearly rule out circumstance number one, for there seems to be no severe, extreme life changes such as the death of a relative. However, there is evidence to substantiate Wolpe's other conditions of severe anxiety, not only in response to work and authority, but also anxiety connected with the third category of "failure to control interpersonal situations."

The initial therapeutic assumption that the Wolpean behavior therapist would make is that the anxiety precedes the depression and that by treating the anxiety the depression would disappear. While no doubt therapists of other orientations would quickly, and correctly, point out that there are profound issues of poor self-esteem, poor self-image, and lack of confidence, the behavioral therapeutic interventions are based on Wolpe's assumption that the depression is a consequence of, and follows, anxiety. The therapeutic work is to isolate those stimulus conditions which set off the anxiety. In the case of Bob, there are two major, although overlapping areas. One is the extreme anxiety he feels with people in general, and with women in particular. The second is the anxiety generated by his being dominated by others in interpersonal relations or, in other words, his lack of assertiveness.

Therapy in his case would take the following form. First, a program of systematic desensitization to interpersonal relations with women. The therapist would first teach him the relaxation procedures, as a general aid to anxiety and as a specific step in the systematic desensitization process. Next is the construction of the scales of anxiety in relating to women and the construction of a hierarchy of approaching women. The last stage would be the actual reconditioning. The hierarchy, at least in the beginning stage, would be toward building interpersonal relations with women on a nonsexual basis. The general themes are to start approaching, in imagination, women who are known to the client who are less available and therefore less threatening and proceed to approaching known women who might be available and then women who are not known. In other words, to increase approach behaviors to women, hopefully feel increasingly comfortable, and progressively less anxious.

He would become desensitized, at first in his imagination, and react with less anxiety to meeting women, a condition which often preceded the onset of his depressive state. One such hierarchy (abbreviated) might be as follows (from the least anxiety producing to the most anxiety producing):

1. Stand at a distance of ten feet from the middle-aged woman who hands out the office supplies.
2. Stand five feet away from this woman.
3. One foot away from this woman.
4. Ask her for a package of paper clips.
5. Take the paper clips from her.
6. Approach the younger section secretary (married), ask her to take a memo.
7. Ask this secretary to come into my office to take a memo.
8. Approach the other secretary (young and unmarried) and ask her to take a memo.
9. Ask her to take a second memo.
10. Ask her to come to my office to take a memo.
11. Ask her to obtain some office supplies for me.
12. In the cafeteria in the building, sit at the table of the older waitress.
13. Sit at the table of a younger waitress.
14. Sit at the table of the youngest and most attractive waitress.
15. Give this waitress the order for lunch.
16. Ask the waitress "What is good today?"
17. Ask the waitress if she would recommend the roast beef.
18. Speak to the young lady in the next section office.
19. Etc.

The reader can grasp the idea. With Bob Billings, there would be two additional steps that the therapist might consider. The first would be the institution of a series of steps of "in vivo desensitization" where Bob might actually carry out steps, in real life, analagous to (or even identical to) the steps in the desensitization hierarchy that were imaginal.

Bob has also had trouble with being dominated by people, i.e., standing up to them. He would receive a course of assertiveness training, as outlined, among others, by Rose (1977), and, considering this man and his isolation, preferably in a group setting. This would include participation in a group where the leader and other group members would model behavior and coach the client, where there would be a trial of assertiveness behavior (behavioral rehearsal), some covert practice procedures, some homework assignments, and the filling of some contingency contracts (Rose, 1977, p. 188 ff). In addition, the group would also provide Bob with feedback when he carried out the "in vivo" exercises. The use of group procedures, regardless of the therapeutic orientation of the behavior therapist, has often proven successful with depressed patients (Lewinsohn, *et al.*, 1970).

Again, consistent with the Wolpean behavior therapy model, the interventions deal with the manifest material, in particular to "desensitize" or reduce the ability of the stimulus situation to elicit anxiety and anxiety responses to the client, anxiety responses which are often followed by depression.

The Treatment of Bob Billings's Depression by an Operant Behavior Analysis Approach

The operant therapist would be less likely to consider depression a conditioned emotional response following the anxiety triggered by certain stimuli. He would analyze the entire contingency situation of the individual and place much more emphasis upon the *consequences* of the depression, as well as the antecedent stimulus factors. In particular, he would try to determine if the depression were being reinforced, or if there were a sudden extinction of reinforcement, or if the depression was escape or avoidance behavior (i.e., negatively reinforced), if the behavior were producing aversive consequences (was being punished, hence the drop in rate, and the extinction trial), to see if there were a lack of behavior, or any of the other possibilities discussed in this chapter in the section on the operant explanations of depression. He would administer the initial interview discussed earlier (see Chapter 3). We shall now present Bob Billings's responses to that questionnaire (in a *very* condensed form for much of the material has already been presented).

INTERVIEW WITH BOB BILLINGS

Q: What is the problem?

A: I have been feeling really down, feel lousy.

Q: Lousy?

A: Yes . . . since—I don't know when . . . I was in Indian Woods Hospital, my doctor put me there because I was depressed . . . I thought of killing myself . . . [there were very long pauses between words] I kept taking longer and longer to get out of the house, to go to work. Weekends I would sit around, not do much . . . used to go out once in a while, see friends . . . now see parents maybe once a month . . . watch a lot of TV . . . sleep a lot during weekends . . . [more details of depression] . . .

Q: How bad did you feel? Just how depressed would you say you are?

A: Very depressed . . . [silence] . . . even thought of killing myself, and that is against my religion, a deadly sin . . . [probe] yea, I still go to church every Sunday, take confession . . . that's how I got to the hospital, you know, as I told you, my priest sent me to a doctor who sent me to a shrink who sent me to the hospital . . .

Q: You felt out of control?

A: [No answer.]

Q: Tell me about your hospital experience.

A: [Relates story of hospitalization, medication, release against medical advice.]

Q: Family background?

A: [Family history as discussed above in brief case summary.]

Q: [After client states problem, history of problem and some other historical information—about three-fifths through the interview] You are coming here for help. Assuming we work together, and everything goes well, the therapy is successful, what would things be like for you?

A: What? How?

Q: [Repetition of this question is often necessary, for the concept of "things working out well" is strange to clients, especially depressed clients.]

Q: What would your life be like? What would you be doing? Can you describe what you would be doing?

A: I'd be back to my normal self.

Q: What was that like?

A: I'd be going to work each day. I'd come home, go out to things . . . I'd be free of fears and tensions . . . [here, additional information volunteered on client being tense for as long as he can remember] . . . I'd grow.

Q: Grow?

A: I'd be doing more things, get more interests, I'm in a rut. . . . I'd also be more, more willing to stand up to people, not let them push me around [said with affect, not of anger but of extreme resignation, depression, self-reproach]. I'd also someday . . . soon . . . like to meet a girl . . . maybe get married [therapist probed here, obtained history of sparse social and sexual contacts with women, denial of homosexuality].

Q: Can you tell me what a typical day is like for you? [Note: An excellent query to use with many clients but especially with depressed clients].

A: Well, now that I'm not working . . . I get up late . . . drink coffee, instant coffee. . . . I sleep late, I sometimes have trouble falling asleep . . . sleep lightly . . . yes, sometimes wake up in middle of night and cannot fall back asleep. . . . I often skip meals . . . try to remind myself to eat three times a day . . . a bother. . . .

Q: [After more details on depression elicited from client] What are your strengths?

A: [Silence, then] Like to read . . . like music, used to exercise a lot [probe], bike, swim [at the Settlement House pool] . . . walk . . . I'm a good friend . . . one, especially to Sam—known since grade school. He's married with three children. . . . I'm faithful, honest, religious. [Note: Additional material obtained negative physical history.]

Q: Is there anything we left out?

A: No.

Q: Anything you'd like to ask me?

A: No.

Q: Well, if there is, or something comes up, please ask me.

A: What are you going to do?

Q: Well, I suggest that we get a better picture of how you spend your day, what your life is like. Would you be willing to keep some records like a log similar to the ones you keep in the chem lab?

A: Yes.

Q: I suggest that you keep a record of your days . . . make one entry an hour. Of course, if you're doing the same thing for several hours, such as watching TV, one entry would be all right. I'd also like you to rate your mood, with 10 = no depression, high, 0 = the pits, and 5 = half and half, somewhat depressed, somewhat not. We're interested not so much in the differences between, say, 7 and 8, but between 7 and 2. It's just to get an idea.

A: Makes sense to me.

Q: Also, I'd like you to record *everything* you eat, and underline the time you eat it in red.

A: O.K.

Q: I'd suggest you do this, without changing your current routine, for the next three days, and then bring it in on Saturday. [After further discussion, which we shall condense here, there was agreement that on the fourth day, at least once a day, Bob would go out of his house and go to the corner store and make a purchase—at least a newspaper, but also one or more items if needed. He was to record these in his logs.] O.K.?[10]

A: Fine, see you on Saturday (this appointment was held on Tuesday). Thank you.

---

[10] During the interview, when there was a discussion of suicide, the therapist explained that he made a "contract" with all new patients that they would agree not to kill themselves. If they felt suicidal, or if they felt like or did anything suicidal (deliberately not spelled out for the patient), they were to call the therapist, at any hour of the day or night. Bob's reaction to this, as is the reaction of many clients, was somewhere between incredulity and amusement. However, Bob—as do all clients as a precondition for therapy—agreed. This tactic of making a "no suicide" contract has been utilized by a number of therapists. In addition to the obvious function of communicating to the client that where there is talk of suicide that suicide is a real potential, there is also the message that the therapist is *hearing* the client, is taking him seriously, and that he, the therapist, is concerned enough about the client and cares that he lives. Furthermore, of course, the client is no longer without an ally and friend; there is help available.

An examination of the logs that Bob kept for the three days (see pp. 205–206) following the initial interview shows a low rate of behavior (the retarded behavior of depression), low mood, and, in behavioral terms, almost a dearth of reinforcements due primarily to a lack of behavior that would elicit reinforcement. Bob did not leave the house for the two days (and had only one brief and unsatisfying telephone call to his parents), so that there was no contact with others to break the withdrawal or the low behavior cycle. His food intake was also poor.

No doubt therapists of many differing theoretical orientations could make a number of interpretations and speculations regarding Bob's inner state. No doubt that they would have been correct. However, the main operant therapeutic task is to break this extinction cycle, to have Bob engage in behavior that would produce some reinforcements and thus to break the extinction cycle.[11] It is also obvious that there is no more necessity for further record keeping for baseline or assessment purposes. The purpose of recording from this point on is to provide feedback to the client and the therapist. At the next session, wisely scheduled four days later instead of one week, the logging requirements were kept the same but the client and the therapist agreed that Bob would make an effort made to (1) eat at least two meals a day, actually planning the food menu the day before, and (2) engage in at least one activity outside the house each day, for example, going to the grocery store. The logic here was to involve him in a nonthreatening, somewhat impersonal interaction with another human being (in this case, a store clerk) and then gradually "shape" his behavior, through successive approximations, meeting with people in relationships increasingly more personal and thus more

---

[11] Using a different theoretical analysis and description, a recent excellent work on the psychoanalytic psychotherapy of depression urges the same action (see Arieti and Bemporad, 1978).

DAILY LOGS—ROBERT BILLINGS

WEDNESDAY, 7 MARCH

Time	Where	Who there	What I wanted	What I got	Mood	Comments
10:30 AM	Bed	Self	To get out of bed	Stayed in bed, half awake for over 30 minutes	2	
11:30	Kitchen	Self	Drink coffee	—	3	Not hungry
12–3 PM	Living Room	Self	Watch TV	TV	4	Feel O.K.
3:00	Kitchen	Self	Eat	*2 slices toast, coffee*	4	O.K.
3–5:30	Living Room	Self	Watch TV	Napped	4–5	Felt tired when I got up
6–7	Kitchen	Self	Eat	*TV chicken dinner*	4	—
7–11	Living Room	Self	Watch TV—got mail	Quiet	4	Feel O.K.
11:00	Bed	Self	Go to sleep	Slept off & on	3	Tired

THURSDAY, 8 MARCH

Time	Where	Who there	What I wanted	What I got	Mood	Comments
11:00	Bed	Self	Got up	Got up	4	Felt tired
11:30	Kitchen	Self	Eat	*1 slice toast and coffee*	4	Felt a little better after eating
12–4	Living Room	Self	TV	TV	4–5	—

(Rest of day the same.)

meaningful. The first step was the one visit a day to the store (the first day he made *two* visits, for on the first visit he "forgot" to buy a newspaper). We can see the log of this day:

SUNDAY, 11 MARCH

Time	Where	Who there	What I wanted	What I got	Mood	Comments
11:00	Bed	Self	Get out of bed	Got up immedi-ately	5	Felt better
11:30	Kitchen	Self	Eat	*Toast, juice*	5	
12:00	Living Room	Self	TV, Dress	Dress	5	
1:30	Store	Self and clerk	Buy groceries	Bought groceries	6–7	Felt better
2–7	Living Room	Self	TV	TV	6	
8:00	Store	Self and clerk	Buy paper	Paper	6	Felt better
9:00	Kitchen	Self	Prepared dinner; eat	TV dinner	6	Felt better after eating
10– 1:00 AM	Living Room	Self	TV	TV	5–6	
1:00 +	Bed				5	

The next steps in the therapy went rather rapidly. Further recordings were drastically shortened and finally omitted within eight weeks of starting therapy. The next step was Bob's idea. He suggested that one meal a day be eaten at a restaurant, a suggestion the therapist heartily seconded. However, Bob—not unlike many depressives—set an initial goal for himself that was too high, but one that he eventually fulfilled. The restaurant was to be in the downtown area. Bob then spent the next few days getting up at

11 A.M., eating some toast and coffee, and then showering, shaving, and dressing preparatory to taking the bus downtown. This ritual consumed most of the day. He arrived at the chosen restaurant after a short bus ride, at about four—too early, so he said, for dinner. He began to have a cocktail before dinner. (Bob and the therapist agreed on one as there was no history of drinking. For some depressives, alcohol—a central nervous system depressant—only serves to heighten the downward spiral of depression.)

Bob dragged out his one cocktail till after five, then had his dinner. As part of the treatment program he began some brief conversation with a cocktail waitress—actually, she was the more aggressive—and, after several months, they went to a movie on her day off. Before the date, Bob and the therapist discussed some of the anxieties he felt, particularly relating to his lack of experience and his lack of assertiveness. The movie had been suggested as an activity (as it had been used by countless young people long before behavior therapy) for it was a structured activity. There would be only a short time for conversation before the movie, and the movie itself would be something to talk about, or at least provide the beginnings of conversations afterwards. (In a sense, in a situation with depressed and other individuals with deficient interpersonal dating repertoires, it is useful to think back to the problems of beginning daters, i.e., adolescents. Despite the age difference, many of Bob's problems were similar to those of individuals who did not go through or successfully complete this stage of development.)

Bob and the therapist did some role playing (behavioral rehearsal) before the date that helped relieve some of Bob's anxieties.

In the next session after the date, Bob and the therapist reviewed what had gone on. Bob and his date both enjoyed the movie and went out for something to eat afterwards. Keeping up his end of the conversation was comparatively easy, for this very talkative woman hardly let Bob get a word in sideways.

There followed several other dates, approximately one week apart. Bob suggested that he would like to "try to fix his place up," an area of new concern undoubtedly stimulated by his new friendship with the waitress. He began a systematic cleanup of his small apartment, an activity which involved a number of trips to the local hardware store (actually more than was absolutely necessary), which offered a good chance to meet with men and talk about neutral matters, such as paints, tools, and appliances.

After several more weeks in therapy, more dates and increasing activity outside his apartment, Bob decided to risk the appointment with the company doctor which was necessary to resume work. While he was still visibly anxious— his voice would tremble and he would sometimes almost shake with nervousness—the company doctor (a nonbehaviorist!) suggested that he come back to work gradually, to "get your toes wet." Bob readily agreed. The first week he went to work for two hours in the afternoon (1 P.M. to 3 P.M.). The next step was to go all morning, 9 A.M. to noon. The accompanying behavioral chore was to get up on time in the morning, a task Bob dealt with both by setting the alarm clock and by having his girlfriend call him. He then faded out the girlfriend's call after one week, using only the alarm clock to get himself out of bed.

The above opening and middle phases of treatment give a flavor of the operant behavioral analysis approach to the treatment of depression. The emphasis is on analyzing the environmental contingencies and then intervening with specific behavioral assignments. The theory is that the change in the behavior will cause change in affects or, in other words, when you get behavior going you stop the extended extinction trial, either to increase the level of behavior or to elicit more reinforcements from the environment. Certainly this was the case with the treatment of Bob's depression.

Certainly there was a rise in Bob's spirits, and a lessening of the affects of sadness, gloominess, and so forth, when he engaged in additional behaviors which secured for him the reinforcements that were so lacking in his life. The reader will notice that in this approach, as well as in the repondent approach, the emphasis was put on the external, the "observable." There was almost an absence of discussion of "internal" events. There was a minimum of introspection, and the talk of the emotions felt by Bob—such as depression and anxiety—were traced to the environmental contingencies that "caused" the depression. The therapist in treating this case "behaviorally" was most certainly aware of things going on "internally" but he followed the theory that concentration upon the "external" could have the effect of initiating some behavior that could be reinforced, and the reinforcement would increase the behavior, thus breaking the extinction process that characterizes reactive depressions with retarded behavior. However, it is precisely the concentration on the external, with the emphasis on breaking the extinction cycle, that is both the strength as well as the weakness of the strictly operant approach. Bob's behavior did go up; he did start getting out and doing things, and he did meet a woman with whom he began a relationship. He also returned to work.

However, what sometimes happens in cases such as this one is that the rate of behavior goes up but the client still feels worthless. He may be performing a behavior, but inside he feels sad and pessimistic. Some workers would say that he is, in effect, still depressed.

It is our experience that if these feelings are not worked with, the depressive episodes might very well recur (especially since depressive episodes are often self-limiting, and improvements attributed to behavioral interventions might just be "spontaneous remissions".) In addition to changing his behavior, Bob must change the way he views himself, the way he views the world, the way he interprets phenomena—in short, for behavioral changes to remain permanent, there must also be changes in the cognitive realm.

A COGNITIVE-BEHAVIORAL APPROACH[12]

There are many similarities, both in form and in intent, between the operant-behavioral and the cognitive-behavioral initial interviews.

The purpose of the interview in both cases is to gain information in the areas of diagnosis, past history, present life situation, and psychological problems. The outstanding difference seems to be that the cognitive therapist is also interested in the client's attitudes toward, and motivation for, therapy and almost from the beginning tries to get across to the client that faulty thinking processes are playing some part in his disorder. Bob, before entering the office of the cognitive behaviorist, would have taken a Beck Depression Inventory, which would give the therapist a numerical score, categorizing the depth and degree of depression. (This inventory is reapplied throughout the therapy to assess progress, or lack of progress, in the case.) Bob also would have been given a "Hopelessness Scale." (These instruments are described in Beck et al., 1979.)

The cognitive-behavioral therapist would also aim toward selecting "target symptoms" as a focus for immediate work. These "target symptoms" would be not only the behavioral but also the affective, motivational, cognitive, and "physiological or vegetative" aspects of depression (Beck et al., 1979). The operant behaviorist, instead of talking of "motivation," would talk about the consequences of being nondepressed as contrasted with the present situation of being depressed.

[12] The following description of the course of treatment draws heavily from Beck et al. (1979, pp. 87–116).

This initial interview would also introduce, on a conscious, didactic basis, some of the elements of the cognitive-behavioral approach, alerting the client that the way he thinks will be as much of a focus of the therapy as the behavioral assignments.

For example, it would be pointed out that Bob's view of himself as worthless leads directly to the idea that therefore other people would be justified in not associating with him. Thus, rather than being snubbed and rejected by them, Bob will just avoid them. Of course, Bob wants these human contacts (or at least, is highly ambivalent about them), but his negative view of himself is a faulty premise to justify others' avoidance of him and his avoidance of others. It is precisely this kind of illustration of faulty cognitions, of faulty thinking, that the cognitive therapists add to the behavioral exercises.

Bob's therapist might open the initial interview by asking if Bob had any ideas or apprehensions about the interview, about coming for help. The therapist would ask these questions to elicit whether Bob had any misconceptions about the therapy or the therapist. If so, the therapist would correct them and point out to Bob how his misperceptions and/ or his faulty cognitions often lead him to make false assumptions and then, like many clients, to *act* on these assumptions as if they were true.

Whether or not there *were* these false assumptions, cognitions, or misperceptions, the therapist would then ask Bob to talk about the problem(s) with which Bob would like some help, a step identical to the initial questioning of other behavior therapists.

The therapy sessions in the cognitive-behavioral approach to treating depression would have two parts. The first is the "agenda" for the interview, i.e., what is to be discussed. The second is the "homework" assignments to be done and reported on during the next interview. Cognitive-behavioral therapy tends to be more structured than many other kinds of behavior therapy. The agenda for the first few sessions would be to examine the various aspects of Bob's depression, including judging the possibility of suicide. The "homework" for the first session or so is identical in concept with the operant behaviorist—to obtain an idea of the patient's day or activity level. Bob would keep a schedule of his activities, to assess how active he is, in objective terms.

In the second and third sessions, Bob and his therapist would review the activity schedule and agree on some behavioral task—called by Beck a "mastery and/or pleasure activity"—actually the same behavioral homework assignment only under a different name. In the detailing of Bob's problem, the therapist would be more active in eliciting Bob's "thoughts" (particularly how he felt, his affective states) both during periods of activity and nonactivity, during periods of nondepression as well as depression (obviously, there might be considerable overlap among these four conditions).

Both the cognitive-behaviorist and the operant-behaviorist therapist would schedule increasing activities as we have listed above, such as Bob's going out to the store. Starting with approximately session number four, Bob would be asked to write down, for later discussion, *specific* cognitions that preceded unpleasant consequences and affects for him. He would be asked to list incidents in the past week when he felt depressed, or angry, or guilty (Beck et al., 1979). The relations of these incidents to preceding and to consequent cognitions would be closely examined.

In further sessions, as Bob's level of activities rose, following the treatment plan, there would be considerable time spent on problematic situations and cognitions, and there would also be a focus on *functional*, pleasant situations and cognitions. In other words, not only would there be programming for success experiences (through the method of successive approximations, i.e., small steps) but there would be feedback, from the therapist to Bob and from Bob to himself, on these *successes* as well as on Bob's failures. Undoubtedly, some of the dysfunctional cognitions discussed *would* be anger, hostility, sadness, self-criticism, self-defeating statements to himself, and—gradually—an examination by Bob of his "automatic thoughts." These "automatic thoughts," as discussed above, are just below the threshold of consciousness and would be the next "target" of the cognitive restructuring efforts, following and along with the restructuring of the *conscious* thoughts.

These "automatic thoughts," as well as the conscious thoughts and the affects that the client feels, are also keys to contingency situations, to be examined in their own right to determine if there are distortions in cognitions, such as black and white (polarized) thinking, overgeneralization, and so forth. A particular point of focus would be where Bob thinks self-critical thoughts, especially where these self-critical thoughts are possibly the "excuse" for not taking action and are the basis for further depression. Particularly worthy of attention of both Bob and his therapist are the statements of the client that he "should" do something (again the utilization of K. Horney's concept of the "tyranny of the Shoulds" or, in dynamic terms, excessively punitive superego messages, messages that bar actions, that trigger further depressive ideation, or are the beginning of a chain of dysfunctional cognitions).

The remainder of a structured course of therapy would be a redefining of goals; of "wants" as opposed to "shoulds." The cognitive work would parallel and, hopefully, facilitate the undertaking of more and more behavioral assignments outside the sessions, accompanied by (or preceding) a lifting of the sadness and self-blaming thoughts. In short, an improvement in mood which we might also call a lessening of the depression.

This approach is called "cognitive-behavioral" for it features elements of both the behavioral and the cognitive therapies. As we stated earlier, improvement in the behavioral aspects of depression is often accompanied by changes in affects and cognitions, but cognitive-behaviorists believe, as we do, that these changes may be short-lived *unless* there is also accompanying change in the cognitions of the client. However, there is considerable overlap, in the actual treatment of a depressive, among the behavioral, cognitive, and affective elements. It is our feeling that the exploration of cognitive elements in the behavioral treatment of depression is particularly appropriate, for in the affective disorder of depression these feelings are often the result of an insufficient ecology of reinforcement, hence the extinction cycle, and the result of antecedent stimuli which elicit anxiety and then depression (in the Wolpean model). Depression usually involves both low rates of behavior and difficulties in the cognitive sphere, especially of concentration and focussing.

There are many specific "target" symptoms that could be the focus of intervention with Bob Billings. The worker might very well have begun with a strictly operant-behavioral approach and then, when the level of behavior rose, added the cognitive dimension. However, the increasing body of evidence being compiled by the cognitive-behavioral researchers and clinicians indicates that a simultaneous, early (when possible) use of *both* cognitive and behavioral approaches seems to provide the optimal therapeutic benefit. It is a very promising new dimension of research and treatment of the psychiatric disorders in general, and depression in particular.

COMMENT

In this chapter we have contrasted the respondent, operant, and cognitive approaches to the treatment of depression as an example of the differences and the developments under way within the behavioral treatments. These approaches are by no means mutually exclusive but overlap. The behavioral approaches seem to be extremely useful in restoring functioning in depressed clients. That by itself may be sufficient with some clients so that there will be an improvement in the affective and the cognitive aspects of the depression. With some clients, though, it may be necessary to make a direct therapeutic intervention upon these affects and upon these cognitions. Then the cognitive-behavioral methods of Beck and his associates seem to be effective. Since "history" is a variable (a contingency) in behavioral therapies, investigations of past history—particularly of loss and especially of such traumatic early losses as the early death of a parent—may be indicated. This of course is an application of the more traditional psychotherapies, especially the psychodynamic. In serious cases, medication may be indicated. Research by Beck and others shows that, with the seriously depressed and the chronic depressed, psychotherapy combined with medication seems to be the most effective treatment.

Depression is a complicated, widespread, and probably increasing phenomenon. The behavioral therapies represent a positive contribution to what should eventually become a multifactorial approach to treatment of depression. According to Akiskal and McKinney (1973), there will be a push towards a "unified hypothesis" that will integrate the psychological theories with genetic, biochemical, and neurophysiological methodologies.

This brief examination of depression has served to illustrate that in both theory and practice the behavioral therapies are in a constant state of evolution and development. In Chapter 7, we shall briefly review some of the new areas of application as well as the expansion of the focus of intervention from the individual client to the couple, family, small group, larger social collectivities and, finally, the greater society itself.

Chapter 7

Recent Developments in the Behavior Therapies

INTRODUCTION

In the first five chapters of this book, we have described the behavior therapies, stressing their changing nature. In Chapter 6 we presented various behavioral approaches to the treatment of depression to illustrate these perspectives in actual clinical practice. In this chapter we shall survey the expansion of the behavior therapies beyond the traditional areas of treatment.

There has been increasing experimentation in applying behavioral treatment methods both to broader problem areas and to new client groups. As new procedures were developed, they were applied in areas where the more traditional methods seemed to be less than optimally effective. Sometimes the behavioral methods were used by themselves; sometimes they were used in combination with other more conventional methods to effect more successful interventions. Some of these new areas include the medical management of pain, headaches, insomnia, and other conditions as well as in the area of physical rehabilitation. Another area of development has been in the nature of the client group served. We have previously described behavioral interventions in the one-to-one, therapist-client dyad, and in Chapter 4 we discussed briefly the use of behavioral methods in groups. The behavior therapists have also expanded their interventions to larger units.

Extending the Behavior Therapies to New Client Groups

CHILD THERAPY AND CHILD GUIDANCE

Just as the child guidance movement has been called a particularly American institution, so has behavioral therapy with children been a primarily American venture. As we stated in Chapter 2 above, there were early attempts by Watson and Raynor (1920) and by Jones (1924), as well as by other workers, to use behavioral methods with children. In the early days of the application of behavioral principles, particularly those following a respondent model, the main emphasis was on the deconditioning and counterconditioning of children's problems to eliminate undesirable behaviors. However, with the rise of the operant orientation, there was increasing emphasis upon the modification of the environment to effect changes in the children's behavior rather than the direct changing of the children's behaviors themselves. In contrast to other child therapy procedures, which concentrated upon the inner world of the child, the behavior therapies focussed on the environment of the child, in particular changing parental expectations of the child and modifying parents' behavior. Parents were considered to have the potential to change the environment to correct their children's problematic behaviors.

Similarly, the focus of treatment changed from remediation to prevention, from child guidance to "parent training". At the same time, there was a change of emphasis from correcting problematic situations to teaching "healthy" behaviors, including a growing emphasis upon working not only with "problem" families but with intact and "nonproblem" families on the management of the "normal" problems of raising children.

In working with problems of younger children, many behavior therapists will not see the child at all but concentrate on changing the attitudes and behaviors of the parents, intervening into the system. With older children (five and up), the treatment includes not only parent training but also teaching the child "self-control" (Graziano, 1975). Many of the adult intervention procedures emphasizing "self-control" have proved increasingly applicable to children, a valuable development in those situations where the family itself is too pathological to permit change.

Parent Training

Changing the focus of treatment from remediation of a child's pathology to retraining of the parents (education of the parents) has been facilitated by the directness of the behavioral approach, which focuses on the observable, in contrast to other views of parent and child relationships as a more convoluted and complex psychological system. While the language used—such as positive reinforcement, punishment, extinction, schedules of reinforcement, etc.— may appear awkward and mechanistic, nevertheless, it is fairly accurate in describing what goes on. Both parent and child find it extremely reassuring to concentrate on the "here and now," rather than delve excessively into rather vague, mentalistic areas. The specific and direct behavioral procedures also frequently have an immediate positive effect of giving the parents a "handle," giving the parents something to do, to put into effect, thus enabling them to begin to break the chains of the undesired behavior. The immediate feedback that is built in also helps to effect an immediate positive change. Completing even a very small positive step can provide encouragement and incentive to continue working toward completing these goals. Switching the emphasis from individual pathology to the interactions of the parent-child system and, even further, to the entire family system stresses the behaviors to be sought rather than eliminated, emphasizing the norm of health rather than the norm of pathology.

For an introduction to behavioral work with children and with parent training, we shall suggest a few of the many works available. Rettig (1973a) provides a course in behavioral approaches to children, which utilizes a "behavior management workbook" (Rettig, 1973b) consisting of a number of charts where parents may specify "target behaviors," keep a close observation on their own intervention procedures, and also a weekly diary. Rettig emphasizes observation to strengthen desired behaviors and to weaken inappropriate behaviors.

Miller (1975), in a handbook entitled *Systematic Parent Training: Procedures, Cases and Issues,* utilizes a systems approach. His book provides an extremely good overview of behavioral principles in the first few chapters. While it is primarily intended for professionals, this book could readily be used by parents.

The Miller book has been enriched by a *Handbook for Therapists* (Miller and Miller, 1977), a guidebook with specific forms and well-described procedures many of which could be readily adapted for use with typical social work clients, in addition to being applicable for parent education. There are assessment forms for the therapist to "check up" on himself as well as parental forms so the clients themselves can assess the effectiveness of the therapy.

These volumes also contain extremely useful information for developing of carryover procedures, so that future problems can be avoided or dealt with less stressfully. There is also a social learning test, biographical forms, and other useful procedures and techniques. The two volumes, Miller (1975) and Miller and Miller (1977), together form some of the best examples of the application of behavioral principles to parent training.[1] Comprehensive overviews may be found in Wahler (1976) and in Gambrill (1977, particularly Chapter 9, "Behavioral Intervention with Children, Adolescents and Their Families," ibid., pp. 280–356). Gambrill focuses not only on training parents in skills such as recording, observation, contingency contracts, etc., but also offers specific instructions so that parents can "offer models of appropriate behavior" to their children.

While all of the above books tend to mention aversive procedures and punishment procedures, the only aversive procedure suggested as desirable is the very limited use of time out. Almost universally, these volumes stress the use of positive reinforcement and reinforcement procedures in changing child behavior, parent behavior, and teacher behavior.

The Behavioral Treatment of Couples

Many therapeutic approaches have expanded their scope outward from the individual to larger groupings, particularly the family and couples. Liberman (1970) points out that the advantage of this new trend is that the focus of major change is on the more specific interpersonal environments rather than on the vaguer intrapsychic dynamics. Liberman stressed that these interpersonal transactions were

---

[1] For seriously disturbed autistic children, consult the work by Kozloff (1973). For other works of value, we suggest the volume by Mash, Hamerlynck, and Handy (1976) dealing primarily with theory, and a companion volume by Mash, Handy, and Hamerlynck (1976) dealing with applications of behavioral principles to parenting. See also McIntyre (1970), Patterson (1971), and Krumboltz and Krumboltz (1972).

easily translatable into behavioral terms such as reinforcement and modeling, and that the behavioral approach had the further advantage of describing those interactions in concrete and observable terms, which facilitated the application of specific empirically oriented interventions.

The behavioral literature in couple therapy has tended to differentiate between the couple's interactional problems and sexual problems, in our opinion, artificially. However, since there is at the moment no integrated model for treating sexual and interactional problems simultaneously, we shall discuss each in turn.

Interaction problems. An early influential behavioral writer is Richard Stuart (1969). Stuart, in stressing the positive and the workable, stated that the existing patterns of interactions observed between couples were not accidental. No matter how dysfunctional and unhappy they may appear, their interactions are the best balance the couple has managed to work out. He stressed that most married couples wish to enjoy reciprocally rewarding relationships. That is, each individual wants to get something out of the marriage, a "something for something" (*quid pro quo*) (Lederer and Jackson, 1968.) Many marriages, however, are held together not by reciprocally pleasing interactions but by negative reinforcement or coercion (Patterson and Hops, 1972.)

Stuart stated that a chief therapeutic task was to modify the interactions so each partner can provide more rewards or more positive reinforcement for the other. Interventions should utilize operational procedures and goals, the first of which is training the couple in the "logic of the approach," which means redefining their problems as interpersonal behaviors rather than intrapsychic dysfunctioning. For example, common complaints, such as "He is inconsiderate," may be stated specifically as "He wants to have sex when I am tired." "She is not sensitive to my feelings" may be "She tries to provoke conversation when I need to be alone for a while." "He doesn't respect me" may mean "He carelessly tracks mud on the floors I spent all afternoon washing and waxing."

In Stuart's early work, he highlighted structured exchanges, such as partners using token economies with each other. He has recently modified his approach to emphasize programmatic treatment consisting of a number of steps which include negotiating goals and enhancing communication patterns between the partners as well as behavioral contracting. Stuart favors a procedure which he called "caring days," where each partner, on successive days, engages in behaviors reinforcing to the other (Stuart and Lederer, in press, cited in Stuart, 1976).

Other workers (Weiss et al., 1974; Weiss, 1975) also emphasized training couples to negotiate contracts with each other. Similarly, Azrin et al. (1973) emphasized a quick-training program for marital couples. A close examination of Azrin's procedures will show that Azrin, a man trained in animal research procedures, uses such nonbehavioral, abstract terms as "happiness contract," "catharsis counseling procedures," and "reciprocity awareness procedures."

Jacobson and Martin (1976) stress the importance of behavioral procedures, but they also emphasize that these procedures seem to be more effective when combined with more traditional procedures. Jacobson (1977) and Jacobson and Margolin (1979) report the superiority of behavioral treatment which focuses on problem-solving and contingency contracting rather than on straight behavioral exchange of reinforcing behaviors.

In short, the behavior therapy of couple problems is an area currently going through a great deal of change. There seems to be an increasing combination of some of the more behavioral contracting approaches with the more "nonbehavioral" therapies, particularly those based on communication procedures, such as those spelled out by Watzlawick and his associates (1967).

BEHAVIORAL TREATMENT OF SEXUAL DYSFUNCTIONS

As we stated in Chapter 2 above, most of the advances in contemporary sexual therapy have been attributed to Masters and Johnson (1966; 1970), who built upon the work of Joseph Wolpe (1954).[2]

Not too long ago, discussing sexual problems tended to be avoided by both client and therapist. However, we have noticed that since the popularization of Masters and Johnson procedures it has become increasingly frequent not only to talk about these problems but for couples who are dissatisfied with each other and who have psychological and personality problems to label their problems "sexual problems." In addition, because of the direct nature of the behavioral treatments of sexual problems, because of the great amount of publicity they generated, and above all, because these procedures promise success in short, intensive treatment, "sexual dysfunctions" (real or mislabeled) have become an increasingly popular admission ticket to clinics and to therapists' offices.

It is most important that the therapist do a careful differential diagnosis and screening of both individuals and couples who present themselves with sexual dysfunctioning problems. Although these procedures are very applicable when there is a sexual problem, it has been our experience that the majority of troubled couples have interactional and sometimes personality problems in addition to the sexual behavior problems. It is, sometimes, hard to tell which is "cause" and which is "effect." Nevertheless, in the rou-

---

[2] A good review of behavioral approaches to the treatment of sexual problems may be found in Gambrill (1977) and in Annon (1974; 1975.) A recent cogent overview of treatment of the more conventional diagnostic categories may be found in Walen et al. (1977). In addition, a description of certain techniques such as imagery may be found in Husted (1975), of multiple behavioral approaches in Sayner and Durrell (1975), and female masturbation techniques in Barbach (1975; 1980).

tine application of the behavioral treatment approaches one may often overlook what is actually going on between the couple.[3]

Even though the presenting problem may be a "sexual dysfunction," that is, allegedly the problem of just one person (i.e., nonorgasmic return with a female or impotence or premature ejaculation with a male), these often turn out to be couple problems. As with marital interaction problems, the appropriate unit of treatment is the couple. It is our feeling that the behavioral procedures offer a good approach for exploring the interactional problems between two people.

With the development of behavioral procedures to treat sexual problems, many conditions which previously were thought to be intractable have been found to be responsive to treatment. For example, clearly specified treatment procedures are available for dealing with premature ejaculation and with nonorgasmic return (previously wrongly described as frigidity). However, there have also been failures with these procedures, many of them due, we believe, to overlooking the spectrum of problems that usually go hand in glove with the sexual problems. Regardless whether one takes a behavioral or a nonbehavioral approach, it is artificial to separate the interactional from the sexual problems of a couple.

BEHAVIORAL TREATMENT OF THE FAMILY UNIT

As is well known by experienced clinicians, whether a problem is perceived as an individual's or as a couple's, intervening will have an effect not only upon that individual

---

[3] One condition that tends to be overlooked is that one of the pair may be depressed. As we discussed in Chapter 6, loss of libido is a classic symptom of depression and is often overlooked by "sex therapists" who are not trained in more basic therapeutic procedures.

or couple but on everyone in the family system. The homeostasis of the family group will be upset and part of therapy is the establishment of a new homeostasis, a new equilibrium for the better functioning of the unit as a whole.

In the treatment approaches designed specifically for the behavioral treatment of the couple (e.g., Knox 1971; 1975), it is apparent that the behavioral approach is highly compatible with a systems approach. Basically, a systems approach is an overall organizing framework or set of synthesizing concepts. Behavioral methods may be a useful adjunct to interventions with the system as a whole. The advantage of the behavioral approaches is that they suggest specific procedures for change. Indicative of this trend is the work of Alexander and Barton (1976) entitled "Behavioral Systems Therapy for Families," featuring an analysis of the family process and the specification of procedures such as self-monitoring and monitoring of significant others and the use of behavioral contracts and of behavioral problem-solving techniques.

The behavioral approaches to the treatment of families are currently in their early stages of development. They have much to contribute in direct and observable procedures, utilizing the techniques described in Chapters 2 to 5. This includes analyzing the interactions of the family, of parents as well as children, in terms of antecedents, behaviors, and consequences and their accompanying affects and cognitions, rather than in vague, intrapsychic concepts. This provides a "handle" for intervention (see the work of Wahl et al., 1974). In our opinion behavioral approaches in the treatment of the family will become increasingly fused with other theoretical approaches. The purely behavioral therapies, such as Alvord's token economy with children (1973), may be used by themselves with fairly intact families, but for families with more disturbed interactions, these behavioral interventions will have to be combined with more traditional therapeutic procedures (Betty Vos, personal communication, 1978).

BEHAVIORAL INTERVENTIONS IN SMALL GROUPS

The burgeoning applications of behavioral procedures to group treatment may be viewed from two perspectives. The first is the application of behavior therapy to the treatment of clients and patients in groups, analogous to the growing group therapy movement in conventional psychotherapy.

The second is the increasing use of behavioral principles with non-client groups, such as those focusing on assertive training and social skill training, and in the management of institutions and their staffs.

Sheldon Rose (1972; 1977) has pioneered in the application of behavioral principles to groups and to supervision. His works form a basic primer for the understanding of behavioral methods in these areas. From his early concentration on the use of respondent procedures such as relaxation training, and the operant procedures such as reinforcement and punishment, Rose has increasingly used procedures based on modeling and cognitive concepts, such as cognitive restructuring. There is also increasing use of groups focussing on the ''nonproblematic''—i.e., functioning people who wish to examine and improve some area of their lives. Typical of the latter is Rose's extensive work with mothers and fathers around ''parenting.'' Rose's latest book (1980) contains chapters on assertion training, work with the elderly in problem-solving, work with welfare parents (sic), prevention of obesity, skill training for students, social skill training, training for deaf clients in community activities, discussion groups for older, institutionalized men, communication and problem-solving skills for couples, and training for paraprofessionals.

While a more thorough discussion of the group approaches is beyond the scope of this book, we believe that the group approaches represent an area where the behavioral methods will be used increasingly. In addition to the works of Rose cited above, a group at the University of Wisconsin publishes a lively newsletter, *Behavior Group Therapy* (see Appendix), and there is now an annual review of applications of behavioral principles to groups (see also Appendix).

Behavioral Intervention in Schools

There is a surprising misconception that behavioral approaches to education have consisted mostly of programmed learning. Partially this may be due to the misreading of Skinner's masterful work, *The Technology of Teaching* (1968.) This and similar works have spawned the misperception that behaviorists have intended that teaching machines take over the task of educating children. Nothing could be further from the truth. Skinner and others have stressed that programmed learning has been designed to take care of the routine tasks of learning, enabling each student to proceed at his or her own pace and releasing the teacher to give individual attention to children as they need it. Furthermore, Skinner has consistently stated that programmed learning procedures are applicable primarily to the teaching of *facts* and not to the teaching of moral or ethical issues.

Of more relevance to the social worker, though, is that the school is an environment that has long been the host for interventions based on learning theory. John Dewey emphasized the management of the learning environment.

Intervention in the school setting may be somewhat artificially divided into two categories: The first includes changing the behavior of students. The second deals with the changing of the behavior of teachers. There have been, of course, combinations.

A good example of the former is the work by Sulzer and Mayer, *Behavior Modification Procedures for School Per-*

sonnel (1972), which concentrates upon procedures to raise the frequency of desired behavior in the classroom and lower the frequency of undesired behavior and presents procedures for carrying out the program. Later behavioral work has progressed from the modification of children's behavior to an analysis of the interaction of teachers and students with an emphasis on introducing modeling and other instructional methods. More recent works on behavioral modification in the schools (O'Leary and O'Leary, 1976) have stressed movement towards student self-management, self-determination of goals, and ways of carrying them out.

The literature on the changing of teachers' behavior focuses on the demonstration of practical methods to change children's behavior and to change contingencies in the environment to facilitate learning. Research has shown that problems may be effectively handled through a concentration upon the environmental contingencies.[4]

Teaching both teachers and students the application of behavioral methods concentrates highly upon applying the A–B–C method of analysis, both of dysfunctional behavior and the consequences of potentiating or raising desired behavior. For example, a teacher examines a student's disruptive behavior of speaking out "at random" and thus disrupting the class. She may find that *her* response (yelling at the student) is *maintaining* the unruly behavior she is trying to eliminate.

The areas covered within the category of school interventions have been very large. Even a cursory look at the sub-

---

[4] Part of the effectiveness of behavioral methods to change teachers' behaviors and attitudes is a nonjudgmental attitude, in addition to the observable intervention procedures that a teacher can use. One technique is the acknowledgement of the reality of the problems. A work by Carter with a title that has never failed to evoke immediate responses from teachers is his book, *Help! These Kids Are Driving Me Crazy!* (1972).

ject index in Reese (1978) will reveal not only a wide variety of topics at all levels of education but a vast array of suggested procedures. There are instructions on dealing with specific problem topics such as arithmetic, handwriting, languages, music, as well as lack of attention to work, daydreaming, acting out, school phobia, and others. Intervention procedures have featured behavioral contracting, token economies, stimulus control procedures, and a plethora of behavioral procedures.

There are some cautions to be exercised in the application of behavioral methods in the classroom. First of all, it may be tempting to apply behavioral procedures as a package. It is strongly advised that the behavioral method be applied only after a careful analysis and assessment of each individual. We remind the reader of the difference between topographic and functional definitions of behavior (see Chapter 3, above). Each individual is different, and obviously one person's reading disability does not serve the same functions as another person's.

Another issue is the question of generalization and maintenance (O'Leary and O'Leary, 1976, pp. 497–501). Behavioral methodology may be used to effect behavioral change in children in one particular classroom or set of classrooms. However, many times the behaviors do not spread from classroom to classroom; sometimes they do not go from subject to subject within the same classroom, and sometimes there is difficulty generalizing the behavior from the school to the home. Generalization and maintenance of behavioral changes has been a problem of all therapies. It is obvious that the child cannot be treated isolated in the school. If generalization or maintenance of changes is to take place, this must be carefully programmed and planned as part of the intervention procedures. For example, if school and home problems overlap, the child cannot be treated solely in the school. In more dynamic terms, we would say that behaviors have to be "internalized." In behavioral terms, we would say that behavioral changes must be maintained.

If resources are limited or the parents are not cooperative, one *can* work solely in the school setting. There is a lot to be said for a behavior that is changed only within a classroom if that change facilitates learning. If learning is a criterion measure of intervention, then the behavioral methods may be said to be quite successful, for it has been shown repeatedly that learning has taken place and has been facilitated through the use of behavioral methods at all levels of education, from preschool to graduate school, and with many populations, including exceptional children, both the gifted and the mentally handicapped.

One way of maintaining behavioral change, of course, is to change the environment, both in the school through teacher training and in the home through the involvement of parents in the therapeutic-corrective procedures. This is again similar to breaking down the artificial boundaries that exist between the institution and the outside world. Just as the environment of the discharged psychiatric patient too often does not provide needed reinforcement, so the environment of the problematic child outside school generally does not either. There must be planning in both situations for gratification of the client's needs.

If behavior is changed but not maintained, then the therapist must examine ways of maintaining behavior. Depending upon the nature of the situation, the difficulty of the problem, and other factors, the behavioral methods may, again, be used as a complement to other more traditional procedures.

The evidence of the effectiveness of the behavioral methods in improving the school situation, especially in the short run, is overwhelming. The remaining task is the area of maintaining behavioral changes. This task may necessitate the development of cross-model methods, discussed at length in the final chapter.

APPLICATION OF BEHAVIORAL PROCEDURES TO LARGER SOCIAL GROUPINGS

In an early article tracing the history of behavior shaping, Goodall (1972) stated that in 1935 the "target subjects" were animals and the behavior shapers were experimental psychologists who were interested only in responses. The research took place mostly in college psychology labs utilizing Skinner boxes and token incentives. By 1960 treatment had expanded to individuals, and the behavior shapers were primarily clinical and school psychologists whose "target subjects" had serious emotional disturbances, learning disability, mental retardation, and other conditions. For a long time behaviorists worked quite successfully with the most serious of conditions, apparently because these were the only clients they could get. Nonbehavioral therapists tended to keep the less disturbed and the "healthier" clients for themselves, passing along to the behaviorists those difficult clients with whom they could not deal.

By 1965 the "target subjects" were small and large groups and families; the behavior shapers had expanded to include psychologists, teachers, special therapists, parents, and social workers; and the "target environments" were expanded to prisons, classrooms, halfway houses, homes, and institutions. The behavior therapy models were suitable to be taught to paraprofessionals as well as professionals.

By 1970, according to Goodall, the emphasis had changed from treatment to prevention, and the targets were whole schools, neighborhoods, counties, and the general public. The behavior shapers were no longer only "professional psychotherapists" such as social workers and psychologists but included administrators, etc. The target responses were both mild disturbances and normal behavior. The settings were mental health centers, welfare agencies, and businesses.

In expanding the focus of intervention from individuals to larger groupings the emphasis of treatment changed from the pathological to the normal. Partly this reflected B.F. Skinner's own interest in social reform. Skinner, in *Walden Two* (1948), envisioned communes that were model societies. Skinner's teaching on communes was later put into practice by Kinkade (1973), who told with a great deal of honesty and interest the efforts at establishing a commune called "Twin Oaks," in Louisa, Virginia.

Goodall's view is that by the year 2001 the target subjects will be everybody, everybody will be a behavior shaper, everbody will live in a happy, productive society. This reflects the prophesies of Skinner, especially in his controversial book, *Beyond Freedom and Dignity* (1971.) We shall, in a moment, discuss the ultimate focus of Skinner's attention—the behavior modification of an entire society—but first we shall talk about some of the intermediate changes.

Social Work Application of Behavioral Principles to Larger Social Groupings

The profession of social work has always been concerned with the larger social scene. For years social work schools have offered courses in "community organization". More recently the other psychotherapeutic professions have followed suit; the development of community psychology and social and community psychiatry is indicative of the understanding of these professionals that they must work with more than just the individual.

This broader focus has long been a concern of behavior

therapists. Perhaps consonant with the learning theory basis of behavioral intervention, many of them see themselves not as "therapists" but as educators, often as co-consultants with their clients in planning remedial and/or educational programs, particularly involving these larger client groupings (Schwartz, 1972).

The behavioral approaches have been utilized with delinquents and troubled children. One of the earliest and most successful prototypes is a home called "Achievement Place" at the University of Kansas (Phillips, 1968.) Achievement Place espoused a "teaching-family" model. Initially based on a token economy, the focus changed to democratic determination by the residents of the policies and procedures in the institution. (For an interesting critique and commentary on Achievement Place, see Levitt et al., 1979.)

Cohen and Filipczak (1971) worked with hard-core adolescent delinquents and, through the use of a number of behavioral procedures, produced hardworking students. After the institution closed, these hardcore delinquents remained out of trouble for at least two years. However, a five-year follow-up showed that all but one was back in trouble with the authorities (John Conrad, personal communication). This does not mean that the behavioral approaches were ineffective. On the contrary; follow-up studies of nonbehavioral institutions show that the effects often do not last as long as two years. This means that there is a useful beginning technology that has been developed that needs to be expanded, particularly in the areas of generalization and maintenance of the effects. Once again, this may indicate a necessity for combinations with other kinds of treatment approaches.

Other procedures have been used in foster homes (Stein and Gambrill, 1976), homes for the aged (MacClanahan, 1973; Schwartz and Blackman, 1977), and mental hospitals

(Stahl and Leitenberg, 1976). Stahl and Leitenberg review treatment procedures used in chronic mental hospital wards from the initial emphasis on token economies to the individualized behavioral programs used with some patients in long-term wards. In their view, behavioral reinforcement programs seem to be more effective than other treatment programs, but "in and of themselves they cannot be considered panaceas" (ibid., p. 235). They caution that chronic patients who have been in the hospital a number of years often have lost their outside support systems; while such a patient's existence inside a chronic ward may be improved, there may be difficulty in placing him back into the community. (The dumping of mental patients from chronic wards into local facilities where they are maintained on medication can hardly qualify as a "treatment" or "cure" for mental patients.) Stahl and Leitenberg recommend procedures for working with the environment outside of the hospital but this still represents a chronic problem of high priority for mental health workers of all theoretical orientations.

The impact of behavioral treatment methods on community mental health work has been great. Liberman et al. (1976) stress that the behavioral methods can be effective, especially when individualized to deal with a patient's personal extra-hospital environment. They are specific, they offer tangible means and procedures, and they can be evaluated. They facilitate the change in treatment approach from merely supporting the patient in staying out of the hospital to helping him cope with the outside environment. Procedures such as modeling and the use of individually tailored intervention programs have been used with promising rates of success.

Just as parents have been taught to be "therapists" for their "disturbed" children, paraprofessionals and nonprofessionals have also been taught to be effective in community mental health interventions, demonstrating the usefulness of behavioral procedures in this area. There has been a great deal of emphasis recently on the use of paraprofessionals in various treatment facilities. However, the usual procedure is for highly trained and highly theoretical practitioners (often the most highly paid and the most distant from the client) to set up the treatment philosophy, and it is often left to paraprofessionals to translate concepts based on intrapsychic and unconscious motivation into working principles for practical interventions, for example, with ex-mental patients in the community. Through ongoing seminars in behavioral procedures, staff and clients may be trained step-by-step in methods of self-observation, record keeping, and self-administered interventions (self-control procedures).

A similar development has been the application of behavioral principles to help increase the involvement of welfare recipients in organizations that govern their destiny (Miller and Miller, 1970). Other studies include various efforts to increase self-help abilities, to facilitate racial integration, to control pollution, to conserve energy, to reduce litter, and to increase the use of mass transportation (Kazdin, 1977).

There have been studies done on increasing peoples' performance on the job and helping people to obtain employment (Azrin, Flores, and Kaplan, 1975).

So far in this chapter we have discussed the application of the behavioral principles to new target populations. New problem areas have also been explored, some that have not previously been considered the province of social workers and others where social workers (along with psychotherapists and intervenors of other theoretical persuasions) have not previously met with success. Of course, the two areas often overlap. It can sometimes be hard to distinguish which is a new client group and which is a new problem area. Nevertheless, we shall now review some of these developments in these areas.

Introduction of the Behavioral Approaches into New Problem Areas

THE TREATMENT OF OBESITY

Obesity is an extremely complex problem involving both physiological and psychological factors. There have been many theories offered for the condition of obesity. A review article by Leon and Roth (1977) lists several dozen. Similarly, there are many ways to treat obesity, all of which at some point or another must include dieting. However, conventional treatments for obesity have been outstandingly unsuccessful and there has been increasing attention paid to the behavioral approaches. Behavioral approaches have been seen as offering promise for success where other interventions have not succeeded (Leon, 1976).

An early theoretical article (Ferster et al., 1962) placed the therapeutic emphasis on the stimulus control of eating behavior. These procedures were successfully tested by Stuart (1967b), who later devised a manual for dieting which was published in both professional and lay editions (Stuart and Davis, 1972.) This imaginative book, *Slim Chance in a Fat World: Behavioral Control of Obesity,* aptly addresses some of the problems and psychological quandaries of the obese person.

The success of Stuart's work encouraged experts in bariatrics (the medical specialty for the treatment of obesity) to acclaim behavioral treatment of obesity, rejecting conventional psychiatric remedies for the new behavioral methods (Stunkard, 1972). By 1973, Abramson (1973) was able to list forty case reports and experimental studies, including some examples of aversive conditioning, and respondent as well as operant approaches.

Most of the behavioral approaches have attempted to use

strictly operant procedures, although a recent excellent work has added cognitive procedures (Mahoney and Mahoney, 1976).

There continues to be a veritable explosion of behavioral books on weight loss, making it difficult to summarize the literature.[5]

The behavioral procedures seem to offer great promise for weight reduction. However, once again the problem is not just losing the weight but *maintaining* the weight loss. The early enthusiasm has given way to a more careful consideration of the evidence. Stunkard and Mahoney (1976), reviewing the many behavioral approaches, concluded that they seem to be promising and useful treatments but stressed the complexity of the problem of obesity and the tendency of some workers to overlook the biology of body weight, metabolism, genetics, physical activity, and other complicating factors. The components of the treatment have to be isolated, there must be measures of effectiveness and, most important, there must be procedures developed to maintain the weight loss. In a later statement, Stunkard concluded that follow-up studies have shown that "behavioral therapies have been no more effective than traditional therapies" (Stunkard, 1977, p. 349.) Early reports, he said, were based on "mean weight changes" which "skewered the curious finding that persons who lost weight in behavior therapy tended to regain it after treatment while those who did not lost weight during treatment did so thereafter (ibid., p. 349). Recently Stunkard and Penick (1979) repeated their caution about the over-optimism of the earlier approaches on the basis of a five-year follow-up of 27 of thirty-two pa-

[5] A bibliography by Loro (1978) listed 182 references on weight reduction and obesity taken from the psychological abstracts. This obviously does not include behavioral weight control measures included in the medical literature. A cursory examination of the sample of the 182 references reveals each study referring to a number of other references, so that the literature is, in essence, absolutely enormous.

tients by telephone. (Four patients who had been successful in losing large amounts of weight died before the second follow-up. Two of the deaths may have been related to obesity but two others were unrelated. One patient underwent intestinal bypass surgery followed by a large weight loss and was not included in the five-year follow-up).

Most patients continued to lose weight for one year following treatment but began to regain the weight during the next four years.

While most follow-up studies of weight loss show that the loss is not maintained, this does not mean that behavioral methods for reducing overweight should be abandoned. It means that more work must be done on maintaining the loss. While Stunkard and Penick say that this is a new frontier for research in behavior modification, we suggest a different interpretation of the evidence. The data clearly indicate that behavioral methods are the most effective for taking weight off but, in common with all other treatments for obesity, have been comparatively ineffective in *keeping* the weight off. We feel that this is another area where behavioral and nonbehavioral treatment techniques, including intrapsychic methods of change, might be wedded, with more emphasis upon biochemical and biological aspects along with changes in cognitions, self-statements, and self-image.

Behavioral Interventions into Anorexia Nervosa

At the other end of the continuum from obesity is anorexia nervosa, a complex condition which is extremely frightening to parents and to therapists. In anorexia nervosa there is involuntary dieting, sometimes alternating with binge eating, reflexive vomiting, amenorrhea (lack of menstrual periods), and extreme weight loss. Individuals with anorexia nervosa, generally teenage girls who begin by dieting, fast to the extent where they literally starve themselves. This aversion to food can be extremely serious and, if left untreated, can result in severe complications and even death. Although once thought to be rare, it appears to be becoming more prevalent. A recent overview by Bemis (1978) finds that the symptoms in anorexia nervosa may include a body weight loss of at least 25 percent (generally occurring prior to twenty-five years of age), usually no other psychiatric disorder, and a number of other symptoms such as amenorrhea (lack of menstrual periods), lanugo (hairiness), lowering of pulse rate, overactivity, and periods of overeating, even gorging. Many of the young women with anorexia nervosa tend to be introverted, conscientious, and highly intelligent. It is difficult to make any definitive statements about the families of anorexic patients in premorbid condition.

Each theoretical approach seems to have a different explanation for anorexia nervosa. The psychoanalyst Hilde Bruch (1973; 1978), a noted authority in this area, postulates a disturbance in the earlier mother/child relationship with a regressive pull to childhood, along with a rejection of food. She feels there is lack of ego boundaries between the dieting child and the mother and ''a robot-like compliance'' by the child to parents and to teachers.

In addition to the many psychoanalytic interpretations, a number of biological factors have been identified as possible causes; for example, VandeWiele (1977) proposes that anorexia nervosa is a result of a specific hypothalmic disorder.

Regardless of the etiology, treatment approaches have been generally unsuccessful. Anorexia was first approached by behaviorists following a successful intervention by Bachrach et al. (1965), whose treatment procedures included reinforcing eating by having nurses approach and talk with the patient while she ate, shaping weight gain.

Agras et al. (1974) also described a typical behavioral intervention, stressing the use of positive and negative reinforcement and the provision of feedback.

In 1974 Bruch issued a warning, if not an outright diatribe, against the use of behavior modification, which appeared in the influential *Journal of the American Medical Association*. She declared that claims for the "efficacy" of behavior modification had been over-optimistic, mistakenly focusing attention on the eating behavior *per se* without adequate attention to the underlying "dynamics." All patients had indeed gained weight in the hospital but lost it soon after discharge. Anorexia nervosa patients will eat under persuasion or force or threats or positive reinforcements—anything to "eat their way out of the hospital" (Bruch 1974, pp. 14–21). Weight gain can be effective only if it is part of an integrated treatment program. Bruch stresses the need for long-term follow-up of anorexia nervosa patients.

Stunkard and Mahoney (1976), in assessing behavioral treatments, define anorexia nervosa as a serious condition at the end of a long behavioral chain. They agree with Bruch that the behavioral approaches to anorexia so far seem to be used primarily on seriously ill hospitalized patients. However, they claim that their effectiveness even in this critical pass is a major therapeutic advance. But they agree with Bruch in faulting the behavioral approach for not providing carryover procedures.

It is our opinion that the treatment of anorexia nervosa in essence is a two-phase problem. One is the cessation of the extreme dieting efforts and the regaining of weight to end the life threat. This often can be done effectively in the hospital using behavioral methods. When the patient is back in the natural environment, other therapeutic interventions are necessary to supplement the behavioral methods. We agree with Bemis that no single theory can explain the etiology or the treatment of anorexia nervosa and that intervention must be multi-modal (Bemis, 1978, p. 611).

Further Applications of the Behavior Therapies

Introduction into New Problem Areas: Behavioral Medicine

Obesity has been defined either as a medical condition or as a psychological or moral problem (gluttony is one of the seven deadly sins). Similarly, many of the other target conditions of behavioral interventions, such as enuresis and nicotine addiction, may be classified either as "medical" problems or as "psychological" or "moral" disorders. While most of us consciously reject dualism, much of our clinical thinking *does* draw an arbitrary line between "body" and "mind." Hence, we have "medical" or we have "psychological" problems.

The "psychosocial" area has always been the realm of social workers, psychologists, and other nonmedical therapists. Recently, however, there has been an extension of behavioral methods into the treatment of what was previously considered physical or organic disease. Shapiro and Surwit (1976) note that the discipline called "psychosomatic medicine" dates from the use of the term by Dunbar in 1943. However, the links between body and mind have been attributed to the *personality* of the patient. While the theoretical orientation has been psychoanalytic and psychodynamic, in our opinion this approach seems to utilize many unnecessary hypothetical constructs; personality, per se, has not been very useful as a predictive variable.

Shapiro and Surwit contrast psychosomatic medicine and the behavioral model, pointing out that in the latter the "target for therapy [is] the *environment* of the individual rather than his or her personality" (Shapiro and Surwit, 1976, p. 74, emphasis added.) They note that the de-emphasis upon personality and the emphasis upon environment have given rise to a new discipline, which Birk (1973) has named "behavioral medicine." Whereas in the medical model symptomatic behavior represents a dysfunction or some underlying pathological disease process, the behavioral model stresses the relationship between behavior and its consequences. Such behaviors as coughing may be defined as an "operant" or a behavior that is maintained by its effect in the environment (e.g., the cough may be reinforced by attention) rather than as a symptom of infection.

There are aspects of most diseases which are under environmental control. For example, in recent studies of the relationship between stress and physical illness, it is becoming apparent that environmental factors contribute to stress. Similarly, social support (support systems) may *relieve* some of the stress. The nonmedically trained social worker or psychotherapist is uniquely capable of detecting the effects of these environmental factors upon illness.

"Behavioral medicine" is a potential area for development, especially for nonmedical therapists such as social workers and psychologists. There is an assumption that behavioral change will take place in two ways: Through focusing upon the environment of the individual and/or through focusing upon the individual's control of that environment and of his own physiological and autonomic functioning. In addition, cognitions—peoples' perceptions of disturbances—have proven to be highly influential on the course of any illness.

Some critics may regard these problems, such as stress-related illness, as mostly "psychogenic" and dismiss the cures as patients with "hysterical" disorders as contrasted with people who are "really sick"—i.e., those with organic problems (Gentry, 1975, p. 130). In recent years there has been an emphasis in the medical literature on possible psychological causes for physical pain, particularly backaches, headaches, earaches and facial pain, conditions in which it is often hard to pinpoint physical causes even when they exist. Physicians are increasingly referring patients for psychotherapy for these conditions, after telling the patient that the pain *is* "all in your mind." This may or may not be true. In these cases, it is extremely important for the therapist to make a careful assessment and come to his own conclusions. If the therapist concludes that the pain is primarily organic, further medical consultations should be pursued. It may be helpful for the therapist to be involved in setting up these consultations and intervening on behalf of a patient who has been made to feel he is imagining his pain and is discouraged by not being believed, as well as by his continuing physical distress. A patient always has a hard time rising above a recorded diagnosis of "psychological origin."

It is obvious that before any intervention there has to be a very thorough assessment and diagnosis of the disease, a good life history, physical examination and laboratory tests as needed, an assessment of anxiety and stress and, of course, in all cases a ruling out of organic causation or complications. Behavioral intervention in this area is a collaborative team effort with physicians, nurses, technicians, and others. The nonmedically trained therapist must be prepared to regard the physician as the chief of the intervention team. However, since physicians are organically trained and tend to think in terms of physical and organic causation, part of the job of the behavior therapist might well include some education of the physicians and other members of the team. It is suggested that the behavioral interventions are most appropriate where the symptoms may be under environmental control and/or where the patient has experienced previous failure of surgical or pharmacological methods, and where there is no other alternative medical intervention. It may also be that, of course, the behavioral methods can be used to supplement other interventions (Knapp and Peterson, 1976).

We shall briefly mention some areas where behavioral interventions have been used. For more details, we recommend Knapp and Peterson (1976), Price (1974), Gentry (1975), Bakal (1979), and Davidson and Davidson (1980.) We shall also discuss biofeedback, a technique we feel is of great promise.

BEHAVIOR THERAPY OF MEDICAL PROBLEMS

There are emotional aspects to many "physical" problems. For example, studies have shown that hypertension is extremely susceptible to social conditions (e.g., blacks moving from rural to urban areas suffer a rise in hypertension.) There have been numerous behavioral interventions in hypertension involving the use of biofeedback, relaxation procedures, psychotherapy, environmental modification, placebo, sleep, exercise, singly and in combination.[6]

Furthermore, the use of behavioral procedures is indicated for people with high stress who seem to be cardiac-prone "type A" patients. Treatments of hypertension are described in Shapiro and Surwit (1976), and the use of relaxation procedures in cardiology in Benson (1977).

Similarly, behavioral treatment of asthma and other diseases of the respiratory system has been undertaken. Asthma can be counterconditioned with classical conditioning techniques, but since asthma attacks are so closely tied in with emotions and the environment of the patient, behavioral procedures have also been used to alter interactions between asthmatics and their "significant others" in the immediate environment. Summaries of these procedures may be found in Shapiro and Surwit (1976), Price (1974) and Knapp and Wells (1978.) (The latter study reviews twenty-four case studies and experiments.)

Dermatological problems responsive to behavioral inter-

---

[6] For an excellent bibliography listing dozens of behavioral interventions for treating hypertension see Ragland (1977).

vention are excessive scratching and hives (Knapp and Peterson, 1976.) Two social workers used stimulus-control procedures with a seventeen-month-old girl resistant to treatment of extensive burns (Shorkey and Taylor, 1973). They taught the child to discriminate treatment periods from socializing periods by the use of different colored gowns; responding differently to these cues, within an extremely short time the child stopped resisting treatment and improved.

Among the gastrointestinal problems treated, in addition to obesity, anorexia nervosa, eneuresis, and encropesis (fecal incontinence), are emesis and ruminative vomiting, electrolytic imbalance, diarrhea, constipation, and excessive sphincter pressure.

Similarly, a number of gynecological problems, especially dysmenorrhea, have been treated by behavioral procedures such as relaxation and systematic desensitization. A major advantage of these procedures is, of course, that they do not use drugs.

In the area of neurological disorders there are many conditions refractory to behavioral procedures such as seizures (Mostofsky and Balaschak, 1977), spasmotic colitis, conditions associated with cerebral palsy such as drooling, speech disorders (Bakal, 1979), tension and migraine headaches (Bakal, 1975; Blanchard et al., 1978), and sleep disorders (Bootzin, 1977; Ribordy and Denney, 1977).

There have been a number of applications in physical rehabilitation, especially with neuromuscular problems (Fordyce 1976a; 1976b; Michael, 1970). Behavior therapists have been especially helpful to the medical team in dealing with the emotional and physical management of the patient (Berni and Fordyce, 1977).

One such problem is the management of pain. Pain is usually considered a medical problem (Fordyce, 1976a), but whether the pain has a physical organic cause or is "psychogenic" is often an arbitrary distinction. There are behavioral aspects of all pain and behaviors connected with pain such as groaning, moaning, etc. In addition, pain sometimes has definite consequences for the patient in the situation. In addition to warning the patient that he is in danger, the pain itself can affect the environment around the patient, and the environment around the patient affects the pain. Fordyce (1976a; 1976b), a leading worker in this area, has stated that much of the therapy is designed to help the patient to stop engaging in pain related behaviors and to start engaging in well behaviors (1976b, p. 147.)

Of course, attention must be given to the medical aspects of pain, and a differentiation made between acute (short-term) pain and chronic (long-term) pain. There is a greater chance of a systematic alteration of the patient's environment in the case of chronic pain as sequences develop. Some pain may be called "operant pain" (Fordyce, 1976a, p. 41ff). The environment can directly and positively reinforce pain behavior, and it can indirectly but positively reinforce pain behavior by avoidance of aversive consequences, or by lack of reinforcement when the patient does engage in well behavior (Fordyce, 1976b, p. 45).

People often respond to the sufferer in a way that reinforces pain, by attending to the patient when he is in pain and ignoring him when he is not. Thus, consciously and unconsciously, pain may serve a function, enabling the patient to receive attention that he does not receive through "healthy" behavior.

Needless to say, the condition of pain is also closely associated with distress and depression, as described in Chapter 6 above (Fordyce, 1976b, pp. 161-162).

In treating pain behaviorally, the first goal, the medical situation permitting, is to eliminate the pain behavior or, rather, to eliminate the consequences dependent upon pain behavior. The patient not only needs to get rid of pain behavior but needs to learn "well behavior" as a desired alternative and how to generalize or maintain the well behavior. Generalization should be part of the treatment planning (Fordyce, 1976b, p. 163).

In behavioral management of pain there must be an acute assessment of the patient's support system: What are the reinforcers? What is the time pattern? What increases pain behavior? What decreases pain behavior? What do others do? There are also specific procedures involving the scheduling of medication and its relationship to patient demand, and the establishment of a program of exercises, and management of the exercises and the procedures to allow for generalization of the activities (see Fordyce, 1976a; 1976b).

We emphasize again that the behavioral aspect of pain may be only one facet of a general medical-neurological condition. It is imperative that any behavioral intervention be done in cooperation with, or under the direction of, a responsible physician.

BIOFEEDBACK

Biofeedback is a general term applied to a number of procedures. In these procedures an aspect of an individual's physiological functioning is monitored and he receives feedback in the form of an auditory or a visual signal. He may then respond to that signal in such a way to change the physiological function which, in turn, changes the signal (Rimm and Masters, 1979, pp. 448-449). The example given by Rimm and Masters is of a client suffering from tension headaches. A therapist will apply electrodes to the client's forehead, which pick up very minute amounts of electrical activity. When the patient's muscles contract, the apparatus amplifies electrical discharges and a tone is emitted. The client may change the tone through procedures of relaxation (Rimm and Masters, 1979, p. 449).

Biofeedback, a form of "self-control," is a recent discovery despite evidence that Eastern holy men have long been able to control involuntary bodily functions.[7] The implication is that people suffering from a variety of problems such as hypertension, spastic colon, rapid heartbeat, headaches, etc., can control these conditions without drugs (Jonas, 1973). Rimm and Masters (1979, p. 450) list about two dozen areas of application including alpha brain activities, epileptic brain activities, heart rate, galvanic skin response, blood pressure, skin temperature, stomach acidity, and functional diarrhea.

While early reports of biofeedback were extremely optimistic, later commentators have been less enthusiastic. First of all, a number of early findings were not replicated (Miller and Dworkin, 1974). Secondly, the whole area of biofeedback is much more complex than originally conceptualized (Blanchard and Epstein, 1977). Thirdly, biofeedback procedures require a heavy investment in equipment, technical knowledge to run this equipment, and facilities to house it. Relaxation training, which produces comparative results, is inexpensive, easy to teach and to learn, and requires little, if any, equipment other than a good comfortable chair.

APPLICATION OF BEHAVIORAL PRINCIPLES TO SOCIETY

So far in this chapter we have discussed applications of behavioral principles to new problems and to new client groups. It is inevitable that the principles of operant conditioning which have been so successfully applied to individuals and to small groups would be considered for applica-

---

[7] As pointed out by Shapiro and Surwit (1976), people for years, especially holy people in India, have trained themselves to bring "involuntary" bodily functions under their "psychological" self-control.

tion to the larger society as a whole. Skinner has always been interested in social planning for the larger society, as evidenced by *Walden Two* (1948). However, the statement by Skinner that provoked most controversy was *Beyond Freedom and Dignity* (1971). In this book, Skinner states that "freedom" and "dignity" are abstract concepts that have been used aversively as a way of maintaining social control, despite their alleged overt meaning of heightening man's freedom from control. Skinner states that man has always been controlled; the objective of an ideal society is not to eliminate control but to make it positive rather than aversive. This can be done through manipulation of the environments so as to create a society based on positive reinforcements rather than punishment, restraints, or negative reinforcements.

To state that Skinner's book provoked outbursts of indignation and rage, along with some support, is a gross understatement.[8]

It is the opinion of this author that the writing of *Beyond Freedom and Dignity* was an important and positive act. We feel that Skinner's notion is true in that we are not, or should not be, free to pollute and destroy our environment. Yet the notion that man is so much a product of the environment as Skinner presents him and so little responsive to

[8] Skinner estimates that the reviews were 80 percent negative. An excellent thoughtful review, both pro and con, is by Wheeler (1973). A volume that reflects the primarily negative response is by Geiser (1976). Many reviews were outright vicious. The lead review of *Time* Magazine on September 20, 1971, headlined "B.F. Skinner says: We can't afford freedom," showed a picture of Skinner along with a pigeon pecking at a pingpong ball, a rat pressing a lever, a person pressing a programmed teaching machine, and a picture of a bucolic scene. The article was subtitled "Skinner's Utopia: Panacea or Path to Hell?" Rabbi Richard Rubenstein was quoted as saying, "That is an important and terrifying book but is less a blueprint for the golden age than for the 'theory and practice of hell.' " This last remark was particularly invidious since *The Theory and Practice of Hell,* by Eugene Kogon (1950) is a well-known book detailing the miseries of the Nazi concentration camps.

his "inner" life is indeed difficult to contemplate except by the most radical behaviorists.

Richard Sennett, in the New York Times Book Review (October 24, 1971), stated that there were *three* B.F. Skinners: The first is the experimenter, the laboratory psychologist, and there is general agreement, even among Skinner's most ardent critics, that Skinner's work in this area is valuable and relevant. The second B.F. Skinner is a utopian writer, as evidenced by his book *Walden Two*. The third Skinner, as witness *Beyond Freedom and Dignity,* is the "moral philosopher." Sennett avers that Skinner is really a nineteenth-century small-town philosopher, quite innocent of the complexities of society and of the broader sociological realities of people living together. Sennett states that Skinner seems to be unaware of society's effect upon people and downcries Skinner's statement that dignity is simply a matter of positive reinforcement.

The search for a better society has long been part of the heritage of social work. The early social work reformers would feel much kinship with some of the ideas of B.F. Skinner. While a further discussion of *Beyond Freedom and Dignity* is beyond the scope of this book, the work is extremely important, and the reaction and debate it produced, including Skinner's own response in the form of *About Behaviorism* (1974), may be even more important than the book itself. Certainly, it is a book that will continue to have important implications as human society becomes increasingly technological and as people become increasingly alienated.

Concluding Comments

We have discussed in this chapter some of the extensions of the behavioral approaches, first in some new client groups and then in some new substantive areas.

Behavioral interventions are not restricted to the one-to-one patient-therapist format but go out to the patient's environment, to training parents, to treating couples, expanding to the family, the small group, and then larger groupings, eventually the society as a whole. New areas where the behavioral approaches can be used are many, including physical health and the treatment of disorders of many systems of the body and the treatment of pain. We also discussed biofeedback.

It is obvious that interventions into new problem areas and interventions with new client groups often overlap. While the behavioral approaches by themselves have not proven to be the panacea that some first thought they were, it is felt, and the author agrees, that the specifics of the behavioral approaches, concentrating on observable and definable procedures, have a great deal to offer in a number of these areas. There are, however, some limitations to the behavioral approaches, as well as some ethical issues. These we shall discuss in the final chapter.

Chapter 8

The Current Status and Future Implications of the Behavior Therapies

In the past few decades, we have seen a veritable explosion of writings and research on the behavior therapies. There has been a growth not only in behavioral techniques but in the range of problems amenable to behavior therapies, as well as a broadening of the client groups for these procedures. There has also been a continuing critical reappraisal of the behavior therapies. While part of this reappraisal is healthy self-criticism by behavior therapists, part is a response to the strident attacks of behaviorists on other models of helping, particularly the psychodynamic. In addition, many of the earlier behavioral claims for success have not been substantiated. Follow-up studies have shown that many of the changes achieved have not held up. Thus the current picture in the behavior therapies is one of success but also constant change, development, and reformulation of procedures and growing awareness of the need for theories as well as procedures.

The diversity of the behavior therapies is not fully appreciated by people with minimal experience or outdated views. The respondent, or Pavlovian, approaches, especially as enriched by the contributions of Wolpe, concentrated primarily upon changing behavior itself. Some authors (Rimm and Masters, 1979, p. 421) have said that the Wolpean desensitizing approach essentially places the patient in a passive role, requiring little activity from him in changing his target behavior. In contrast, the Skinnerian approach basically views the client as an active participant within an A-B-C framework. Intervention is undertaken with the individual and with all of his contingency relationships. The conflicts between the Skinnerian and classical views for a while divided the ranks of American behaviorists, but the importance of this schism has lessened considerably in importance. The broadening of the behavior therapies to include the Skinnerian conceptualization extended the focus of behavior therapists from the treatment primarily of phobias to a wide range of human problems. Behavior therapists also began to apply Skinnerian concepts to a whole group of situations which are part of everyday life rather than solely to those classified "problematic" or clinical in nature. These include areas of teaching, learning, and training, and extend into many settings such as factories, schools and businesses. We elaborated upon these extensions of behavioral concepts in Chapter 7.

This expansion resulted in a vast burgeoning of experimental laboratory and clinical work on a number of problems previously handled by other means or completely ignored. In their recent work on behavior therapy, Rimm and Masters included a three-page "Index of Disorders" which includes academic problems, bedwetting, cardiac arrythmia, dating (anxiety related to), dermatitis, eating problems, hair twirling, insomnia, mutism, pain, psychogenic blindness, racial prejudice, sadism, sleepwalking, stage fright, urine (psychogenic retention of), weight loss, writer's block, and writer's cramp (Rimm and Masters, 1979, pp. 513-515.) This list reflects the ingenuity and imagination of hundreds of workers who seem to be constantly expanding the use of various combinations of behavioral methods into newer and newer areas as the effectiveness of these methods becomes increasingly verified.

The behavioral methods have achieved some successes and some failures, and in the process of development and application, the behavioral methods themselves have been changed. Both the Pavlovian and the Skinnerian approaches concentrated upon the external environments of the individual; both represented, in a sense, an extreme situationalism. However, Skinnerians soon expanded their approach from an emphasis upon environmental manipulation to teaching the individual to analyze the contingencies controlling his behavior and then himself to arrange the contingencies that would control his own behavior. This approach is called "self-control." The nature of behavioral intervention changed from the clinical situation to the learning situation, from "healing" to "education." The self-control approach, helping the client to become his own behavior analyst, soon showed that it was not enough merely to help a client eliminate maladaptive behavior; one had to help him learn new, more adaptive behaviors and equip him with the ability to handle similar situations in the future (Skinner, 1953). In other words, the behavioral focus came to include not only remediation but prevention (Schwartz and Goldiamond, 1975).

Equipping clients with specific behavioral procedures to deal with problematic situations was certainly an improvement upon the old-fashioned—often moralistic—emphasis upon "will power," "drive," "motivation," including "resistance," that therapists might use to place the onus of failure not upon themselves but upon their clients. However, it became apparent that the individual is not merely an organism reacting to controlling conditions (including his own history) but is an active force, inconsistent, inconstant, ever changing.

Our access to the factors operating within the individual

is limited to such techniques as psychophysiological measures, consciousness-altering methods such as hypnosis, and to the examination of verbal behavior. The classes of variables that make the human a very active participant in his own contingency relationship matrix also include what he thinks and feels, his cognitions and his affects. These areas therefore became quite important to those behaviorists who began to expand their focus, to increase their work in "self-control," and to try to understand the central, more pressing, and more important aspects of human functioning. In other words, the extreme emphasis on the externals, the extreme emphasis on the environment(s), had reached its limits. Some behaviorists began to realize that it *was* important to go *inside* the organism, into the "black box," to consider those vague, metaphysical, terribly difficult to research but terribly relevant and necessary factors to consider.

This rediscovery of the relevance of the "internal" meant a change in research methods, too.[1] In addition, there was the realization that automatically applying a specific method for a specific problem was simplistic, that what was seemingly the same presenting problem, such as stuttering, could actually be two distinct and separate problems. One stutterer might be expressing hostility; another

---

[1] This author feels that behaviorists as a group—in a laudable effort to minimize speculation—have given too narrow a meaning to the word "empiricism." Too often it was used as a justification to study only the external and the available, to gather more and more precise data on increasingly trivial and peripheral matters.

As work in clinical behavior therapy expanded, it soon became apparent that the findings from the animal laboratories and from the human-operant laboratories could not always be translated directly to individuals in the natural and the clinical settings. Human individuality was too great a factor to allow predictability without some element of error, often a very large element of error. We might be able to predict for a *group of humans,* but for *this particular human* in *this situation,* our probablistic statements, would often not be too much better than educated guesses.

regressive behavior; and a third merely demonstrating a lack of learned skills. The effort to develop specific procedures for specific problems might be commendable, but applying procedures to problems without a careful study and assessment denies the individual's uniqueness and probably will be ineffective.

While the behavioral methods have been increasingly applied to new areas, including some that have proved intractable to previous therapies, the behavioral methods themselves have changed. There has been increasing interest by a growing number of behavior therapists in investigating cognitions, emotions, and symbolic processes. Behaviorists as a group wish to remain empirically oriented, but the focus of behavioral work has increasingly included the "internal," in a scientific analysis of its interplay with the "external." Thus, following the chapters in this book on the respondent and the operant models, we included a discussion of the relevance and importance of cognitions, of examining the way the clients think, how they view the world and themselves.

The Behavior Therapies: Persisting Issues for Social Work

The Issues of "Control"

While the behavior therapies have a positive contribution to make to the practice of clinical social work, their methods are by no means all-encompassing or all-powerful, as their most outspoken adherents claimed. These limitations lend perspective to the oft-cited complaint that behavior therapists attempt to "control" their clients. This argument is specious on several accounts. First of all, the issue of "control" always arises in therapy of *any* kind. The important question is not whether there is or is not control but whether the control is of a positive and not an aversive nature (Rogers and Skinner, 1956.) Most controls are seen, rightly or wrongly, as aversive. However, control is not the opposite of freedom, and the opposite of freedom is not "lack of control." (For example, there is marked "lack of control" in certain psychotic states such as schizophrenia, which are certainly not instances of freedom.)

All kinds of therapy are characterized by control. However, the behavioral approaches make the nature of that control overt and manifest. By helping the client to achieve as much control over his own life as possible, behaviorism works in helping him to increase his own self-determination, a goal long dear to social work practitioners (Perlman, 1965).

The behavioral approaches, by making the procedures specific and by spelling out the goals to be achieved and the steps to be taken, by transferring the responsibility for programming and therapy as much as possible to the client, in essence heighten—not lessen—client "control" and thus enhance the client's self-determination (see Schwartz and Goldiamond, 1975, for a fuller discussion.) The signing of a therapeutic contract, making the procedures and goals manifest, is in keeping with basic social work principles.

The charge that behavior therapy is manipulation is related to the issue of "control." Again, *all* therapists influence their clients. It is in the nature of the therapist-patient situation that the therapist is a highly influential person in the life of the client. Even the nondirect psychotherapist Carl Rogers was shown to be influencing his patient through systematic reinforcement of some content and either extinguishing or not paying attention to other content introduced by the client (Truax, 1967). Wachtel (1977, p. 276) distinguishes between "influence," which is a part of all relationships, and "abused power or control," which Wachtel sees as "both an exaggeration and a perversion of influence.'' All competent therapists are aware of their influence and recognize it as an integral part of the conduct of therapy. It is the directness with which a therapist consciously influences his client that varies from one theoretical orientation to another. Part of the problem around the issue of control is that the behaviorist's methods and procedures are so overt and so clearly spelled out that in some situations they have proved to be quite powerful. Powerful techniques *can* be more easily abused, either consciously or not so consciously, and they can be more abusive than less powerful techniques. To avoid abuse and manipulation, behavior therapists use a *contract* between the client and the worker specifying procedures as well as goals. The more manifest and overt the procedures used, the less likely they are to be abused.

THE ISSUE OF SELF-DETERMINATION

Another persistent issue is the question of who is determining the goals of the therapy—the social work issue of *self-determination*. This issue is often confounded by the categorizing of the behavior therapies as deterministic. (Schwartz and Goldiamond, 1975, pp. 273-278). Of course, the psychoanalytic theories are also deterministic. Determinism, however, is not to be confused with fatalism. Fatalism is the belief that one can do nothing to change a preordained sequence of events and eventual outcome (Shaw, 1972.) Determinism means that, given certain arrangements of factors, the outcome is predictable. People are constantly changing and able to change these arrangements of factors and variables (Skinner, 1971).

As we stated above, in much contemporary behavior therapy, the therapeutic process is governed by behavioral contracts which are the direct statement of the goals of the client. While it is a task very early in the therapy to establish the contract, it may very well be that in these early stages definite goals cannot be established, in which case the contract is "to make the contract." It may be that after achieving one set of goals the client will then be able to move on to other kinds of problems, in which case client and worker renegotiate the contract. Contracting does not necessarily mean that there is a time limit placed on the number of therapeutic sessions, although some recent developments in casework do emphasize specific limits on the number of interviews and the scope of the therapy. It is important to recognize that the behavioral approaches are *not* synonymous with short-term or time-limited therapies.[2] Behavior therapy may extend over a long period of time, encompassing a large number of client contacts.

Frequently the critics of behavioral practice have not looked at the realities of contemporary behavior therapy practice (Schwartz, 1975, p. 371). Contrary to the way they are often portrayed in the media and by their critics, most behaviorists do not use punishment procedures. Furthermore, most behaviorists very consciously utilize relationship factors, although they believe that relationship—while necessary—is not a sufficient basis for change (Klein et al., 1969). However, "the competent and caring behavior therapist, like the competent and caring psychodynamic therapist, is sensitive to his clients first and his theories second" (Schwartz and Goldiamond, 1975, p. 15).[3]

The goal of "self-control" is to train a person to be his own behavior analyst. In addition, the exploration of cognitive and affective factors tends to help the client to develop

---

[2] This misconception may also be a result of the rather strident claims of some behavior therapists. While a behavior therapist might apply specific procedures to eliminate specific symptoms, and often do this in a very short time, as behavior therapists have taken on more complex problems, the average time of therapy has increased (Klein et al., 1969).

[3] Another statement of the importance and relevance of relationship to the behavior therapies may be found in Goldfried and Davison (1976), especially Chapter 4, "The Therapeutic Relationship," p. 55–80.

"insight." Insight means becoming aware not only of one's contingency relationships but also of what is happening "inside" him. There is evidence that the increasing tendency of having the client examine his own cognitions and how they are influencing his life adjustment, combined with assessing the effect of the behavioral procedures, does produce a kind of insight. Unfortunately, the term "insight" is used in the original and somewhat outdated sense, in terms of unconscious intrapsychic conflicts and instinctual origins of behavior (Yelloly, 1972, pp. 126–127). Previous research has shown that only a small part of the casework process is spent on developing insight (Reid, 1967; Mullen, 1968; Davis, 1973).

The overtness of the behavioral procedures plus the emphasis upon client awareness not only reduces the amount of possible manipulation by the therapist and increases the client's self-control but also facilitates the generalization of the therapy effects into other situations. This is one of the ways the behavior therapist uses to enhance transfer of learning. There is agreement among most behavior therapists that the problems of generalization and maintenance of change require additional attention.

The broadening of focus from one-to-one contacts in the therapist's office into the natural environment and into group situations tends to further generalization of therapy gains. Ironically, this transfer out of the office back into the natural environment is a return to some of the earlier methods in social work, particularly social casework. Much of what are reported as "new developments" sounds astonishingly like the writings of Mary Richmond and of the early Chicago Settlement House work of Jane Addams.

Combat and Coexistence

I should like to report that currently there is an ongoing dialogue and a growing tendency towards adapting the most effective aspects of each of the various therapeutic approaches into a comprehensive approach to helping. Unfortunately, this is not so. Many behaviorists find themselves embattled and defensive, as well as openly attacking, while psychodynamic therapists similarly find themselves under fire and defensive. Much energy is spent in fruitless squabbling, in attack and counterattack rather than in positive exchange.

The acrimony is mutual and the assaults by behaviorists on the psychodynamic adherents and vice versa have been equally vicious and sometimes irrational. Many behaviorists are still mouthing the earlier antipsychoanalytic arguments of Eysenck (1964) and Rachman (1965). Similarly, many of the attacks on behaviorism are still based on and aimed at the 1920's branch of Watsonian behaviorism, made by individuals who do not realize the permutations undergone by American behaviorism, such as the displacement of the predominantly stimulus-response orientation of Watson and Wolpe, first by the operant conditioning of B.F. Skinner and more recently by the social learning-modeling approach of Bandura and the recent work of the cognitive-behavior therapists. This was recognized by the American Psychiatric Association Task Force on Behavior Therapy (1973) when it stated, "Analysts [should not] attack in the 1970's the straw man of the over-simplified view of the early strict behaviorists of the 1920's."[4] Critics of behavior therapy often do not realize that many contemporary behaviorists *do* see the whole man, within the ecology of his contingency relations, as well as his "inner" world. Behaviorists *do* isolate target behaviors but, then again, so do psychodynamic practitioners "partialize" (Schwartz, 1977). The behavioral approach is not a cookbook application of routinized, stereotypic inhumane procedures but a

---

[4] The same Task Force also states: "behavior therapists [should not base] their attacks in the 1970's on the psychoanalytic theories of the 1920's" (ibid.).

careful analysis and planning of each patient's treatment. It is highly individualized and humane, oriented toward helping each individual understand as well as change his behaviors and, more recently, his thoughts and his feelings.

Part of the difficulty in communication may be semantic. Because of the different origins of the psychodynamic and behavioral viewpoints, the novice reader often has difficulty with the unfamiliar language of the behavioral literature. The reports in behavioral journals tend to be extremely short, factual, and oriented toward the procedures. Because the journals tend to be edited by experimental psychologists, some dynamically oriented readers say, not without justification, that these reports sound as if they were written about rats or pigeons rather than people. What is too often left out of these "data-based" articles is that behavior therapy, like all therapies, is based primarily on the relationship between a warm, caring, empathic therapist and a troubled client. In other words, it is a human encounter between two human beings. If a behaviorist tends to treat a client as if he were a laboratory rat, his procedures will reflect this antihuman orientation and the therapy will be a failure. More likely than not, he will probably not be able to retain his clients.

The contemporary behavior therapists, particularly those trained within the humanistic orientation of the profession of social work, tend to engage in therapy that increasingly resembles the more traditional therapies, but with a greater emphasis upon empirical procedures, evaluation, and accountability. This is not to state that behaviorally oriented social workers have exclusive control over these "virtues" while dynamically oriented therapists do not. It is this author's feeling that there is increasing emphasis in all therapies toward accountability, toward empiricism, toward the up-to-date application of knowledge gleaned from a number of sources, both within social work and outside related fields.

There is increasing evidence that certain features are central to successful treatment in many therapies that are theoretically quite different. In a recent study contrasting behavioral and dynamic therapies (Sloane et al., 1975), researchers pointed out that, while there were noticeable differences in style, orientation, and stated goals of each of the therapies, clients in each group improved significantly. Some of the shared elements were a therapist who took time with the patient, showed an interest, took a biographical psychiatric history, formulated the patient's problems, attempted to reconstruct possible original causes of the disorder, looked for continuing causes of the difficulty, and aimed to produce a change that would benefit the client. Furthermore, both kinds of therapists corrected misconceptions, clarified objectives, answered questions, used few technical terms, perhaps used abreaction (releasing emotion through the recall of repressed material) and discussed both the strengths and weaknesses of the theory and practice of that method. Both therapists used suggestion. Clients in both groups stated that the qualities they admired in each group of therapists were empathy and genuineness, a high degree of interpersonal contact and therapist warmth. In fact, successful clients in both groups rated the "personal interaction with the therapist as the single most important part of their treatment" (Sloane et al., 1975, pp. 225–226).

In comparing the behavioral approaches with other approaches, predominantly the psychodynamic, Strupp noted that, while we do not know what precisely went on between Freud and his clients, it is his opinion "that Freud never practiced psychoanalysis in the manner advocated in his writings, and [that] today more than ever there exists a vast hiatus between actual psychoanalytic practice and enshrined principles" (Wachtel, 1977, pp. xii–xiv). Strupp also stated that any reconciliation of approaches has been delayed by "polemics" on such "slogans and clichés" as the medical model, symptom substitution, diagnosis, the unconscious, spontaneous remission, and others (ibid.). He observed that unfortunately both behavior therapists and psychodynamically oriented therapists are ignorant of each other's approach and work in terms of stereotypes. In Strupp's view, very appropriate for this concluding chapter, "a psycho-therapeutic system . . . is not a dogma but a set of provisional hypotheses in need of testing, refinement, and further testing. When perceived as dogma, concepts and terms become reified with disastrous consequences" (Wachtel, 1977, p. xiii).[5]

Future Directions

It seems ironic that the behavior therapies so far have not lived up to their promise in those areas where they seem to have been most promising, such as the treatment of enuresis, smoking, obesity, and some of the addictions. However, they have shown increasing promise as an adjunct or complementary set of techniques in such areas as depression. However, the changes in the behavior therapies have led to a new generation of behaviorists (Schwartz, 1977). Many practitioners who are now assuming positions of leadership, in behavioral psychology, in psychiatry, and certainly in social work, are individuals who have been trained in psychodynamic psychology but who, through disenchantment with their earlier training, have now approached and evaluated behaviorism for what it may contribute. This new generation is not wedded to a rigid behavioral philosophy but has no hesitation in adopting some of the precepts and procedures of a discipline that originated

[5] Strupp also cautions against the exaggerated empiricism of the extremist behaviorist who may not acknowledge phenomena if he can't measure them. For example, the most meaningful information is in the often vague and difficult-to-measure factors of the client and therapist relationship (Strupp, in Wachtel, 1977, p. xiv).

in animal experimentation, particularly its empiricism, objectivity, and specification of procedures. The practitioner of the future should not be bound by any ideological straitjacket but should be free to choose several orientations, within ethical limitations, that will produce the best result for his client.

The behavioral approaches can make a substantial contribution to the armamentarium of social work therapists adequately trained and flexible enough to use a number of different therapeutic modalities. It has become fashionable to mock eclectics as "people with both feet planted firmly in mid-air" (Schwartz, 1977, p. 375). Yet as the orientation to behavior therapy has broadened and become more effective by the inclusion of cognitive restructuring and the use of other procedures, so we feel that the practice of social work will similarly benefit by the inclusion of a number of these helping orientations, including the humanistic (Krill, 1978). Goodall (1972, p. 62) has pointed out that many of the younger behavior modifiers have really challenged the establishment and have much in common with younger radicals. "I suspect if it weren't for their own curtains of mutually exclusive jargons and mutually reinforcing labels, the humanist and the behaviorist might be surprised at how near they are to being bedfellows."[6]

In conclusion, we are not advocating that in future practice any useful approach be abandoned or that any single approach be emphasized to the exclusion of all others. We do, however, feel that the behavioral approach, especially the functional-analytic, contingency analysis of Skinner, as modified by the self-control and the cognitive behavioral approaches, has a great deal to offer to a cross-model approach to therapy. Psychotherapeutic practice is in a state

[6] For further amplification of the relationship of behavior therapy and the "humanistic" view, see Wandersman et al., 1976.

of constant flux and may very well come to include not only the approaches listed above but others such as psycho-pharmacology.

The criteria for the future should be effectiveness, efficiency, and low cost, all within a humanistic framework, regardless of the label applied to the approach or its origin, be it behavioral, psychodynamic, humanistic, or what you will. As the growing literature indicates, it may be that a combination of one or more procedures from one or more disciplines or orientations might be the most effective intervention in any given situation. It may also be that at some times within the therapeutic situation the therapist may have to switch not only from one technique or approach to another but from one complete *model* to another. It is not uncommon, when examining what behavior therapiest *actually* do as contrasted with what they *say* they do, to find that a great deal of the interview is conversation and not the application of "specific procedures" such as positive reinforcement or systematic desensitization (Wachtel, 1977).

Above all, procedures should be regarded as tentative and changeable. We are all interested in ethical, empirically proven mehtods. We all want to know what works. Therapy must be humane and, hopefully, cost-effective, with benefits over the long run as well as in the immediate present (Schwartz, 1977, p. 377).

The practice of therapy is currently in a period of great change. We see this as a positive phenomenon. The potential contribution of the behavioral therapies is one of the factors contributing to this change. If we teach effectively, we shall endow future generations of practitioners with the critical facilities to enable them to evaluate and revise their practice on an ongoing basis, discarding that which is ineffective or unethical and retaining that which is effective, ethical, and practical. The contributions of the contemporary behavior therapies will be a prominent part of the future therapy models.

How to Utilize the Literature on Behavioral Approaches to Therapy

The novice or newcomer to the behavioral therapies faces an almost overwhelming task in making his or her way through the now burgeoning behavioral literature. Even an introductory volume such as this book has a rather large working bibliography attached to it.

To make a path through this landslide of publications, it is advisable that the individual have some preliminary knowledge of some of the basic tenets of behaviorism. This would include the respondent model (Chapter 2) the operant model (Chapter 3) and the newer modeling and cognitive-behavioral methods (Chapter 5).

We suggest that one can enter the behavioral literature through any one of the following ways or by any combination, such as approaching a specific behavioral journal, or browsing through one of the several literature abstracts, or by scanning a number of annual reviews and handbooks which provide the useful service of summarizing the previous year's research. We shall discuss several of these approaches in turn.

Annual Reviews

The annual publication *Behavior Therapy: Theory and Practice* is one excellent source of information. These volumes are edited by Cyril M. Franks and G. Terence Wilson, both of Rutgers University, and published annually by Brunner/Mazel of New York City. The annual, first published in 1973, started as a collection of articles. However, as the series has developed, the editors' commentaries connecting the articles have grown longer and longer, increasingly reviewing and summarizing the literature, at the cost of decreasing the articles reprinted. A worthwhile tradeoff, in my opinion. The annuals usually begin with an overview of the past year's research, followed by debates on theoretical issues. There are usually chapters on procedures such as systematic desensitization or behavioral assessment, on therapy with particular client groups, sections on new subjects such as behavioral medicine and social applications. There are chapters on specific problems such as the addictions, sexual disorders, marriage, industry, as well as discussions on generic problems such as generalization. Each issue also contains a number of case studies of novel and useful procedures on either new or common problem areas. Each of the chapters is followed by a highly selective, relevant, and above all, very recent bibliography particular to that topic in the article. At the end of the volume, there is a list of references mentioned in the commentary. The bibliography in volume 6 (1978) ran thirty-five single-spaced pages. The commentaries connecting the chapters are by themselves extremely concise overviews of the current state of behavior therapy, and this is useful to the beginner as well as to the more experienced practitioner.

Another annual, organized in a slightly different manner, is *Progress in Behavior Modification,* published by Academic Press in New York, with changing editorship. Most libraries have this annual on serial order. This publication differs from the Franks and Wilson volumes in that there are usually only seven articles but each of these articles is a review article. For example, in volume 4 there are review articles on obesity, on extensions to social situations (the Kazdin article quoted in this book), on community settings, on demand characteristics, on biofeedback, on "parents as behavior therapists," and on implosive therapy. Previous volumes review depression, ethical issues, the token economies, modeling therapies, aversion therapy, hypnosis, and a number of other behavioral issues. Each chapter is followed by an extensive bibliography reviewing previous studies and publications. Once again, there is a strong emphasis upon recent publications.

Another set of annuals, also published by Academic Press, is *Advances in Behavior Therapy*. These tend to be proceedings of the Association for the Advancement of Behavior Therapy. Each volume contains approximately fifteen to twenty articles. The articles tend to include a review of the most recent literature. For example, in volume 4 (1973), there are articles on delinquency, mental retardation, cognitive factors, programming language, community mental health centers, automation, a review article on token economies, sexual disorders, and a number of other topics. There is even an article on modification of "self-concept." Once again, bibliographies are extensive.

There are other annual reviews which are less likely to be available and are highly specialized; for example, there is an annual review of *"Biofeedback and Self-Control,"* published by Aldine Press in Chicago.

A more recent annual, perhaps reflecting a growing trend toward specialization, is *Behavioral Group Therapy: An Annual Review,* edited by Dennis Upper and Steven Ross. It so far has been published in 1979 and 1980 by Research Press (Box 3177Y, Champaign, IL 61820). Each volume contains an overview of theoretical issues, practice problems, and new applications, in addition to extensive bibliographies as well as summaries of the literature on applications of behavior therapy principles to groups.

JOURNALS

The number of journals with behavioral orientations is rapidly expanding. This, we feel, is a somewhat mixed blessing as the proliferation of journals tends to result in a decrease in quality. The following journals are those we find most relevant.

Behavior Therapy is the official organ of the Association for the Advancement of Behavior Therapy. Volume 1 was published in 1970; currently the journal appears five times a year. This comprehensive journal contains carefully selected theoretical articles, case studies and reports, and brief research notes. The focus is on short articles and on short summaries of interesting—though more specialized—works. The addresses of the authors from whom one may obtain more information are also included.[1] This journal tends to include a number of case histories, and while adhering to an empirical basis, tends to be more eclectic than most behavioral journals. Among behavioral journals this journal, in particular, has been most forthright in publishing articles with constructive criticism of behavior therapy.

The *Journal of Applied Behavior Analysis* has appeared four times yearly since 1968 and is currently published at the State University of New York in Stony Brook. It represents basically an operant conditioning viewpoint. The articles are experimentally meticulous, usually illustrations of single-organism research. Sometimes the articles sacrifice relevance for neatness of research design. While this jour-

---

[1] *Behavior Therapy* often lists the articles accepted in advance of their publication so that interested readers may write to the authors for preprints.

nal has tended to concentrate upon school problems and problems of the mentally handicapped, recent issues have also featured articles on medical procedures, clinical problems, and social issues such an antilittering.

More traditional journals include *Behaviour Research and Therapy* (volume 1 in 1963, published in Great Britain) and the *Journal of Behavior Therapy and Experimental Psychiatry* (first edition in 1970, published in the United States and edited by Joseph Wolpe). These are clinically oriented, the former being more respondent than operant, with the latter featuring many more operant approaches. A good many of their articles are abstracted in the *Annual Review*. They are both highly recommended.

Behaviorism (volume 1 in 1972), is a journal edited by both philosophers and psychologists. It is highly theoretical, and the articles are sometimes very difficult to read. While it is definitely for the advanced student of behaviorism (a background in philosophy is also helpful), many of these articles are worth reading.

A somewhat new journal is *Behavior Modification* (first edition 1977), which tends to be a fairly conventional, operant-oriented journal with varied content.

Cognitive Therapy and Research (volume 1 in 1977), a journal stressing the cognitive-behavioral approach, is published by Plenum Press in New York and edited by Michael J. Mahoney. This journal attempts to provide comparative studies of cognitive-behavioral methods and, obviously, is a schism from the more conventional, radical behavioral view as expressed in the *Journal of Applied Behavior Analysis,* although there is an overlap between articles in this journal and in *Behavior Therapy*. However, the articles in this journal tend to focus much more on the "softer" cognitively oriented issues within the behavioral framework.

Another journal that may be helpful, though not always readily available, is *Behavioural Analysis and Modification* (formerly the *European Journal of Behavioural Analysis and Modification.*) Each issue contains several articles on treatment research, with differing commentators followed by a rebuttal by the author of the article, thus providing a useful dialogue on various relevant, contemporary issues. While the number of topics covered is, by necessity, small, because of the debate and dialogue they are covered in depth. Bibliographic references tend to be excellent and, unlike most other journals, usually extend beyond the American literature.

HANDBOOKS AND BOOKS ON BEHAVIOR THERAPY

Another approach to enter the behavioral literature is through one of the several handbooks published on behavior therapy methods. Many of these handbooks are extremely comprehensive and provide good overviews of the literature. The drawback, of course, is that these references are limited to the time of approximately six to eight months prior to publication date. One good example is Gambrill (1977), with 23 chapters and over 1,000 pages of text, and a bibliography over 90 pages long. There are excellent surveys of the literature and illustrations for the various techniques and the various procedures. Gambrill's book is quite comprehensive, providing an excellent encyclopedic overview.

The *Handbook of Behavior Modification and Behavior Therapy,* edited by Leitenberg (1976), has eighteen chapters covering alcoholism, the eating disorders, physiological functions, neuroses, depression, schools, delinquency and other topics, as well as an overview chapter. The text is economically written and the review of the literature is comprehensive.

The *Handbook of Behavioral Assessment* (1977), edited by Siminero, Calhoun and Adams is one of a series of books published by Wiley on the psychological approaches in general, and behavioral approaches in particular. The book first discusses behavior assessment including instrumentation, then progresses to general approaches to assessment such as interviews, self-reports, and psychophysiological procedures. A third section covers the assessment of specific behavior problems including anxiety, addiction, sexual problems, social skills, marital conflict and accord, child behavior problems, and psychotic behavior. Each of the chapters is accompanied by an up-to-date bibliography.

The second edition of Rimm and Masters *Behavior Therapy: Techniques and Empirical Findings* (1979) is a very comprehensive textbook including a bibliography over forty pages long, which is selective and current, in addition to an "index of disorders" that covers a large number of problems from academic problems to writers' cramp. A similar index of behavioral conditions may also be found in Agras (1978).

Human Behavior: Analysis and Application by Reese (1978) is an excellent introductory textbook that explains the basic principles of behavior analysis and application. It contains good overviews of the respondent and operant models and self-control, but unfortunately neglects the cognitive change model. It is concisely written, highly understandable, with good illustrations and examples which clarify these sometimes complicated concepts. I have used this edition, as well as the first edition (now outdated), in my classes at the University of Chicago with a great deal of success.

Another series of books contains the proceedings of the annual International Conference on Behavior Modification. These are held each spring in Banff, Canada. Each conference generally focusses on a specific problem area. The first, in 1969, was on "Ideal Mental Health Services"; other volumes have focused on programs for youth, schools, new methodologies, families and parenting. A recent volume (Stuart, 1977) was concerned with behavioral self-management; another (Davidson and Davidson, 1980) focused on behavioral medicine. The proceedings from the Banff conference, now published annually by Brunner/Mazell in New York, are excellent source books.

NEWSLETTERS

Three very useful newsletters come to mind immediately. The *Behavior Therapist* is distributed to the membership in the Association for the Advancement of Behavior Therapy. In addition to providing news of association business, it also lists new publications, workshops, research in progress, and a host of other worthwhile features.

A second newsletter that shows every promise of surviving (for the mortality rate among newsletters is high) is *Behavior Group Therapy,* published at the University of Wisconsin, Madison, and edited by Sheldon Rose, a leading practitioner and theorist in the application of behavior therapy and cognitive-behavioral approaches to group practice. This newsletter contains abstracts, references, and reports on research and work in progress, in addition to short original articles. Anyone using groups or contemplating integrating behavioral methods into his/her work with groups should look into this publication.

As we noted in Chapter 5, investigations into cognition are increasing and will continue to increase. This is evidenced by the excellent annual newsletter—continually expanding in size and scope—*Cognitive-Behavior Modification,* edited by Donald Meichenbaum of the University of Waterloo, Ontario, Canada. Listing just about all research in the cognitive and cognitive-behavioral areas, it is voluminous, comprehensive, and intelligently edited. It is obtainable from Donald Meichenbaum, Ph.D., Psychology Department, University of Waterloo, Waterloo, Ontario, Canada N2L,3G1. It is well worth the few dollars it costs.

Another publication that is helpful is the *Psychological Abstracts,* readily available in most academic and institutional libraries. One drawback is that there tends to be a lag of several years between publication date and the time the abstracts appear.

AUDIO CASSETTES

Several firms publish reviews of literature in the form of audio cassettes. A leader in this area is BMA Audio Cassettes, a division of Guilford Publications, 200 Park Avenue South, New York 10003. The BMA catalog lists cassettes on various topics, for example, a series on cognitive behavior therapy edited by Donald Meichenbaum that touches upon phobic disorders, sexual disorders, depression, obesity, anxiety, impulse disorders, and others. These eight cassettes sell, at least at the time of this printing, for $84. While this may seem expensive, the quality of the recordings is very high. Individuals or agencies may consider joining and pooling their resources to buy these cassettes. This publisher also has cassettes on biofeedback, principles of behavior analysis, behavior therapy, behavior self-management, clinical hypnosis, rational emotive therapy, stress behavior, and behavioral medicine, and a number of other topics. They also record conferences. This author has had the experience of not being able to attend important conferences, only to find that the cassette tapes purchased for $50 to $75 provided the significant presentations of the conference. While it is true that one does not get the between-session gossip, the costs of the cassettes are, in most cases, less than one day's expenses at a conference. It is not beyond probability that distribution of cassette tapes may render attendance at some of these conferences more as a social rather than a professional occurrence.

BEHAVIORAL PUBLICATIONS IN SOCIAL WORK

While several behavioral journals are being contemplated in social work, there does not seem to be at the moment a specific behavioral outlet in social work. There is an organization called the "Group for the Study of Behavioral Methods in Social Work," which meets annually, simultaneously with the Annual Program Meeting of the Council for Social Work Education. This is an interest group comprised of a number of people teaching behavioral methods at various colleges. They sometimes publish bibliographies and other material. One of the founders of this group, Professor Clayton T. Shorkey, periodically publishes bibliographies for behavioral methods in social work. His last bibliography (dated March, 1978) is fifteen pages long and represents—at least to this author—a complete coverage of the behavioral material in social work done by social workers. Professor Shorkey is at the School of Social Work of the University of Texas at Austin, Texas.

Another publication increasingly featuring behavioral material is *Social Work Research and Abstracts,* published by the National Association of Social Workers. This journal, in addition to reports of original research and review articles, has abstracts of the current literature that are cross-indexed, not only by specific behavioral method itself, but by characteristic of target group. For example, the issue of volume 14, no. 4 (Winter 1978) has an article on communication theory, and an article by Ed Thomas on single-case experimentation. In the index they list behavioral disorders, behavioral intervention, behavior modification, behavior therapy, as well as entries under specific topics such as assertiveness training. The time lag between publication and abstracting seems to be less than a year in nearly all cases. This is an excellent publication useful to social workers and psychotherapists of all theoretical persuasions.

References

ABRAHAM, K. "Notes on the Psychoanalytic Investigation and Treatment of Manic Depressive Insanity and Allied Conditions." In W. Gaylin (ed.), *The Meaning of Despair.* New York: Science House, 1968.

ABRAMSON, E. E. "A Review of Behavioral Approaches to Weight Control." *Behaviour Research and Therapy,* 1973, *11,* 547–556.

ADAMS, S., AND ORGEL, M. *Through the Mental Health Maze: A Consumer's Guide to Finding a Psychotherapist, Including a Sample Consumer/Therapist Contract.* Washington, D.C.: Health Research Group, 1975.

AGRAS, W. S. "Behavior Modification in the General Hospital Psychiatric Unit." In H. Leitenberg (ed.), *Handbook of Behavior Modification and Behavior Therapy.* Englewood Cliffs, New Jersey: Prentice-Hall, 1976.

AGRAS, W. S. "The Token Economy." In *Behavior Modification: Principles and Clinical Applications,* (2nd ed.) W.S. Agras (ed.). Boston: Little, Brown & Co., 1978.

AGRAS, W. S.; BARLOW, D. H.; CHAPIN, H. N.; ABEL, G.; AND LEITENBERG, H. "Behavior Modification of Anorexia Nervosa." *Archives of General Psychiatry,* 1974, *30,* 279–285.

AKISKAL, H. S., AND McKINNEY, W. T. "Depressive Disorders: Toward a Unified Hypothesis." *Science,* 1973, *182,* 20–29.

ALBIN, R. S. "Depression in Women: A Feminist Perspective." *APA Monitor,* 1976, *7,* p. 27.

ALEXANDER, J. F., AND BARTON, C. "Behavioral Systems Therapy for Families." In D. H. L. Olson (ed.), *Treating Relationships.* Lake Mills, Iowa: Graphic Publishing Company, 1976.

ALVORD, J. R. *Home Token Economy: An Incentive Program for Children and Their Parents.* Champaign, Ill.: The Research Press, 1973.

AMERICAN PSYCHIATRIC ASSOCIATION TASK FORCE ON BEHAVIOR THERAPY. *Behavior Therapy in Psychiatry.* Washington, D.C.: American Psychiatric Association, 1973.

ARIETI, S., AND BEMPORAD, J. *Severe and Mild Depression.* New York: Basic Books, 1978.

ARKAVA, M. L. *Behavior Modification: A Procedural Guide for Social Workers.* Missoula, Montana: University of Montana, Department of Social Work, 1973.

AYLLON, T. "Intensive Treatment of Psychotic Behaviour by Stimulus Satiation and Food Reinforcement." *Behaviour Research and Therapy,* 1963, *1,* 53–61.

AYLLON, T., AND AZRIN, N. H. *The Token Economy: A Motivational System for Therapy and Rehabilitation.* New York: Appleton-Century-Crofts, 1968.

AZRIN, N. H.; FLORES, T.; AND KAPLAN, S. J. "Job-Finding Club: A Group-Assisted Program for Obtaining Employment." *Behaviour Research and Therapy,* 1975, *13,* 17–27.

AZRIN, N. H., AND FOXX, R. M. *Toilet Training in Less Than a Day.* New York: Simon and Schuster, 1974.

AZRIN, N. H.; NASTER, B. J.; AND JONES, R. "Reciprocity Counseling: A Rapid Learning-Based Procedure for Marital Counseling." *Behaviour Research and Therapy,* 1973, *11,* 365–382.

BACHRACH, A. J.; ERWIN, W. J.; AND MOHR, J. P. "The Control of Eating Behavior in an Anorexic by Operant Conditioning Techniques." In L. P. Ullman and L. Krasner (eds.), *Case Studies in Behavior Modification.* New York: Holt, Rinehart and Winston, 1965.

BAER, D. M. "A Case for the Selective Reinforcement of Punishment." In C. Neuringer and J. L. Michael (eds.), *Behavior Modification in Clinical Psychology.* New York: Appleton-Century-Crofts, 1970.

BAER, D. M., AND SHERMAN, J. A. "Reinforcement Control of Generalized Imitation in Young People." *Journal of Experimental Child Psychiatry*, 1964, *1*, 37–49.

BAKAL, D. A. "Headache: A Biopsychological Perspective." *Psychological Bulletin*, 1975, *82*, 369–382.

BAKAL, D. A. *Psychology and Medicine: Psychobiological Dimensions of Health and Illness*. New York: Springer Publishing Company, 1979.

BANDURA, A. *Principles of Behavior Modification*. New York: Holt, Rinehart and Winston, 1969.

BANDURA, A. (ed.). *Psychological Modeling: Conflicting Theories*. Chicago: Aldine-Atherton, 1971.

BANDURA, A. *Aggression: A Social Learning Analysis*. Englewood Cliffs, N.J.: Prentice-Hall, 1973.

BANDURA, A. "Self-Efficacy: Toward a Unifying Theory of Behavioral Change." *Psychological Review*, 1977a, *84*, 191–215.

BANDURA, A. *Social Learning Theory*. Englewood Cliffs, N.J.: Prentice-Hall, 1977b.

BANDURA, A. "On Paradigms and Recycled Ideologies." *Cognitive Therapy and Research*, 1978a, *2*, 79–104.

BANDURA, A. "The Self-System in Reciprocal Determinism," *American Psychologist*, 1978b, *33*, 344–358.

BARBACH, L. G. *For Yourself: The Fulfillment of Female Sexuality*. Garden City, N.Y: Doubleday, 1975.

BARBACH, L. G. *Women Discover Orgasm: A Therapist's Guide to a New Treatment Approach*. New York: The Free Press, 1980.

BECK, A. T. *Depression: Causes and Treatment*. Philadelphia, Pa.: University of Pennsylvania Press, 1967.

BECK, A. T. "Cognitive Therapy: Nature and Relation to Behavior Therapy." *Behavior Therapy*, 1970, *1*, 184–200.

BECK, A. T. "The Phenomena of Depression: A Synthesis." In D. Offer and D. X. Freedman (eds.), *Modern Psychiatry and Clinical Research: Essays in Honor of Roy Grinker, Sr.* New York: Basic Books, 1972.

BECK, A. T. *Cognitive Therapy and the Emotional Disorders.* New York: International Universities Press, 1976.

BECK, A. T., AND MAHONEY, M. J. "Schools of 'Thought' " (Comment on Wolpe, 1978.) *American Psychologist,* 1979, *34,* 93–98.

BECK, A. T.; RUSH, A. J.; SHAW, B. F.; and EMERY, G. *Cognitive Therapy of Depression: A Treatment Manual.* Philadelphia, Pa.: Center for Cognitive Therapy, 1978.

BECK, A. T.; RUSH, A. J.; SHAW, B. F.; AND EMERY, G. *Cognitive Therapy of Depression.* New York: The Guilford Press, 1979.

BEMIS, K. M. "Current Approaches to the Etiology and Treatment of Anorexia Nervosa." *Psychological Bulletin,* 1978, *85,* 593–617.

BENSON, H. *The Relaxation Response.* New York: William Morrow & Company, 1975.

BERGIN, A. E. "The Evaluation of Therapeutic Outcomes." In A. E. Bergin and S. L. Garfield (eds.), *Handbook of Psychotherapy and Behavior Change: An Empirical Analysis.* New York: John Wiley, 1971.

BERNI, R., AND FORDYCE, W. E. *Behavior Modification and the Nursing Process* (2nd ed.). St. Louis: The C. V. Mosby Company, 1977.

BERNSTEIN, D., AND BORKOVEC, T. D. *Progressive Relaxation Training: A Manual for the Helping Professions.* Champaign, Ill.: Research Press, 1973.

BIKLEN, D. P. "Behavior Modification in a State Mental Hospital: A Participant-Observer's Critique." *American Journal of Orthopsychiatry,* 1976, *46,* 53–61.

BIRK, L. (ed.). *Biofeedback: Behavioral Medicine.* New York: Grune & Stratton, 1973.

BLANCHARD, E. B., AND EPSTEIN, L. H. "The Clinical Usefulness of Biofeedback." In M. Hersen, R. M. Eisler, and P. M. Miller (eds.), *Progress in Behavior Modification: Volume 4.* New York: Academic Press, 1977.

BLANCHARD, E. B.; THEOBALD, D. E.; WILLIAMSON, D. A.; SILVER, B. V.; AND BROWN, D. A. "Temperature Biofeedback in the Treatment of Migraine Headaches." *Archives of General Psychiatry,* 1978, *35,* 581–588.

BONIME, W. "The Psychodynamics of Neurotic Depression." In S. R. Arieti (ed.), *American Handbook of Psychiatry: Vol. 3.* New York: Basic Books, 1966.

BOOTZIN, R. B. "Effects of Self-Control Procedures for Insomnia." In R. B. Stuart (ed.), *Behavioral Self-Management: Strategies, Techniques and Outcomes.* New York: Brunner/Mazel, 1977.

BORENZWEIG, H. "Social Work and Psychoanalytic Theory: A Historical Analysis." *Social Work,* 1971, *16,* 7–16.

BORMAN, L. D. *Explorations in Self-Help and Mutual Aid.* Evanston, Ill.: Center for Urban Affairs, Northwestern University, 1975.

BRITT, M. F. *Bibliography of Behavior Modification 1924–1975.* Durham, N.C.: Cerebral Palsy and Crippled Child Hospital of North Carolina, 1975.

BRUCH, H. *Eating Disorders: Obesity, Anorexia Nervosa, and the Person Within.* New York: Basic Books, 1973.

BRUCH, H. "Perils of Behavior Modification in Treatment of Anorexia Nervosa." *Journal of the American Medical Association,* 1974, *230,* 1419–1422.

BRUCH, H. *The Golden Cage: The Enigma of Anorexia Nervosa.* Cambridge, Mass.: Harvard University Press, 1978.

BUCKLEY, N. K., AND WALKER, H. M. *Modifying Classroom Behavior: A Manual of Procedures for Classroom Teachers.* Champaign, Ill.: The Research Press, 1970.

CARPENTER, F. *The Skinner Primer: Beyond Freedom and Dignity.* New York: The Free Press, 1974.

CARTER, R. D. *Help! These Kids Are Driving Me Crazy.* Campaign, Ill.: The Research Press, 1972.

CAUTELA, J. R. "Covert Sensitization." *Psychological Reports,* 1967, *20,* 459–468.

CAUTELA, J. R. "Covert Reinforcement." *Behavior Therapy,* 1970, *1,* 273–278.

CAUTELA, J. R. "Covert Extinction." *Behavior Therapy,* 1971, *2,* 192–200.

CAUTELA, J. R. "Rationale and Procedures for Covert Conditioning." *Advances in Behavior Therapy: 1972.* New York: Academic Press, 1972.

CAUTELA, J. R.; FLANNERY, R. B.; AND HAMLEY, E. "Covert Modeling: An Experimental Test." *Behavior Therapy,* 1974, *5,* 494–502.

CAUTELA, J. R., AND GRODEN, J. *Relaxation: A Comprehensive Manual for Adults, Children, and Children with Special Needs.* Champaign, Ill.: The Research Press, 1978.

CHAIKLIN, H. "Discussion and Comment." In M. F. Shore and S. E. Golann (eds.), *Current Ethical Issues in Mental Health.* Rockville, Md.: National Institute of Mental Health, 1973.

CHRISTOPHERSON, E. R.; ARNOLD, C. M.; HILL, D. W.; AND QUILITICH, H. R. "The Home Point System: Token Reinforcement Procedures for Application by Parents of Children with Behavior Problems." *Journal of Applied Behavior Analysis,* 1972, *5,* 485–497.

COHEN, H. L., AND FILIPCZAK, J. *A New Learning Environment: A Case for Learning.* San Francisco: Jossey-Bass, 1971.

CONRAD, J. Personal Communication. May, 1975.

COSTELLO, C. G. "Depression: Loss of Reinforcers or Loss of Reinforcer Effectiveness?" *Behavior Therapy,* 1972a, *3,* 240–247.

COSTELLO, C. G. "Reply to Lazarus." *Behavior Therapy,* 1972b, *3,* 251–253.

DAVIDSON, P. O. (ed.). *The Behavioral Management of Anxiety, Depression and Pain.* New York: Brunner/Mazel, 1976.

DAVIDSON, P. O., AND DAVIDSON, S. M. (eds.). *Behavioral Medicine: Changing Health Lifestyles.* New York: Brunner/Mazel, 1980.

DAVIS, I. "Caseworker's Use of Influence in Counseling Parents." Unpublished doctoral dissertation, University of Chicago, 1973.

DAVISON, G. C., AND STUART, R. B. "Behavior Therapy and Civil Liberties." *American Psychologist*, 1975, *30*, 755–763.

DOLEYS, D. M. "Behavioral Treatments for Nocturnal Enuresis in Children: A Review of the Recent Literature." *Psychological Bulletin*, 1977, *84*, 30–54.

DOLLARD, J., AND MILLER, N. E. *Personality and Psychotherapy: An Analysis in Terms of Learning, Thinking and Culture*. New York: McGraw-Hill, 1950.

D'ZURILLA, T. J., AND GOLDFRIED, M. "Problem Solving and Behavior Modification." *Journal of Abnormal Psychology*, 1971, *78*, 107–126.

D'ZURILLA, T. J., AND GOLDFRIED, M. "Cognitive Processes, Problem-Solving, and Effective Behavior." In M. R. Goldfried and M. Merbaum (eds.), *Behavior Change Through Self-Control*. New York: Holt, Rinehart & Winston, 1973.

ELLIS, A. "The Basic Clinical Theory of Rational-Emotive Therapy." In A. Ellis and R. Grieger (eds.), *Handbook of Rational-Emotive Therapy*. New York: Springer Publishing Company, 1977a.

ELLIS, A. "Rational-Emotive Therapy: Research Data That Supports the Clinical and Personality Hypotheses of RET and Other Modes of Cognitive-Behavior Therapy." *The Counseling Psychologist*, 1977b, *7*, 2–42.

ELLIS, A. "On Joseph Wolpe's Espousal of Cognitive-Behavior Therapy" (Comment on Wolpe, 1978). *American Psychologist*, 1979, *34*, 98–99.

ELLIS, A., AND GRIEGER, R. (eds.). *Handbook of Rational-Emotive Therapy*. New York: Springer Publishing Co., 1977.

EPSTEIN, S. "Toward a Unified Theory of Anxiety." In B. Maher (ed.), *Progress in Experimental Personality; Volume 4*. New York: Academic Press, 1967.

EVANS, R. I. *B. F. Skinner: The Man and His Ideas*. New York: E. P. Dutton, 1968.

EYSENCK, H. J. "The Effects of Psychotherapy: An Evaluation." *Journal of Consulting and Clinical Psychology*, 1952, *16*, 319–324.

FERGUSON, J. M., AND BIRCHLER, G. R. "Therapeutic Packages: Tools for Change." In W. S. Agras (ed.), *Behavior Modification: Principles and Clinical Applications* (2nd ed.) Boston: Little, Brown and Company, 1978.

FERSTER, C. B. "Classification of Behavioral Pathology." In Krasner and L. P. Ullman (eds.), *Research in Behavior Modification.* New York: Holt, Rinehart and Winston, 1965.

FERSTER, C. B. "Animal Behavior and Mental Illness." *Psychological Record,* 1966, *16,* 345–356.

FERSTER, C. B. "An Experimental Analysis of Clinical Phenomenon." *The Psychological Record,* 1972, *22,* 1–16.

FERSTER, C. B. "A Functional Analysis of Depression." *American Psychologist,* 1973, *28,* 857–870.

FERSTER, C. B.; NURNBERGER, J. I.; AND LEVITT, E. B. "The Control of Eating." *Journal of Mathetics,* 1962, *1,* 87–109.

FERSTER, C. B., AND SKINNER, B. F. *Schedules of Reinforcement.* New York: Appleton-Century-Crofts, 1957.

FESTINGER, L. "Behavioral Support for Opinion Change." *Public Opinion Quarterly,* 1964, *28,* 404–417.

FIEDLER, F. "A Comparison of Therapeutic Relationships in Psychoanalytic, Nondirective, and Adlerian Therapy." *Journal of Consulting Psychology,* 1950, *14,* 426–445.

FISCHER, J., AND GOCHROS, H. L. *Planned Behavior Change: Behavior Modification in Social Work.* New York: The Free Press, 1975.

FORDYCE, , W. E. *Behavioral Methods for Chronic Pain and Illness.* St. Louis, Mo.: C. V. Mosby Company, 1976a.

FORDYCE, W. E. "Behavioral Concepts in Chronic Pain and Illness." In P. O. Davidson (ed.), *The Behavioral Management of Anxiety, Depression and Pain.* New York: Brunner/Mazel, 1976b.

FRANKL, V. E. *Man's Search for Meaning: An Introduction to Logotherapy.* New York: Washington Square Press, 1959.

FRANKS, C. M. (ed.). *Behavior Therapy: Status and Appraisal.* New York: McGraw-Hill, 1969.

FRANKS, C. M. "Pavlovian Conditioning Approaches." In D. J. Levis (ed.), *Learning Approaches to Therapeutic Behavior Change*. Chicago: Aldine, 1970.

FRANKS, C. M., AND WILSON, G. T. *Annual Review of Behavior Therapy: Theory and Practice, 1976*. New York: Brunner/Mazel, 1976.

FRANKS, C. M., AND WILSON, G. T. *Annual Review of Behavior Therapy: Theory and Practice, 1978*. New York: Brunner/Mazel, 1978.

FRANKS, V., AND BURTLE, V. (eds.). *Women in Therapy: New Psychotherapies for a Changing Society*. New York: Brunner/Mazel, 1974.

GAMBRILL, E. D. *Behavior Modification: Handbook of Assessment, Intervention and Evaluation*. San Francisco: Jossey-Bass Publishers, 1977.

GAMBRILL, E. D., AND RICHEY, C. A. "An Assertion Inventory for Use in Assessment and Research." *Behavior Therapy*, 1975, *6*, 550–561.

GEISER, R. L. *Behavior Mod and the Managed Society*. Boston, Mass.: Beacon Press, 1976.

GENDLIN, E. T. *Focusing*. New York: Everest House, 1978.

GENTRY, W. D. "What Is Behavior Modification?" In W. D. Gentry (ed.), *Applied Behavior Modification*. St. Louis, Mo.: C. V. Mosby Co., 1975.

GERMAIN, C. B. "An Ecological Perspective in Casework Practice." *Social Casework*, 1973, *54*, 323–330.

GLISSON, D. H. "A Review of Behavioral Marital Counseling: Has Practice Tuned Out Theory?" *The Psychological Record*, 1976, *26*, 95–104.

GOLDFRIED, M. R., AND DAVISON, G. C. *Clinical Behavior Therapy*. New York: Holt, Rinehart & Winston, 1976.

GOLDIAMOND, I. "Self-Control Procedures in Personal Behavior Problems." *Psychological Reports*, Monograph Supplement 3–V17, 1965, *17*, 851–68.

GOLDIAMOND, I. "Toward a Constructional Approach to Social Problems: Ethical and Constitutional Issues Raised by Applied Behavior Analysis." *Behaviorism*, 1974, *2*, 1–84.

GOLDIAMOND, I. "A Diary of Self-Modification." *Psychology Today,* 1973, *7,* 95–101.

GOLDIAMOND, I. "Coping and Adaptive Behaviors of the Disabled." In G. L. Albrecht (ed.), *Socialization in the Disability Process.* Pittsburgh: University of Pittsburgh, 1975.

GOODALL, K. "Shapers at Work." *Psychology Today,* 1972, *6,* 53–62, 132–138.

GRANT, D. A. "Classical and Operant Conditioning." In A. W. Melton (ed.), *Categories of Human Learning.* New York: Academic Press, 1964.

GRAZIANO, A. M. (ed.) *Behavior Therapy with Children.* Chicago: Aldine-Atherton, 1971.

GRAZIANO, A. M. (ed.) *Behavior Therapy with Children, II.* Chicago: Aldine Publishing Co., 1975.

GRINNELL, R. M. "Environmental Modification: Casework's Concern or Casework's Neglect?" *The Social Service Review,* 1973, *47,* 208–220.

GRINNELL, R. M., AND KYTE, N. S. "Modifying the Environment." *Social Work,* 1974, *19,* 477–483.

GRINNELL, R. M., AND KYTE, N. S. "Environmental Modification: A Study." *Social Work,* 1975, *20,* 313–318.

HOMME, L. E. "Perspectives in Psychology—XXIV: Control of Coverants, The Operants of the Mind." *Psychological Record,* 1965, *15,* 501–511.

HOMME, L. E. *How to Use Contingency Contracting in the Classroom.* Champaign, Ill.: The Research Press, 1969.

HORNEY, K. *Neurosis and Human Growth: The Struggle Toward Self-Realization.* New York: Norton, 1950.

HUSTED, J. R. "Desensitization Procedures in Dealing with Female Sexual Dysfunction." *The Counseling Psychologist,* 1975, *5,* 30–37.

JACOBSON, E. *Progressive Relaxation.* Chicago: University of Chicago Press, 1938.

JACOBSON, N. S. "Problem Solving and Contingency Contracting in the Treatment of Marital Discord." *Journal of Consulting and Clinical Psychology,* 1977, *45,* 92–100.

JACOBSON, N. S., AND MARGOLIN, G. *Marital Therapy: Strategies Based on Social Learning and Behavior Exchange Principles.* New York: Brunner/Mazel, 1979.

JACOBSON, N. S., AND MARTIN, B. "Behavioral Marriage Therapy: Current Status." *Psychological Bulletin,* 1976, *83,* 540–556.

JEHU, D.; HARDIKER, P.; YELLOLY, M.; AND SHAW, M. *Behaviour Modification in Social Work.* London: Wiley-Interscience, 1972.

JONAS, G. *Visceral Learning: Toward a Science of Self-Control.* New York: The Viking Press, 1973.

JONES, M. C. "The Elimination of Children's Fears." *Journal of Experimental Psychology,* 1924, *7,* 382–390.

KANFER, F. H. "Self-Management Methods." In F. H. Kanfer and A. P. Goldstein (eds.), *Helping People Change: A Textbook of Methods.* New York: Pergamon Press, 1975.

KANFER, F. H. "The Many Faces of Self-Control, or Behavior Modification Changes Its Focus." In R. B. Stuart (ed.), *Behavioral Self-Management: Strategies, Techniques and Outcomes.* New York: Brunner/Mazel, 1977.

KANFER, F. H., AND KAROLY, P. "Self-Control: A Behavioristic Excursion into the Lion's Den." *Behavior Therapy,* 1972, *3,* 398–416.

KANFER, F. H., AND PHILLIPS, J. S. *Learning Foundations of Behavior Therapy.* New York: Wiley, 1970.

KAPLAN, H. I., AND KAPLAN, H. S. "The Psychosomatic Concept of Obesity." *Journal of Nervous and Mental Diseases,* 1957, *125,* 181–201.

KATZ, M. M.; SECUNDA, S. K.; HIRSCHFELD, R. M. A.; AND KOSLOW, S. H. "NIMH Clinical Research Branch Collaborative Program on the Psychobiology of Depression." *Archives of General Psychiatry,* 1979, *36,* 765–771.

KAZDIN, A. E. *The Token Economy: A Review and Evaluation.* New York: Plenum Press, 1977.

KAZDIN, A. E. "Extensions of Reinforcement Techniques to Socially and Environmentally Relevant Behaviors." In M. Hersen, R. M. Eisler, and P. M. Miller (eds.), *Progress in Behavior Modification: Volume 4.* New York: Academic Press, 1977.

KAZDIN, A. E., AND BOOTZIN, R. B. "The Token Economy: An Evaluative Review." *Journal of Applied Behavior Analysis,* 1972, *5,* 343–372.

KAZDIN, A. E., AND BOOTZIN, R. B. "The Token Economy: An Examination of Issues." In *Advances in Behavior Therapy, Volume 4,* R. R. Rubin et al. (eds.), New York: Academic Press, 1973.

KAZDIN, A. E., AND WILCOXON, L. A. "Systematic Desensitization and Nonspecific Treatment Effects: A Methodological Evaluation." *Psychological Bulletin,* 1976, *83,* 729–758.

KINKADE, K. *A Walden Two Experiment: The First Five Years of the Twin Oaks Community.* New York: Morrow, 1973.

KLEIN, G. "Two Theories or One?" *Bulletin of the Menninger Clinic,* 1973, *37,* 102–132.

KLEIN, M. H.; DITTMANN, A. T.; PARLOFF, M. B.; AND GILL, M. M. "Behavior Therapy: Observations and Reflections." *Journal of Consulting and Clinical Psychology,* 1969, *33,* 259–266.

KLERMAN, G. L. "Clinical Research in Depression." *Archives of General Psychiatry,* 1971, *24,* 305–319.

KNAPP, T. J.; DOWNS, D. L.; AND ALPERSON, J. R. "Behavior Therapy for Insomnia: A Review." *Behavior Therapy,* 1976, *7,* 614–625.

KNAPP, T. J., AND PETERSON, L. W. "Behavior Management in Medical and Nursing Practice." In W. E. Craighead, A. E. Kazdin, and M. J. Mahoney (eds.), *Behavior Modification: Principles, Issues and Applications.* Boston: Houghton Mifflin Company, 1976.

KNAPP, T. J., AND WELLS, L. A. "Behavior Therapy for Asthma: A Review." *Behaviour Research and Therapy,* 1978, *16,* 103–115.

KNOX, D. *Marriage Happiness: A Behavioral Approach to Counseling.* Champaign, Ill.: The Research Press, 1971.

KNOX, D. *Dr. Knox's Marital Exercise Book.* New York: David McKay, 1975.

KOGON, E. *The Theory and Practice of Hell: The German Concentration Camps and The System Behind Them.* N.Y.: Berkley Publishing Corp., 1950.

KOLATA, G. B. "Mental Disorders: A New Approach to Treatment?" *Science,* 1979, *203,* 36–38.

KOZLOFF, M. A. *Reaching the Autistic Child: A Parent Training Program.* Champaign, Ill.: The Research Press, 1973.

KRAPFL, J. E., AND VARGAS, E. A. (eds.). *Behaviorism and Ethics.* Kalamazoo, Mich.: Behaviordelia, 1977.

KRASNER, L., AND ULLMANN, L. P. (eds.). *Research in Behavior Modification: New Developments and Implications.* New York: Holt, Rinehart & Winston, 1965.

KRILL, D. F. *Existential Social Work.* New York: Free Press, 1978.

KRUMBOLTZ, J. D., AND KRUMBOLTZ, H. B. *Changing Children's Behavior.* Englewood Cliffs, N.J.: Prentice-Hall, 1972.

KUNKEL, J. H. *Social and Economic Growth: A Behavioral Perspective of Social Change.* New York: Oxford University Press, 1970.

KUNKEL, J. H. *Behavior, Social Problems, and Change.* Englewood Cliffs, N.J.: Prentice-Hall, 1975.

LAZARUS, A. A. "In Support of Technical Eclecticism." *Psychological Reports,* 1967, *21,* 415–416.

LAZARUS, A. A. "Learning Theory and the Treatment of Depression." *Behaviour Research and Therapy,* 1968, *6,* 83–89.

LAZARUS, A. A. *Behavior Therapy and Beyond.* New York: McGraw Hill, 1971.

LAZARUS, A. A. "Some Reactions to Costello's Paper on Depression." *Behavior Therapy,* 1972, *3,* 248–250.

LAZARUS, A. A. "Multimodal Behavior Therapy: Treating the 'BASIC ID.' " *Journal of Nervous and Mental Disease,* 1973, *156,* 404–411.

LAZARUS, A. A. "Multimodal Behavioral Treatment of Depression." *Behavior Therapy,* 1974, *5,* 549–554.

LAZARUS, A. A. (ed.). *Multimodal Behavior Therapy.* New York: Springer Publishing Company, 1976.

LAZARUS, A. A. "Has Behavior Therapy Outlived Its Usefulness?" *American Psychologist,* 1977, *32,* 550–554.

LAZARUS, A. A. "A Matter of Emphasis" (Comment on Wolpe, 1978)." *American Psychologist,* 1979, *34,* 100.

LEDWIDGE, B. "Cognitive Behavior Modification: A Step in the Wrong Direction?" *Psychological Bulletin,* 1978, *85,* 353–375.

LEDWIDGE, B. "Cognitive Behavior Modification: A Rejoinder to Locke and Meichenbaum." *Cognitive Therapy and Research,* 1979, *3,* 133–139.

LEFKOWITZ, M. M., AND BURTON, N. "Childhood Depression: A Critique of the Concept." *Psychological Bulletin,* 1978, *85,* 716–726.

LEITENBERG, H. (ed.). *Handbook of Behavior Modification and Behavior Therapy.* Englewood Cliffs, N.J.: Prentice-Hall, 1976.

LEON, G. R. "Current Directions in the Treatment of Obesity." *Psychological Bulletin,* 1976, *83,* 557–578.

LEON, G. R., AND ROTH, L. "Obesity: Psychological Causes, Correlations, and Speculation." *Psychological Bulletin,* 1977, *84,* 117–139.

LESSE, S. (ed.). *Masked Depression.* New York: Jason Aronson, 1974.

LEVIS, D. J. "Behavioral Therapy: The Fourth Therapeutic Revolution?" in D. J. Levis (ed.), *Learning Approaches to Therapeutic Behavior Change.* Chicago: Aldine Publishing Company, 1970.

LEVIS, D. J. "Implosive Therapy: A Critical Analysis of Morganstern's Review." *Psychological Bulletin,* 1974, *81,* 155–158.

LEVIS, D. J., AND HARE, N. "A Review of the Theoretical Rationale and Empirical Support for the Estimation Approach of Implosive (Flooding) Therapy." In M. Hersen, R. M. Eisler, and P. M. Miller (eds.), *Progress in Behavior Modification: 4.* New York: Academic Press, 1977.

LEVITT, J. L.; YOUNG, T. M.; AND PAPPENFORT, D. M. *Achievement Place: The Teaching-Family Treatment Model in a Group Home Setting.* Chicago: National Center for the Assessment of Alternatives to Juvenile Justice Processing, University of Chicago, 1979.

LEWIN, K. "Formalization and Progress in Psychology." In K. Lewin, *Field Theory in Social Science: Selected Theoretical Papers.* (Edited by D. Cartwright). New York: Harper Torchbooks, 1951.

LEWINSOHN, P. M. "The Behavioral Study and Treatment of Depression." In M. Hersen, R. M. Eisler, and P. M. Miller (eds.), *Progress in Behavior Modification: 1.* New York: Academic Press, 1975.

LEWINSOHN, P. M.; BIGLAN, A.; AND ZEISS, A. M. "Behavioral Treatment of Depression." In O. Davidson (ed.), *The Behavioral Management of Anxiety, Depression, and Pain.* New York: Brunner/Mazel, 1976.

LEWINSOHN, P. M., AND SHAFFER, M. "Use of Home Observations as an Integral Part of the Treatment of Depression: Preliminary Report and Case Studies." *Journal of Consulting and Clinical Psychology,* 1971, *37,* 87–94.

LEWINSOHN, P. M.; WEINSTEIN, M. S.; AND ALPER, T. "A Behavioral Approach to the Group Treatment of Depressed Persons: A Methodological Contribution." *Journal of Clinical Psychology,* 1970, *26,* 525–532.

LIBERMAN, R. P. "Behavioral Approaches to Family and Couple Therapy." *American Journal of Orthopsychiatry,* 1970, *40,* 106–118.

LIBERMAN, R. P.; KING, L. W.; AND DeRISI, W. J. "Behavior Analysis and Therapy in Community Mental Health." In H. Leitenberg (ed.), *Handbook of Behavior Modification and Behavior Therapy.* Englewood Cliffs, N.J.: Prentice-Hall, 1976.

LIBERMAN, R. P., AND RASKIN, D. E. "Depression: A Behavioral Formulation." *Archives of General Psychiatry,* 1971, *24,* 515–523.

LOCKE, E. A. "Behavior Modification Is Not Cognitive—and Other Myths: A Reply to Ledwidge." *Cognitive Therapy and Research,* 1979, *3,* 119–125.

LONDON, P. *The Modes and Morals of Psychotherapy.* New York: Holt, 1964.

LORO, B. "Bibliography of Behavioral Approaches to Weight Reduction and Obesity from 1962 Through 1976." *Professional Psychology,* 1978, *9,* 278–289.

LOVAAS, O. I.; KOEGEL, R. L.; SIMMONS, J. Q.; AND LONG, J. S. "Some Generalization and Follow-Up Measures on Autistic Children in Behavior Therapy." *Journal of Applied Behavior Analysis,* 1973, *6,* 131–165.

LOVAAS, O. I., AND NEWSOME, C. D. "Behavior Modification with Psychotic Children." in H. Leitenberg (ed.), *Handbook of Behavior Modification and Behavior Therapy*. Englewood Cliffs, N.J.: Prentice-Hall, 1976.

LOVIBOND, S. H. *Conditioning and Enuresis*. New York: Pergamon Press, 1964.

MAHONEY, M. J. "The Self-Management of Covert Behavior: A Case Study." *Behavior Therapy*, 1971, *2*, 575–578.

MAHONEY, M. J. *Cognition and Behavior Modification*. Cambridge, Mass.: Ballinger Press, 1974.

MAHONEY, M. J. "A Critical Analysis of Rational-Emotive Theory and Therapy." *The Counseling Psychologist*, 1977a, *7*, 44–6.

MAHONEY, M. J. "Personal Science: A Cognitive-Learning Therapy." In A. Ellis and R. Grieger (eds.), *Handbook of Rational-Emotive Therapy*. New York: Springer, 1977b.

MAHONEY, M. J. "Reflections on the Cognitive-Learning Trend in Psychotherapy." *American Psychologist*, 1977c, *32*, 5–13.

MAHONEY, M. J., AND ARNKOFF, D. "Cognitive and Self-Control Therapies." In S. L. Garfield and A. E. Bergin (eds.), *Handbook of Psychotherapy and Behavior Change: An Empirical Analysis*. (2nd ed.) New York: Wiley, 1978.

MAHONEY, M. J., AND MAHONEY, K. *Permanent Weight Control*. New York: Norton, 1976.

MAHONEY, M. J. AND THORESEN, C. E. *Self-Control: Power to the Person*. Monterey, Calif.: Brooks/Cole, 1974.

MALOTT, R. W. "Focus." *Journal of Applied Behavior Analysis*, 1974, *7*, inside cover.

MARQUIS, J. N.; MORGAN, W. G.; AND PIAGET, G. *A Guidebook for Systematic Desensitization*. (4th ed.) Palo Alto, Calif.: Veterans Administration Hospital, 1974.

MASH, E. J.; HAMERLYNCK, L. A.; AND HANDY, L. C. (eds.). *Behavior Modification and Families*. New York: Brunner/Mazel, 1976.

MASH, E. J.; HANDY, L. C.; AND HAMERLYNCK, A. (eds.). *Behavior Modification Approaches to Parenting*. New York: Brunner/Mazel, 1976.

MASTERS, W. H. AND JOHNSON, V. E. *Human Sexual Response.* Boston: Little, Brown and Company, 1966.

MASTERS, W. H. AND JOHNSON, V. E. *Human Sexual Inadequacy.* Boston: Little, Brown and Company, 1970.

MATTHEWS, A., AND SHAW, P. "Cognitions Related to Anxiety: A Pilot Study on Treatment." *Behaviour Research and Therapy,* 1977, *15,* 503–505.

McBROOM, E. "Socialization and Social Casework." In R. W. Roberts and R. H. Nee (eds.), *Theories of Social Casework.* Chicago: University of Chicago Press, 1970.

McFALL, R. M. "Effects of Self-Monitoring on Normal Smoking Behavior." *Journal of Consulting and Clinical Psychology,* 1970, *35,* 135–142.

McINTIRE, R. W. *For Love of Children: Behavior Psychology for Parents.* Del Mar, Calif: CRM Books, 1970.

McLEAN, P. "Therapeutic Decision-Making in the Behavioral Treatment of Depression." In P. O. Davidson (ed.), *The Behavioral Management of Anxiety, Depression and Pain.* New York: Brunner/Mazel, 1976.

McLEAN, P. D.; OGSTON, K.; AND GRAUER, L. "A Behavioral Approach to the Treatment of Depression." *Journal of Behavior Therapy and Experimental Psychiatry,* 1973, *4,* 323–330.

MEICHENBAUM, D. "Cognitive Factors in Behavior Modification: Modifying What Clients Say to Themselves." In C. Franks and G. T. Wilson (eds.), *Annual Review of Behavior Therapy, Theory and Practice: 1973.* New York: Brunner/Mazel, 1973.

MEICHENBAUM, D. *Cognitive-Behavior Modification.* Morristown, N.J.: General Learning Press, 1974.

MEICHENBAUM, D. *Cognitive-Behavior Modification: An Integrative Approach.* New York: Plenum Press, 1977.

MEICHENBAUM, D. "Cognitive-Behavior Modification: The Need for a Fairer Assessment." *Cognitive Therapy and Research,* 1979, *3,* 127–132.

MEICHENBAUM, D., AND CAMERON, R. "The Clinical Potential of Modifying What Clients Say to Themselves." In M. J. Mahoney and C. E. Thoresen (eds.), *Self-Control: Power to the Person.* Monterey, Calif.: Brooks-Cole, 1974.

MENDELS, J. *Concepts of Depression.* New York: Wiley, 1970.

MERTON, R. *Social Theory and Social Structure.* (rev. ed.), Glencoe, Ill.: The Free Press, 1957.

MILLER, I. W., AND NORMAN, H. "Learned Helplessness in Humans: A Review and Attribution-Theory Model." *Psychological Bulletin,* 1979, *86,* 93–118.

MILLER, N. E. "Learning of Visceral and Glandular Responses." *Science,* 1969, *163,* 434–445.

MILLER, N. E., AND DWORKIN, B. R. "Visceral Learning: Recent Difficulties with Curarized Rats and Significant Problems for Human Research." In P. A. Obrist, A. H. Black, J. Brener, and L. V. Di Cara (eds.), *Cardiovascular Psychophysiology.* Chicago, Ill.: Aldine, 1974.

MILLER, L. K., AND MILLER, O. L. "Reinforcing Self-Help Group Activities of Welfare Recipients." *Journal of Applied Behavior Analysis,* 1970, *3,* 57–64.

MILLER, W. H. *Systematic Parent Training: Procedures, Cases and Issues.* Champaign, Ill.: The Research Press, 1975.

MILLER, W. H., AND MILLER, N. B. *Therapist's Guidebook to Systematic Parent Training.* Champaign, Ill.: Research Press, 1977.

MILLER, W. R.; ROSELLINI, R. A.; AND SELIGMAN, M. E. P. "Learned Helplessness and Depression." In J. D. Maser and M. E. P. Seligman (eds.), *Psychopathology: Experimental Models.* San Francisco: Freeman, 1977.

MILLER, W. R., AND SELIGMAN, M. E. P. "Depression and Learned Helplessness in Man." *Journal of Abnormal Psychology,* 1975, *84,* 228–238.

MILLER, W. R., AND SELIGMAN, M. E. P. "Learned Helplessness, Depression and the Perception of Reinforcement." *Behaviour Research and Therapy,* 1976, *14,* 7–17.

MORGANSTERN, K. P. "Implosive Therapy and Flooding Procedures: A Critical Review." *Psych. Bulletin,* 1973, *79,* 318–34.

MOSTOFSKY, D. I., AND BALASCHAK, B. "Psychobiological Control of Seizures." *Psychological Bulletin,* 1977, *84,* 723–750.

MOWRER, O. H. "Apparatus for the Study and Treatment of Eneuresis." *American Journal of Psychology,* 1938, *51,* 163–6.

MOWRER, O. H. *Learning Theory and Personality Dynamics.* New York: Ronald Press, 1950.

Mowrer, O. H. "Two-Factor Learning Theory Reconsidered, with Special Reference to Secondary Reinforcement and the Concept of Habit." *Psychological Review*, 1956, *63*, 114–128.

Mullen, E. J. "Casework Treatment Procedures as a Function of Client Diagnostic Variables." Unpublished doctoral dissertation, Columbia University, 1968.

Nay, W. *Behavioral Intervention: Contemporary Strategies.* New York: Gardner Press, 1976.

Novar, L. G. *Self-Control of Smoking Behavior: A Comparative Study of Constructional and Eliminative Approaches.* Unpublished doctoral dissertation, University of Chicago, 1976.

O'Leary, S. G., and O'Leary, K. D. "Behavior Modification in the School." In H. Leitenberg (ed.), *Handbook of Behavior Modification and Behavior Therapy.* Englewood Cliffs, N.J.: Prentice-Hall, 1976.

Patterson, G. R. *Families: Applications of Social Learning to Family Life.* Champaign, Ill.: Research Press, 1971.

Patterson, G. R., and Hops, H. "Coercion, a Game for Two: Intervention Techniques for Marital Conflict." In R. Ulrich and P. T. Mountjoy (eds.), *The Experimental Analysis of Social Behavior.* New York: Appleton-Century-Crofts, 1972.

Paul, G. L. *Insight vs. Desensitization in Psychotherapy.* Stanford: Stanford University Press, 1966.

Paul, G. L. "Outcome of Systematic Desensitization." In C. M. Franks (ed.), *Behavior Therapy: Appraisal and Status.* New York: McGraw-Hill, 1969.

Paul, G. L., and Bernstein, D. *Anxiety and Clinical Problems: Systematic Desensitization and Related Techniques.* Morristown, N.J.: General Learning Press, 1973.

Perlman, H. H. *Social Casework: A Problem-Solving Approach.* Chicago, Illinois: University of Chicago Press, 1957.

Perlman, H. H. "Self-Determination: Reality or Illusion?" *Social Service Review*, 1965, *39*, 410–421.

Phillips, E. L. "Achievement Place: Token Reinforcement Procedures in Home-Style Rehabilitation Setting for 'Pre-delinquent' Boys." *Journal of Applied Behavior Analysis*, 1968, *1*, 213–223.

PHILLIPS, J. S., AND KANFER, F. H. "The Viability and Vicissitudes of Behavior Therapy." *International Psychiatry Clinics,* 1969, *6,* 75–131.

PRICE, K. P. "The Application of Behavior Therapy to the Treatment of Psychosomatic Disorders: Retrospect and Prospect." *Psychotherapy: Theory, Research and Practice,* 1974, *11,* 138–155.

QUITKIN, F.; RIFKIN, A.; AND KLEIN, D. F. "Monoamine Oxidase Inhibitors: A Review of Antidepressant Effectiveness." *Archives of General Psychiatry,* 1979, *36,* 749–760.

RACHMAN, S. "Behavior Therapy and Psychodynamics." *Behavior Therapy,* 1970, *1,* 527–530.

RACHMAN, S., AND TEASDALE, J. *Aversion Therapy and Behavior Disorders: An Analysis.* Coral Gables, Fla.: University of Miami Press, 1969.

RAGLAND, D. R. *Behavioral Approaches to the Treatment of Hypertension: A Bibliography.* (DHEW Publication No. [NIH] 77-1219) Washington, D.C.: U.S. Government Printing Office, 1977.

RAHE, R. H. "Life Changes and Near-Future Illness Reports." In L. Levi (ed.), *Emotions—Their Parameters and Measurement.* New York: Raven, 1975.

REESE, E. P. *Human Behavior: Analysis and Application.* (2nd ed.) Dubuque, Ia.: Brown, 1978.

REID, W. J. "Characteristics of Casework Intervention." *Welfare in Review,* 1967, *5,* 11–19.

REST, E. R. "Rehabilitating Offenders Through Behavioral Change." In B. Ross and C. Shireman (eds.), *Social Work and Social Justice.* Washington, D.C.: National Association of Social workers, 1973.

RETTIG, E. B. *A-B-Cs for Parents: An Educational Workshop in Behavior Modification.* San Marino, Calif.: Associates for Behavior Change, 1973a.

RETTIG, E. B. *ABC: Behavior Management Workbook.* San Marino, Calif.: Associates for Behavior Change, 1973b.

RIBORDY, S. C., AND DENNEY, D. R. "The Behavioral Treatment of Insomnia: An Alternative to Drug Therapy." *Behaviour Research and Therapy,* 1977, *15,* 39–59.

RIMM, D. C., AND MASTERS, J. C. *Behavior Therapy: Techniques and Empirical Findings*. New York: Academic Press, 1974.

RIMM, D. C., AND MASTERS, J. C. *Behavior Therapy: Techniques and Empirical Findings*. (2nd ed.) New York: Academic Press, 1979.

ROGERS, C. R. "Toward a Science of the Person." In T. W. Wann (ed.), *Behaviorism and Phenomenology: Contrasting Bases for Modern Psychology*. Chicago: University of Chicago Press, 1964.

ROGERS, C. R., AND SKINNER, B. F. "Some Issues Concerning the Control of Human Behavior: A Symposium." *Science,* 1956, *124,* 1057–1066.

ROSE, S. D. *Treating Children in Groups*. San Francisco: Jossey-Bass, 1973.

ROSE, S. D. *Group Therapy: A Behavioral Approach*. Englewood Cliffs, N.J.: Prentice-Hall, Inc., 1977.

ROSE, S. D. (ed.). *A Casebook in Group Therapy: A Behavioral-Cognitive Approach*. Englewood Cliffs, N.J.: Prentice-Hall, 1980.

ROSENTHAL, T., AND BANDURA, A. "Psychological Modeling: Theory and Practice." In S. L. Garfield and A. E. Bergin (eds.) *Handbook of Psychotherapy and Behavior Change: An Empirical Analysis*. (2nd ed.) New York: Wiley, 1978.

RUSH, A. J.; BECK, A. T.; KOVACS, M.; AND HOLLON, S. "Comparative Efficacy of Cognitive Therapy and Imipramine in the Treatment of Depressed Outpatient." *Cognitive Therapy and Research,* 1977, *1,* 17–37.

SALEEBEY, D. "Pigeons, People and Paradise: Skinnerian Technology and the Coming of the Welfare Society." *Social Service Review,* 1976, *50,* 388–401.

SALTER, A. *Conditioned Reflex Therapy*. New York: Farrar, Straus and Giroux, 1949.

SAYNER, R., AND DURRELL, D. "Multiple Behavior Therapy Techniques in the Treatment of Sexual Dysfunction." *The Counseling Psychologist,* 1975, *5,* 38–41.

SCHULTERBRANDT, M. S., AND RASKIN, A. (eds.). *Depression in Childhood: Diagnosis, Treatment, and Conceptual Models.* (DHEW Publication No. [ADM] 77–476) Washington, D.C.: U.S. Government Printing Office, 1977.

SCHWARTZ, A. *The Reference Groups of Dieting Obese Women.* Unpublished doctoral dissertation, Columbia University, 1965.

SCHWARTZ, A. "Beyond Freud and Skinner: Behavior Analysis and Social Work Practice in the 1970's." Paper presented at the Third NASW Professional Symposium, New Orleans, La., November, 1972.

SCHWARTZ, A. "The Constructional Approach to Behavioral Practice." Paper presented at the Fourth NASW Professional Symposium, Hollywood-by-the-Sea, Florida, October, 1975.

SCHWARTZ, A. "Behaviorism and Psychodynamics." *Child Welfare,* 1977, *56,* 368–379.

SCHWARTZ, A., AND BLACKMAN, D. *Developing Behavioral Therapies for the Institutionalized Elderly: Final Report.* Chicago: School of Social Service Administration, University of Chicago, 1977.

SCHWARTZ, A., AND GOLDIAMOND, I. *Social Casework: A Behavioral Approach.* New York: Columbia University Press, 1975.

SCHWARTZ, A., AND SCHWARTZ, R. *The Treatment of Sexual Dysfunctioning and Marital Conflict: A Unified Model for the Treatment of Artificially Dichotomized Problems.* Book in preparation, 1982.

SCHWARTZ, G. E. "Biofeedback and the Self-Management of Disregulation Disorders." In R. B. Stuart (ed.), *Behavioral Self-Management: Strategies, Techniques and Outcomes.* New York: Brunner/Mazel, 1977.

SECUNDA, S. K.; KATZ, M. M.; FRIEDMAN, R. J.; AND SCHUYLER, D. *Special Report: 1973—The Depressive Disorders.* Washington, D.C.: U.S. Government Printing Office, 1973.

SEITZ, F. C. "Behavior Modification Techniques for Treating Depression." *Psychotherapy: Theory, Research and Practice,* 1971, *8,* 181–184.

SELIGMAN, M. E. P. *Helplessness: On Depression, Development and Death.* San Francisco: W. H. Freeman & Company, 1975.

SELIGMAN, M. E. P.; KLEIN, D. C.; AND MILLER, W. R. "Depression." In H. Leitenberg (ed.), *Handbook of Behavior Modification and Behavior Therapy*. Englewood Cliffs, N.J.: Prentice-Hall, 1976.

SENNETT, R. Review of *Beyond Freedom and Dignity* by B. F. Skinner. *New York Times Book Review* (Sunday), October 24, 1971.

SHAPIRO, D. *Neurotic Styles*. New York: Basic Books, 1965.

SHAPIRO, D., AND SURWIT, R. S. "Learned Control of Physiological Function and Disease." In H. Leitenberg (ed.), *Handbook of Behavior Modification and Behavior Therapy*. Englewood Cliffs, N.J.: Prentice-Hall, 1976.

SHAW, M. "Ethical Implications of a Behavioral Approach." In D. Jehu, *et al.* (eds.), *Behaviour Modification in Social Work*. London: Wiley-Interscience, 1972.

SHORKEY, C. T. "Behavioral Methods in Social Work Practice: A Comprehensive Bibliography." Mimeo, 1978. (Available from C. T. Shorkey, School of Social Work, University of Texas at Austin.)

SHORKEY, C. T., AND TAYLOR, J. "Management of Maladaptive Behavior of a Severely Burned Child." *Child Welfare*, 1973, *52*, 543–547.

SKINNER, B. F. *Walden Two*. New York: The Macmillan Company, 1948.

SKINNER, B. F. *Science and Human Behavior*. New York: The Free Press, 1953.

SKINNER, B. F. *The Technology of Teaching*. New York: Appleton-Century-Crofts, 1968.

SKINNER, B. F. *Beyond Freedom and Dignity*. New York: Alfred A. Knopf, 1971.

SKINNER, B. F. *About Behaviorism*. New York: Alfred A. Knopf, 1974.

SLOANE, R. B.; STAPLES, F. R.; CRISTOL, A. H.; YORKSTON, N.J.; AND WHIPPLE, K. *Psychotherapy versus Behavior Therapy*. Cambridge, Mass.: Harvard University Press, 1975.

Smith, J. M., and Smith, D. E. P. *Child Management: A Program for Parents and Teachers.* Champaign, Ill.: The Research Press, 1976.

Srole, L. *Mental Health in the Metropolis.* New York: McGraw-Hill, 1962.

Stahl, J. R., and Leitenberg, H. "Behavioral Treatment of the Chronic Mental Hospital Patient." In H. Leitenberg (ed.), *Handbook of Behavior Modification and Behavior Therapy.* Englewood Cliffs, N.J.: Prentice-Hall, 1976.

Stampfl, T. G., and Levis, D. J. "Essentials of Implosive Therapy: A Learning-Theory-Based Psychodynamic Behavioral Therapy." *Journal of Abnormal Psychology,* 1967, *72,* 496–503.

Stampfl, T. G., and Levis, D. J. "Implosive Therapy: A Behavioural Therapy." *Behaviour Research and Therapy,* 1968, *6,* 31–36.

Stanton, A. H., and Schwartz, M. S. *The Mental Hospital.* New York: Basic Books, 1954.

Stein, T. J., and Gambrill, E. D. "Behavioral Techniques in Foster Care." *Social Work,* 1976, *21,* 34–39.

Steinmark, S. W., and Borkovec, T. D. "Active and Placebo Treatment Effects on Moderate Insomnia under Counterdemand and Positive Demand Instructions." *Journal of Abnormal Psychology,* 1974, *83,* 157–163.

Stuart, R. B. "Applications of Behavior Therapy to Social Casework." In E. J. Thomas (ed.), *The Socio-Behavioral Approach and Applications to Social Work.* New York: Council on Social Work Education, 1967a.

Stuart, R. B. "Behavioral Control of Overeating." *Behaviour Research and Therapy,* 1967b, *5,* 357–365.

Stuart, R. B. "Casework Treatment of Depression Viewed as an Interpersonal Disturbance." *Social Work,* 1967c, *12,* 27–36.

Stuart, R. B. "Operant Interpersonal Treatment for Marital Discord." *Journal of Consulting and Clinical Psychology,* 1969, *33,* 675–682.

Stuart, R. B. "Behavioral Contracting with the Families of Delinquents." *Journal of Behavior Therapy and Experimental Psychiatry,* 1971, *2,* 1–11.

STUART, R. B. "Behavior Modification Techniques for the Education Technologist." In R. Saari and F. F. Maple (eds.), *The School in the Community*. Washington, D.C.: NASW, 1972.

STUART, R. B. "An Operant Interpersonal Program for Couples." In H. L. Olson (ed.), *Treating Relationships*. Lake Mills, Ia.: Graphic Publishing Co., 1976.

STUART, R. B. (ed.). *Behavioral Self-Management: Strategies, Techniques and Outcomes*. New York: Brunner/Mazel Publishers, 1977.

STUART, R. B., AND DAVIS, B. *Slim Chance in a Fat World: Behavioral Control of Obesity*. Champaign, Ill.: The Research Press, 1972.

STUART, R. B., AND LOTT, L. A. "Behavioral Contracting with Delinquents: A Cautionary Note." *Journal of Behaviour Therapy and Experimental Psychiatry*, 1972, *3*, 161–169.

STUNKARD, A. J. "New Therapies for the Eating Disorders: Behavior Modification of Obesity and Anorexia Nervosa." *Archives of General Psychiatry*, 1972, *26*, 391–398.

STUNKARD, A. J. "Behavioral Treatment of Obesity: Failure to Maintain Weight Loss." in R. D. Stuart (ed.), *Behavioral Self-Management: Strategies, Techniques and Outcomes*. New York: Brunner/Mazel, 1977.

STUNKARD, A. J., AND MAHONEY, M. J. "Behavioral Treatment of the Eating Disorders." In H. Leitenberg (ed.), *Handbook of Behavior Modification and Behavior Therapy*. Englewood Cliffs, N.J.: Prentice-Hall, 1976.

STUNKARD, A. J., AND PENICK, S. B. "Behavior Modification in the Treatment of Obesity: The Problem of Maintaining Weight Loss." *Archives of General Psychiatry*, 1979, *36*, 801–806.

SUINN, R. M., AND RICHARDSON, F. "Anxiety Management Training: A Nonspecific Behavior Therapy Program for Anxiety Control." *Behavior Therapy*, 1971, *2*, 498–510.

SULZER, B., AND MAYER, G. R. *Behavior Modification Procedures for School Personnel*. Hinsdale, Ill.: The Dryden Press, 1972.

SULZER, E. "Reinforcement and the Therapeutic Contract." *Journal of Counseling Psychology*, 1962, *9*, 271–276.

SUNDEL, M., AND SUNDEL, S. S. *Behavior Modification in the Human Services: A Systematic Introduction to Concepts and Applications.* New York: Wiley, 1975.

SUOMI, S. J., AND HARLOW, H. F. "Production and Alleviation of Depressive Behaviors in Monkeys." In J. D. Maser and M. E. P. Seligman (eds.), *Psychopathology: Experimental Models.* San Francisco: Freeman, 1977.

TAYLOR, F. G., AND MARSHALL, W. L. "Experimental Analysis of a Cognitive-Behavioral Therapy for Depression." *Cognitive Therapy and Research,* 1977, *1,* 59–72.

TEASDALE, J. D., AND REZIN, V. "Effect of Thought-Stopping on Thoughts, Mood, and Corregator EMG in Depressed Patients." *Behaviour Research and Therapy,* 1978, *16,* 97–102.

THIMANN, J. "Conditioned-Reflex Treatment of Alcoholism, I." *New England Journal of Medicine,* 1949, *241,* 368–370.

THOMAS, E. J. (ed.). *The Socio-Behavioral Approach and Applications to Social Work.* New York: The Council on Social Work Education, 1967.

THOMAS, E. J. (ed.). *Behavior Modification Procedure: A Sourcebook.* Chicago: Aldine, 1974.

THOMAS, E. J., AND GOODMAN, E. (eds.). *Socio-Behavioral Theory and Interpersonal Helping in Social Work.* Ann Arbor, Mich.: Campus Publishers, 1965.

THORESEN, C. E., AND MAHONEY, M. J. *Behavioral Self-Control.* New York: Holt, Rinehart & Winston, 1974.

THORNDIKE, E. L. "Animal Intelligence: An Experimental Study of the Associative Processes in Animals." *Psychological Review,* Monograph Supplement, 1898, *2,* No. 8.

TRUAX, C. B. "Reinforcement and Nonreinforcement in Rogerian Psychotherapy." *Journal of Abnormal Psychology,* 1966, *71,* 1–9.

ULLMANN, L. P. "Making Use of Modeling in the Therapeutic Interview." In D. R. Rich and C. M. Franks (eds.), *Advances in Behavior Therapy, 1968.* New York: Academic Press, 1969.

ULLMANN, L. P., AND KRASNER, L. (eds.). *Case Studies in Behavior Modification.* New York: Holt, Rinehart & Winston, 1965.

UPPER, D., AND ROSS, S. M. *Behavioral Group Therapy: 1979.* Champaign, Ill.: The Research Press, 1979.

UPPER, D., AND ROSS, S. M. *Behavioral Group Therapy: 1980.* Champaign, Ill.: The Research Press, 1980.

VANDEWIELE, R. L. "Anorexia Nervosa and the Hypothalamus." *Hospital Practice,* 1977, *12,* 45–51.

VATTANO, A. "Self-Management Procedures for Coping with Stress and Anxiety." *Social Work,* 1978, *23,* 113–119.

VOS, B. Personal Communication. September, 1979.

WACHTEL, P. L. *Psychoanalysis and Behavior Therapy: Toward an Integration.* New York: Basic Books, 1977.

WAHL, G.; JOHNSON, S. M.; JOHANSSON, S.; AND MARTIN, S. "An Operant Analysis of Child-Family Interaction." *Behavior Therapy,* 1974, *5,* 64–78.

WAHLER, R. G. "Deviant Child Behavior Within the Family: Developmental Speculations and Behavior Change Strategies." in H. Leitenberg (ed.), *Handbook of Behavior Modification and Behavior Therapy.* Englewood Cliffs, N.J.: Prentice-Hall, 1976.

WALEN, S. R.; HAUSERMAN, N. M.; AND LAVIN, P. J. *Clinical Guide to Behavior Therapy.* Baltimore, MD.: The Williams and Wilkins Company, 1977.

WALTERS, G. C., AND GRUSEC, J. E. *Punishment.* San Francisco: Freeman, 1977.

WANDERSMAN, A.; POPPEN, P. J.; AND RICKS, D. F. *Humanism and Behaviorism: Dialogue and Growth.* Oxford: Pergamon Press, 1976.

WATSON, D., AND THARP, R. *Self-Directed Behavior: Self-Modification for Personal Adjustment.* Monterey, Calif.: Brooks-Cole, 1977.

WATSON, J. B. *Behaviorism.* New York: Norton, 1924.

WATSON, J. B., AND RAYNOR, R. "Conditioned Emotional Reactions." *Journal of Experimental Psychology,* 1920, *3,* 1–14.

WATZLAWICK, P.; BEAVIN, J. H.; AND JACKSON, D. D. *Pragmatics of Human Communication: A Study of Interactional Patterns, Pathologies and Paradoxes*. New York: Norton, 1967.

WEISS, R. L. "Contracts, Cognition and Change: A Behavioral Approach to Marriage Therapy." *The Counseling Psychologist*, 1975, *5*, 15–26.

WEISS, R. L.; BIRCHLER, G. R.; AND VINCENT, J. P. "Contractual Models for Negotiation Training in Marital Dyads." *Journal of Marriage and the Family*, 1974, *36*, 321–330.

WEISSMAN, M. M. "The Epidemiology of Suicide Attempts, 1960 to 1971." *Archives of General Psychiatry*, 1974, *30*, 737–746.

WEISSMAN, M. M. "The Psychological Treatment of Depression." *Archives of General Psychiatry*, 1979, *36*, 1261–1269.

WEISSMAN, M. M., AND PAYKEL, E. S. *The Depressed Woman: A Study of Social Relationships*. Chicago: The University of Chicago Press, 1974.

WHEELER, H. (ed.), *Beyond the Punitive Society: Operant Conditioning; Social and Political Aspects*. San Francisco: Freeman, 1973.

WHITE, O. R. *A Glossary of Behavioral Terminology*. Champaign, Ill.: The Research Press, 1971.

WHITELEY, J. M. (ed.). "Rational-Emotive Therapy." *The Counseling Psychologist*, 1977, *7*, 2–82. (entire issue).

WODARSKI, J., AND BAGAROZZI, D. A. *Behavioral Social Work*. New York: Human Sciences Press, 1979.

WOLPE, J. *Psychotherapy by Reciprocal Inhibition*. Stanford, Calif.: Stanford University Press, 1958.

WOLPE, J. *The Practice of Behavior Therapy*. New York: Pergamon Press, 1969.

WOLPE, J. *The Practice of Behavior Therapy*. (2nd ed.) New York: Pergamon Press, 1973.

WOLPE, J. *Theme and Variations: A Behavior Therapy Casebook*. New York: Pergamon Press, 1976.

WOLPE, J. "Cognition and Causation in Human Behavior and Its Therapy." *American Psychologist*, 1978, *33*, 437–446.

Wolpe, J., and Lazarus, A. A. *Behavior Therapy Techniques.* New York: Pergamon Press, 1966.

Yates, A. J. *Theory and Practice in Behavior Therapy.* New York: Wiley, 1975.

Yelloly, M. "Insight." In D. Jehu et al. (eds.), *Behaviour Modification in Social Work.* London: Wiley-Interscience, 1972.

Zeldow, P. B. "Some Antitherapeutic Effects of the Token Economy: A Case in Point." *Psychiatry,* 1976, *39,* 318–324.

Index

behavioral treatment of couple problems, 222–23
treatment of obesity, 237
Stunkard, Albert J.:
on treatment of anorexia nervosa,
241
on treatment of obesity, 237, 238,
239
Stuttering, differential theoretical conceptualization as sympton, 5–6
Suggestion: in behavioral and psychodynamic approaches, 264
Suicide:
and depression, 172–73
in youth, 172
under-reporting of, 172
discussion of, in initial interview,
203n
"no suicide" contract, 203n
Suinn, R. M.: anxiety management
training, 140–41
Sulzer, Beth: behavioral intervention
in classrooms, 228–29
Sundel, M.: introductory textbook,
56n
Sundel, S. S.: introductory textbook,
56n
Suomi, S. J.: see Harry Harlow
Symbolic covert control: in self control, 109; see also cognitive therapy
Symptom:
comparison of behavioral and psychodynamic views of, 4–7
as "learned" phenomenon, 4–7
as consequences, 5–6
removal by relearning of alternate
behavior, 6
see also symptom substitution
Symptom subtitution:
comparison of behavioral and psychodynamic views, 4–7
as a continuing issue, 264
Systematic desensitization:
description, 26–33
steps in, 27–33
see also Joseph Wolpe
assessment procedures in, 26–27
description of a session, 31
homework assignments in, 31–32
necessity of client cooperation, 2
spacing of hierarchy items, 32–33

differing views on reasons for its efficacy, 33–37
variations, in vivo desensitization,
37–38, 50
summary of discussion, 50
in depression, 197–98
case illustration, 198–99
Systems theory: and behavioral treatment of families, 266

Teachers behavior: the classroom as
environment, 229, 229 n; see also
schools; Ellen D. Reese
Terminal repertoire:
in initial interview, 65
as goals, 65
see also goals of therapy
Therapist:
as employee of the client, 73
as a model, 120–21
Therapy, goals of: comparison of behavioral and psychodynamic, 3;
see also behavior therapy
Thimann, Joseph: conditioned reflex
treatment for alcoholism, 44–46,
48
Thomas, Edwin J.: as behavioral inno-
vator in social work, 19
Thought processes: 17; see also cognitive therapy
Thought-stopping:
as a coping skill, 141–43
adaptations of, 142
criticisms of, 142–43
Time out:
as procedure to lower behavior, 100
"quiet room," 100
use in sibling rivalry, 100
mentioned, 115
as an aversive procedure with children, 221
Token economy:
general description of, 83–88, 114
advantages of, 84–85
as a motivational system, 84–85
in mental hospitals, 84, 86–88
procedures for establishing, 84–85
problems in application of, 85–88
staff resistances to, 85
issue of "bribery," 85–86
problems of generalization, 86, 88
client reaction to, 86–88